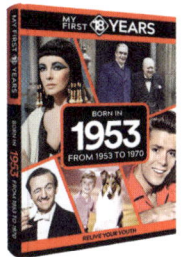
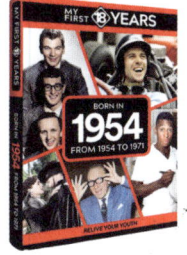

CW01507004

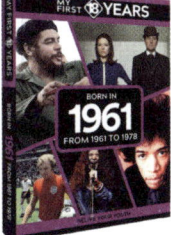
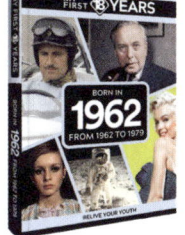
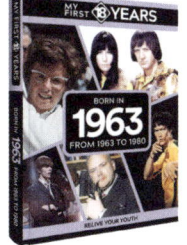

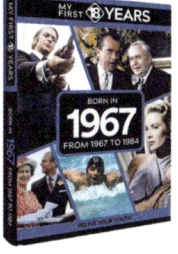

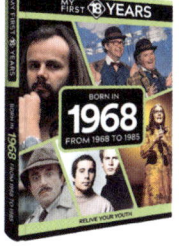

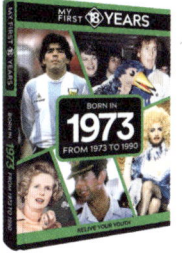
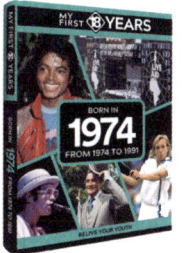
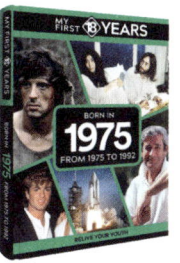

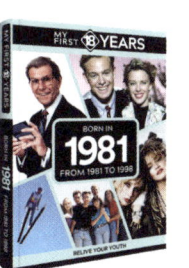
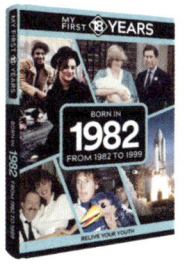
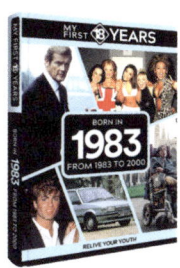
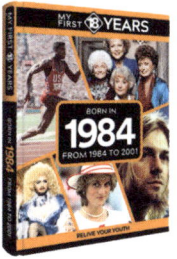

MY FIRST 18 YEARS

BORN IN
1980
FROM 1980 TO 1997

My First 18 Years is a brand of TDM Publishing.
The image, brand and logos are protected and owned by TDM Publishing.

www.mijneerste18jaar.nl
info@mijneerste18jaar.nl

My First 18 Years idea and concept: Thars Duijnstee.
Research and text: Lucinda Gosling, Stephen Barnard, Jeffrey Roozeboom, Katherine Alcock.
Composition and image editing: Jeffrey Roozeboom.
Design: Ferry Geutjes, Boudewijn van der Plas, Jeffrey Roozeboom.
Proofreading: Alison Griffiths.

Every effort has been made to trace the rights holders of all images. If you believe an image has been incorrectly credited, please contact the publisher.

Photos: Sound & Vision, National Archives, Getty images, Mary Evans Picture Library, Shutterstock, BNNVARA, AVROTROS, Veronica, KRO-NCRV, KIPPA, *Mijn eerste 18 jaar* archives.

In writing this series, the authors drew from the following sources: view from 1963-1999, NTS / NOS Annual Review, nueens.nl, vandaagindegeschiedenis.nl, beleven.org, IMDb, Wikipedia, Eye Filmmuseum, Rollingstone.com, image & sound, National Archives, Onthisday.com, Parlement.com. *Complete Book of UK Hit Singles, First Hits 1949-1959* (Boxtree Books), Billboard Books, *Reader's Digest* Music series 1950s-1970s, British Library Newspaper Archive, rogerebert.com

Thanks to: Spotify, Rick Versteeg, Rik Booltink.

The Top 10 list for each year is compiled by Stephen Barnard and is a personal selection of best-selling hits, radio favourites and lesser-known tracks that reflect the popular artists and styles of each year. Some are universally regarded classics, others will be less remembered yet are equally emblematic of the tastes of that year. Each list should provoke many 'Ah yes!' moments, particularly those almost forgotten treasures that are rarely heard even as 'golden oldies' yet tickled the ears in their day.

How to use Spotify playlists:

1. Open Spotify.
2. Click search (the magnifying glass in the image).
3. Click scan (the camera in the picture).
4. Point your camera at the Spotify code in the book.
5. After that, you can play the selected list.

ISBN 978 94 9331 789 5
NUR: 400

SPORT

Ice dream

Bristol-born figure skater Robin Cousins has the year of his sporting life when he takes the gold medal at the Winter Olympics at Lake Placid, New York, on 23rd February, skating a routine of artistic brilliance.

Gold rush for GB

With many countries, including the USA, boycotting the Olympic Games in Moscow in protest at the USSR's invasion of Afghanistan, there are claims that British athletes have greater opportunities in track and field events. Speedy Scot, Allan Wells scoops gold in the 100 metres final, with a time of 10:25, but proves any doubters wrong at a meeting in Cologne less than a fortnight later, where he beats the Americans Carl Lewis and Harvey Glance in the 100 metres with a time of 10:19 seconds. Elsewhere, Daley Thompson wins gold in the decathlon, a medal indicative of his dominance in the event during this period, regardless of who else is competing.

Clash of the tennis titans

The atmosphere on Centre Court is electric at Wimbledon on 5th July as Swedish ice man Bjorn Borg hopes to achieve a fifth, record-breaking men's singles title in a meeting with American 'Superbrat' John McEnroe. The confrontation, between two polar opposites, lasts for five nail-biting sets, including a fourth set tie-break that goes to 16-17, but Borg eventually triumphs and falls to his knees in his now familiar champion's ritual. The match feels like the apogee of tennis's golden era; two genius players with their wooden racquets and their headbands, playing at the height of their powers.

Brute force

British boxer Alan Minter faces Vito Antuofermo in a boxing match for the World Middleweight title, at Caesar's Palace, Las Vegas on 16th March. The pair go the full fifteen rounds, with a split decision result, in Minter's favour. Minter proves his supremacy on 28th June in a bloody rematch from which he emerges undisputed World Middleweight Champion but loses the title to Marvin Hagler later in the year.

18 JAN 1980

Sir Cecil Beaton, photographer, illustrator, and diarist, dies at the age of 76.

25 FEB 1980

Political comedy, *Yes, Minister* with Paul Eddington and Nigel Hawthorne, begins on BBC1.

19 MAR 1980

MV *Mi Amigo*, the ship from which pirate station, Radio Caroline broadcasts, runs aground and sinks in the Thames estuary.

3

1980

Middle-distance duels

Great Britain's prowess in middle-distance running during this period is embodied by the legendary rivalry of Sebastian Coe and Steve Ovett, two runners who break and counter-break each other's records, but whose actual meetings on the track are few and far between; until, that is, the Olympic final of the 800 metres in the Lenin Stadium in Moscow on 26th July. In a race Coe is widely expected to win, Ovett barges to the front of the pack to power down the final 100 metres and win gold (photo). Coe, suffering from what he later describes as a tactical disaster, settles for silver, but four days later, finds the form of his life to win gold in the 1500 metres. Ovett finishes with a bronze.

DOMESTIC
NEWS

Naturist beaches

1st April 1980 Britain gets its first official naturist beach in Brighton. Despite shocking some, the idea proves popular, and soon others open across the country.

Iranian Embassy siege

5th May 1980 A horrified nation watches live on television as the SAS storm the Iranian Embassy in London, ending a six-day occupation of the building by the Democratic Revolutionary Front for the Liberation of Arabistan. Television captures the moment the SAS enter through an upper-storey window to attempt a rescue. Two hostages and five of the six terrorists are killed, the rest of the captives are rescued safely.

British Steel strike

2nd January 1980 The Iron and Steel Trades Confederation call their 90,000 members at British Steel out on strike. The action ends in April with an agreed 16% pay rise, but not before the industry is rocked by the announcement that the Corby plant will close with the loss of over 11,000 jobs. This was in addition to the already advertised 4,500 job closure at Consett in September.

29 APR 1980

Death of Alfred Hitchcock, aged 88, British director with a string of suspenseful movies to his name.

21 MAY 1980

Star Wars Episode V - The Empire Strikes Back opens at cinemas.

13 JUN 1980

he UN calls for South Africa to free Nelson Mandela.

Sixpence withdrawn
30th June 1980 The pre-decimal sixpence, or 'tanner', is withdrawn from circulation. It had survived the initial decimalisation process, with a value equivalent to 2.5 new pennies, but is now set to be withdrawn as the country has adapted to the new currency.

Denmark Place fire
16th August 1980 Tragedy strikes London's Denmark Place, as petty criminal John Thompson seeks revenge for a disagreement with a barman in the Spanish Rooms. Thompson pours two gallons of petrol into the establishment and sets it on fire, killing 37 people in the bar and its neighbouring salsa club Rodo's. Thompson is sentenced to life imprisonment.

Unemployment highs
28th August 1980 Figures released throughout the year show that unemployment is rising quickly across the country. By August unemployment is at 2 million, the highest since 1935, with estimates that it will reach 2.5 million by the end of the year. Inflation also rises to 21.8%.

Hercules the bear
20th August 1980 Hercules the bear goes missing on the island of Benbecula in the Outer Hebrides. The bear, owned by wrestler Andy Robin, is there to shoot a Kleenex commercial when he manages to escape. Missing for 24 days, when he is recaptured, it is discovered that he has almost starved rather than kill any animals on the island, leading to Kleenex's 'Big Softie' campaign.

Alexandra Palace fire
10th July 1980 Alexandra Palace, or 'Ally Pally', is gutted by fire. The fire destroys half the building and only the outer walls and parts of the former BBC studios are preserved.

Third-gen Escort
1st September 1980 Ford launch the third generation of their ever-popular Ford Escort, a model which goes on to become the country's best-selling car of the decade.

Right to buy scheme
3rd October 1980 The new Housing Act becomes law, meaning that tenants of council-owned houses, who have lived there for three or more years, now have the right to buy their homes. These homes are sold at a large discount on market rates and are part of an aspirational policy hoping to see a rise in home ownership across the UK.

27 JUL 1980
England fans riot during England's opening European Championship match in Turin leading police to use tear gas.

1 AUG 1980
Buttevant rail disaster kills 18 and injures dozens of train passengers in Ireland.

3 SEP 1980
Jill Barklem's delightful, illustrated books about country mice, *Spring, Summer, Autumn* and *Winter Story* are published this month.

Marlborough diamond stolen

11th September 1980
The Graff jewellery shop in Knightsbridge is robbed by thieves who take the £400,000 'Marlborough' diamond and several other jewels from the window display. A brave shop assistant follows them to their car and notes the registration, and the following day the thieves are arrested in Chicago. The diamond is never recovered.

Foot comes first for Labour

James Callaghan resigns as Labour leader, and despite the British media believing Dennis Healey will become next leader, it is instead Michael Foot (illustration) following a vote on 10th November. Despite his far-left views, Foot is a leader who many believe can unite the party.

Rendlesham Forest Incident

26th & 28th December 1980 Servicemen at RAF Woodbridge are puzzled by the sight of unexplained lights descending into the nearby Rendlesham Forest. These lights, along with rumours of higher-than-average radiation readings and the panic of local farm animals, become one of the most well-known UFO events in Britain.

WE ARE NOT ALONE

The Queen Mum at 80

The Queen Mother celebrates her 80th birthday this year and on 15th July sets off with Prince Charles in the 1902 State Landau to attend a service of thanksgiving at St. Paul's Cathedral. On 4th August, her actual birthday, she greets crowds who gather outside the gates of her home in Clarence House.

ROYALTY & POLITICS

Shy Di

The relationship between Prince Charles and Lady Diana Spencer becomes public knowledge in September, after Diana is spotted watching the Prince fish on the Balmoral estate. An invite to the Queen's Highland retreat is widely known to be a signifier of something more serious and the following months see press intrusion reach new heights as 'shy Di', who works at a kindergarten, is pursued relentlessly by photographers.

3 OCT 1980

The Housing Act allows council housing tenants to buy their own home.

12 NOV 1980

Voyager 1 space probe reaches Saturn and sends back photographs of its rings of orange and yellow clouds.

14 DEC 1980

Thousands hold a vigil for John Lennon in Liverpool following his murder in New York.

No U-turn for the Iron Lady
Margaret Thatcher makes one of the defining speeches of her career at the Conservative Party conference on 10th October, standing firm against calls from others within her party to make a U-turn on her policy of economic liberalisation in the face of rising unemployment and recession. 'You can turn if you want to,' she says, 'The lady's not for turning.' The powerful phrase is one of Thatcher's most memorable.

FOREIGN
NEWS

Street art
Art is for everyone and not just for the elite, is Keith Haring's motto. In New York he discovered graffiti, which he developed into his very own style. He makes chalk drawings on empty billboards in the subway, draws on the street and becomes known far beyond the national borders. Haring makes paintings, sculptures, paints pieces of canvas, applies decorations to vases and t-shirts. In 1985 he decorated the body of singer Grace Jones and contributed to her video *I'm Not Perfect*.

DO YOU REMEMBER THIS?

Ghetto blaster

Note this
1st April 1980 American Art Fry has had enough: his bookmark keeps falling out of his choir book. He comes up with a way to stick the bookmark to the page with a self-adhesive strip and experiments with the yellow pieces of paper on the notepad at the 3M office. Ultimately, 3M successfully markets the Post-it note.

Tito is dead
4th May 1980 Three days before his 88th birthday, Josip Broz, alias Tito, dies. The founder and President of Yugoslavia, who has long advocated a 'Third Way' between the bickering East and West, will receive the largest state funeral the world has ever seen.

Solidarity recognised
14th August 1980 The protest against layoffs and inflation at the Lenin Shipyard in Gdańsk, Poland, marks the end of communism in the region. The strikers no longer demand 'a bigger sandwich' but solidarity and the recognition of trade unions. On 31st August, the anti-communist trade union Solidarność of Lech Wałęsa is recognised as the first independent trade union in the Eastern Bloc. One year after its founding, one in four Poles is a member, and the political consequences of this breakthrough are immense.

Reagan is President
4th November 1980 In the US presidential election, Americans send the incumbent President Jimmy Carter back home to Georgia. The Republican candidate, former Hollywood film actor Ronald Reagan, will become the next President.

ENTERTAINMENT

Morning campers!
Hi-de-Hi, set in a 1950s holiday camp, begins on 1st January on BBC1. Written by *Dad's Army* creators Jimmy Perry and David Croft, the staff at Maplins are Yellowcoats (inspired by Butlin's real-life Redcoats) and it is a yellow coat that scatterbrained chambermaid Peggy (Su Pollard) covets, but she never seems to quite make it. Instead, she is Cinderella to the entertainment staff (led by Paul Shane's Ted), kept in her place by self-important senior Yellowcoat Gladys (Ruth Madoc) whose xylophone tannoy announcements keep Maplins running like clockwork and whose seductive wiles make manager Jeffrey Fairbrother (Simon Cadell) hot under the collar.

Walkies!
Barbara Woodhouse has been training dogs and horses for decades, with occasional spots on television and radio, but the ten-part series, *Training Dogs the Woodhouse Way*, which begins on BBC1 on 7th January, makes her a household name at the age of 70. Woodhouse has a natural confidence on-screen, bossing around dog owners and teaching the dogs how to 'Si-T' and how to go for 'Walkies!' nicely. A true original, Barbara Woodhouse becomes a television sensation.

Higher or lower?
ITV launches two new game shows to bring cheer to the winter months. *Family Fortunes* hosted by the smooth-talking Bob Monkhouse (photo) begins on ITV on 6th January, while Bruce Forsyth fronts *Play Your Card Right* from 6th February. *Play Your Cards Right* is another winner for Brucie (even though actually winning is more to do with luck than any skill).

Metal Mickey

Metal Mickey, a cute, five-foot-tall, eager to please robot, first appears on *The Saturday Banana* in 1978 before becoming the title character in a new kids' comedy show on ITV, starting 6th September. The versatile Mickey, whose favourite phrase is, 'Boogie, boogie' goes on to release several hit singles in addition to his TV success.

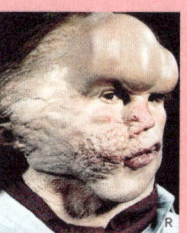

Game to geek out on

Seasoned BBC producer Patrick Dowling devises *The Adventure Game*, and the first of twenty-two episodes airs on 24th May. It's a melting pot of Dowling's interests in early computer adventure games, Dungeons and Dragons and Douglas Adams's *Hitchhiker's Guide to the Galaxy*.

The Elephant Man

David Lynch directs this heart-wrenching story of Joseph Merrick, whose life-limiting deformities made him an object of ridicule and curiosity in Victorian England. John Hurt plays Merrick and Anthony Hopkins is Sir Frederick Treves, the doctor who takes him in at the London Hospital and introduces him to high society.

Diff'rent Strokes

The American sitcom *Diff'rent Strokes* begins on ITV on 24th November. A wealthy New York widower adopts two Harlem boys after the death of their mother.

Pac-Man premieres

22nd May 1980 Launching today is a Japanese-originated video game destined to become one of the best loved and biggest selling in history. Developed by Namco with a design inspired by a pizza with a slice removed, Pac-Man is the first successful attempt to create a video game with to appeal to children and women as well as young adult males. Within two years, Pac-Man attracts over more than 50 million players across the world and inspires a whole new genre of chase-in-a-maze games.

Airplane!

If the 1970s was the decade of disaster movies, then the 1980s is the decade to parody them, and *Airplane!* starring Leslie Nielsen, Peter Graves and Lloyd Bridges is among the first and the best, inspired by films such as *Airport* and *Airport '75* and in particular 1957's *Zero Hour!* It's non-stop jokes and slapstick all the way.

It's a fair cop

Police dramas have been seriously lacking strong female characters, until this year when, like buses, two come along at once. On 11th April, Jill Gascoine is Detective Inspector Maggie Forbes in ITV's *The Gentle Touch* (photo). And on 30th August, BBC1 launch *Juliet Bravo*, with Stephanie Turner as Chief Inspector Jean Darblay, who must fight the prejudice of a male-dominated police force as well as criminals. Both series become hugely popular.

1980

Who Shot J.R.?

On 22nd November, 21.5 million UK viewers tune in to *Dallas* on BBC1 to discover the answer to the whodunnit of the decade. 'Who Shot J.R?' becomes the question on everybody's lips. Four episodes into season 4, the culprit is finally revealed. It's Kristin Shepard, J.R.'s sister-in-law and mistress, who gunned him down in a fit of pique.

Button Moon

Button Moon, which begins on ITV on 8th December, encourages its pre-school audience to follow Mr and Mrs Spoon as they travel to the big yellow button in the sky every episode. Everything on *Button Moon* is created from household objects including the Spoon family's space rocket, which is a converted washing-up liquid bottle.

Flash Gordon

Flash Gordon captures the comic-strip camp of the science-fiction adventure, and is turbo charged by a rollicking soundtrack from rock band Queen thumping along in the background as Flash only has 'fourteen hours to save the Earth' from Max von Sydow's Ming the Merciless. Eminently quotable lines include Brian Blessed's Prince Vultan roaring, 'Gordon's alive!'

Pennysavers

Fine Fare, the UK's third largest super-market, launches a no-frills economy range, with plain white packaging stamped with tea chest-style font.

MUSIC

World Police

20th January 1980 After conquering the UK in 1979 with a masterly fusion of power pop and reggae epitomised by the Sting compositions *Message in a Bottle* and *Walking on the Moon*, the Police take off on their first world tour of 37 cities in nineteen countries.

Sheer Madness

January 1980 Having taken their porkpie-hatted nuttiness from 2-Tone to the Stiff label, Camden Town band Madness begin a decade of chart dominance with *My Girl*, the first of a long stream of comic but faintly melancholy observations of North London life. *Baggy Trousers* follows, a look back at schooldays, while *Embarrassment* dissects the impact of a mixed-race relationship on a close family and their fear of what the neighbours will say.

AC/DC death
19th February 1980 Bon Scott, singer with Australian band AC/DC, dies in London aged 33. Cause of death is given as acute alcohol poisoning. Brian Johnson is named lead singer in his place in April.

Ireland wins Eurovision
19th April 1980 Johnny Logan wins the Eurovision Song Contest for Ireland with the song *What's Another Year*.

Ian Curtis suicide
18th May 1980 On the eve of Joy Division's first tour of the US, singer Ian Curtis commits suicide. Rather than disband, the rest of the group elect to re-form as New Order with new member Gillian Gilbert on keyboards. The new line-up plays its first gig in Manchester in October.

Led Zeppelin disband
25th September 1980 Led Zeppelin drummer John Bonham is found dead by bandmate John Paul Jones at Robert Plant's house near Windsor. He was 32 and had choked in his sleep after a drinking session. The band decide not to continue and make the announcement in December.

Northern echoes
Echoing the early 1960s, the north west of England is once again a hive of music making. Out of Liverpool's club scene - notably Eric's on Matthew Street - come the Teardrop Explodes and the Mighty Wah! while Manchester's Factory record label is a nursery for the likes of the Fall, Joy Division and A Certain Ratio. Another Factory band, Orchestral Manoeuvres in the Dark (photo), quickly sign with Virgin and make an immediate impression with *Enola Gay*, titled after the plane that dropped the atomic bomb on Hiroshima in 1945.

Super troupers
15th November 1980 Abba's seventh album, *Super Trouper*, sets a record for the most pre-orders (one million) ever received for a UK LP. Fans notice a darker tone to their songs, notably the break-up song The *Winner Takes it All*. Bjorn and Agnetha are now divorced and Benny and Anni-Frid's separation is not yet announced.

Sheena hits the big time
2nd July 1980 Scottish teacher and would-be performer Sheena Easton takes part in BBC TV show *The Big Time*, in which she is groomed for a pop career. The exposure boosts the resulting single, *Modern Girl*, and gives her a first hit. US success and a James Bond theme, *For Your Eyes Only*, follow in 1981.

John Lennon shot dead

8th December 1980 John Lennon is shot four times by a smiling fan, Mark Chapman, as he arrives home at Dakota Flats, Manhattan, from a recording session at the Hit Factory. He dies in hospital half an hour later. He had recently released his first album for four years, *Double Fantasy*, and had been undertaking press interviews to promote it. Lennon had celebrated his 40th birthday in October. The shock felt around the world is palpable. Exactly a week after his death, Yoko Ono asks people all over the world to join in a silent vigil in his memory.

MY FIRST 18 YEARS

TOP10 — 1980

1. **Brass in Pocket** *The Pretenders*
2. **Private Life** *Grace Jones*
3. **One Day I'll Fly Away** *Randy Crawford*
4. **To Cut a Long Story Short** *Spandau Ballet*
5. **Don't Stand So Close to Me** *The Police*
6. **Games Without Fronters** *Peter Gabriel*
7. **Three Minute Hero** *Selecter*
8. **It's Different for Girls** *Joe Jackson*
9. **Let's Get Serious** *Jermaine Jackson*
10. **On the Radio** *Donna Summer*

Open | Search | Scan

The other Elvis

Despite a chip-on-the-shoulder stroppiness that made him enemies in the US during 1979, Elvis Costello is proving one of the most influential artists of the post-punk period. His albums *Armed Forces* and *Get Happy!* are classic angry young man fare with accusing lyrics and rapid-fire delivery, while his production work for the Specials and Squeeze has helped both bands get established.

Industry troubles

The pointers are not great for music as the 1980s begin. Two of the biggest names in global music fall victim to take-over, EMI merging with Thorn Electronics and Decca joining the Polygram roster. Rising oil prices increase the cost of vinyl and prompt record companies to cut back on investment. Blank cassette sales soar while record sales drop, leading the music industry to launch a 'home taping is killing music' campaign.

SPORT

A

You cannot be serious?

Living up to his nickname of Superbrat, John McEnroe's furious outburst at umpire Edward James during a first-round match at Wimbledon on 22nd June makes headlines around the world. McEnroe disputes James's call that his serve was out and in full meltdown screams, 'You cannot be serious!?'. It's an incident that confirms McEnroe's hot-tempered notoriety and goes down in the annals of sporting history. Despite the tantrum, McEnroe's genius takes him all the way to the final where he finally unseats five-times champion Bjorn Borg. Borg, despite winning at the French Open this year, acknowledges there is a new king of centre court and announces his retirement early in 1983 at the age of 26.

Marathon men

The first London Marathon takes place on 29th March. 6,747 Runners take part with 6,255 crossing the finish line on Constitution Hill.

Botham's Ashes

During the 51st Ashes series of Test matches between Australia and England, the talismanic all-rounder Ian Botham scores a breathtaking 149 not out during the 3rd Test at Headingley on 16th July, setting Australia a target of 130. Bob Willis then bowls a fearsome spell of 8 for 43 to dismiss Australia for 111. Botham also takes 5-11 in the 4th Test and hits 118 from 102 balls in the 5th. England retain the Ashes 3-1 in what becomes known, quite rightly, as 'Botham's Ashes'.

Rowing revolution

22-year-old Susan Brown, a biochemistry student, becomes the first woman cox in the history of the Oxford-Cambridge boat race when she steers her crew to victory on 4th April.

Davis pots to the top

Steve Davis wins his first World Snooker Championship title at the Crucible Theatre in Sheffield, beating the defending champion Cliff Thorburn in the semi-final and Doug Mountjoy in the final on 20th April by 18 frames to 12. It is the first of eight world championships Davis will win during a decade in which he dominates the sport.

B

---

27 JAN 1981

Rupert Murdoch is permitted to buy The Times without the usual investigation by the Monopolies Commission.

10 FEB 1981

The Coal Board announces plans to close 50 pits employing 30,000 miners.

1 MAR 1981

IRA prisoner, Bobby Sands begins a hunger strike at the Maze prison. He dies on 5th May.

DOMESTIC
NEWS

Yorkshire ripper arrested
5th January 1981 Police arrest 34-year-old lorry driver Peter Sutcliffe on suspicion of being the serial killer known as the Yorkshire Ripper. Sutcliffe has killed thirteen women and attacked seven more. He is found guilty and sentenced to life imprisonment.

The Troubles
1981 sees a continuation of violence associated with the Troubles in Northern Ireland. In the UK there are two major bombings, one at RAF Uxbridge, which is successfully evacuated, and one at the Chelsea Barracks in London which kills two people. A parcel bomb addressed to the Prime Minister is intercepted and defused, and a coal ship, the *Nellie M,* is bombed and sunk by the Provisional IRA. January sees the murders of former MP Sir Norman Stronge and his son James, and an attack on civil rights campaigner MP Bernadette McAliskey who is shot nine time in her home.'

March for jobs
30th May 1981 London plays host to over 100,000 people from across the country as they come together to protest unemployment and economic deprivation in the 'March for Jobs', organised by the Trade Union Congress.

New Cross house fire
18th January 1981 A party at a house in New Cross ends in tragedy as a fire claims the lives of thirteen young people aged 14-22. The victims are black, and many believe the fire to be a case of arson. Moved by the tragedy, 20,000 people take to the streets.

ZX81 computer launches
5th March 1981 The ZX81 is launched by Sinclair Research, intended to provide an affordable at-home computer to the public. It is small and simple and connects to a television set rather than coming with its own screen, with a cheaper cost for those who are prepared to assemble it themselves. 1.5 million devices are sold.

Humber Bridge opens
17th July 1981 Her Majesty Queen Elizabeth II arrives in Hessle for the opening of the Humber Bridge. The longest of its type in the world, the bridge connects Barton-upon-Humber in the south, with Hessle in the north, allowing traffic to flow across the Humber estuary.

27 APR 1981	**8 MAY** 1981	**11 JUN** 1981
Paul McCartney's band Wings breaks-up.	Ken Livingstone is elected leader of the Greater London Council (GLC).	The Queen opens Europe's tallest building - the Natwest Tower in the City of London.

Penlee lifeboat disaster
19th December 1981 A rescue mission off the coast of Cornwall goes badly wrong when the lifeboat RNLB *Solomon Browne* is dispatched to rescue the crew of the MV *Union Star*. Despite reaching the vessel and evacuating some of the men, both ships are soon overcome by the Force 12 gales, and the sixteen men on board are lost. The volunteers aboard the lifeboat all receive posthumous medals for bravery and a devastated community raises £3 million for their village.

A year of riots
1981 sees a wave of riots sweep the country, mostly associated with rising racial tensions. In April the Brixton riots see clashes between the police and black youths which injure 300 people and cause serious damage to property, with riots following in Finsbury Park and Ealing. June sees clashes in Coventry at a National Front march and riots in Peckham, before rioting in Southall follows the deaths of an Asian Muslim family killed by arson in Walthamstow. Riots in Toxteth, Liverpool, and Moss Side, Manchester, are the most prominent across fifteen days of violence that sweep the country.

ROYALTY &
POLITICS

End of an era
Princess Alice, Countess of Athlone, the last surviving grandchild of Queen Victoria, dies on 3rd January at Kensington Palace at the age of 97 years and 313 days.

Shots fired at Queen
On 13th June, the Queen is riding her horse, Burmese, at the annual Trooping of the Colour ceremony, when Marcus Sarjeant fires six blank shots at her. The Queen calmly settles Burmese who is momentarily startled while Serjeant is apprehended and later charged under the 1842 Treason Act. He is sentenced to five years in prison.

Moira reads the news
The BBC's Moira Stuart becomes the first black woman newsreader on television this year. Born in London to Caribbean parents, Stuart is known for her calm, poise, and silken voice.

Charles pops the question
After months of intense speculation, Buckingham Palace announces the engagement of Prince Charles and Lady Diana Spencer on February 24th. The couple pose for the press with Diana wearing a blue skirt suit from Harrods to set off her sapphire engagement ring.

13 JUL 1981	**5 AUG** 1981	**10 SEP** 1981
Martin Hurson is the sixth IRA hunger striker to die.	After touring depressed areas of Merseyside, Michael Heseltine announces a series of measures to help alleviate problems.	Start of Day of the Triffids on BBC1, based on the 1951 science-fiction novel by John Wyndham.

1981

Charles and Di say 'I do'

After six months of frenzied anticipation with the nation in the grip of royal wedding fever, Prince Charles and Lady Diana Spencer marry at St. Paul's Cathedral on 29th July. The 750 million viewers who tune in to watch the wedding finally get their first glimpse of the much-discussed wedding dress, a style which launches a thousand meringue gowns and appears to need a good iron. Nevertheless, it is a glorious spectacle, with all the pomp and pageantry expected and when during the vows a radiant but understandably nervous Diana stumbles over the order of her husband's Christian names, it makes the world love her even more.

Gang of Four

William Rodgers, David Owen, Roy Jenkins and Shirley Williams announce a break from the Labour party with their formation of the Council for Social Democracy on 25th January, the prototype of a new party intended to fight for social justice. The so-called Gang of Four form the SDP and on 16th June announce an alliance with David Steel's Liberal party to fight the next general election as a single organisation.

Anne Frank's diary

1st January 1981 Five months after the death of Anne's father Otto Frank, Anne Frank's original diary is released.

Hostages returned

11h January 1981 The day after Ronald Reagan is sworn in as the 40th President of the US, Iran releases the 52 hostages it has been holding since the storming of the US embassy in 1979. They are set free in return for nearly eight billion dollars of Iranian assets frozen in American banks.

Reagan shot

30th March 1981 Ronald Reagan and four others are shot outside the Hilton Hotel in Washington DC by John Hinckley Jr. A bullet punctures the President's lung and he is close to death on arrival at hospital. Prompt action saves his life.

DO YOU REMEMBER THIS?

Kenner Star Wars figures

---

12 OCT 1981

A report finds that the traditional nuclear family is beginning to fragment as one in eight children live in a single-parent family.

26 NOV 1981

Shirley Williams wins the by-election at Crosby, Merseyside, overturning a Conservative majority of 19,272.

8 DEC 1981

Arthur Scargill is elected president of the National Union of Mineworkers.

Space shuttle
12th April 1981 Six years after the famous handshake between the US and the Soviet Union in space and twenty years to the day since Yuri Gagarin became the first human in space, NASA launches the first space shuttle. This is a reusable spacecraft designed to efficiently transport people and cargo into space. Columbia flies 36 laps around the Earth and lands in California 54.5 hours later.

Attempt on the Pope
13th May 1981 Pope John Paul II is shot twice as he enters St Peter's Square in Vatican City. He survives the assassination attempt by a Turkish gunman, Mehmet Ali Agca, who Pope John Paul II will meet two years later in jail.

AIDS identified
5th June 1981 General practitioner Joel Weisman encounters a number of homosexual young men in his practice, all of whom suffer from a reduced number of white blood cells. A few months later, Weisman publishes a report for the US Centers for Disease Control with immunologist Michael Gottlieb concerning a disease which will soon be known by the acronym AIDS (acquired immunodeficiency syndrome).

Fast and invisible
18th June 1981 The F-117 Nighthawk, the newest American fighter aircraft, is a precision bomber with a remarkably futuristic, angular appearance designed to be difficult to detect with radar. This first aircraft with so-called stealth properties is almost invisible to the enemy.

Sadat assassinated
6th October 1981 Egyptian President Anwar Sadat is assassinated in an attack by the Islamic Jihad during a military parade. It follows a failed coup in June after which he ordered a mass round-up of his Islamist opponents. Vice-President Hosni Mubarak is wounded but takes office as Sadat's successor.

TGV in service
27th September 1981 The first paying passengers board the brand new TGV at Gare de Lyon station in Paris. This *train à grande vitesse* takes travellers at top speeds of around 300 km/h.

 **ENTERTAINMENT**

Nanny
The series *Nanny* starts on BBC1 on 10th January with Wendy Craig as Barbara Gray, a divorcee and new nanny whose itinerant career sees her moving around, taking positions with a succession of dysfunctional upper-class families where she works her Mary Poppins magic on her charges.

1981

De Niro is a knockout
Robert de Niro fully commits to his leading role in Martin Scorsese's master-piece, *Raging Bull*, the story of the rise and fall of boxer Jake LaMotta. He takes up boxing, becoming a serious contend-er, and in order to authentically portray LaMotta's post-boxing descent into a bloated has-been, goes on a gastronomic tour of France and Italy to gain weight. His efforts are not in vain, and he wins the Academy Award for best actor this year.

Thinking aloud
Think Again, presented by Johnny Ball, begins on 16th January and is billed in the *Radio Times* as 'an entertaining excur-sion into an aspect of everyday life that you might be taking for granted'. *Think Again* tackles a wide range of subjects, explaining how everything works from the publishing industry and financial markets to the national grid with Ball managing to be both upbeat and jokey, but also clear and concise; a true leading light of factual entertainment.

Raiders of the Lost Ark
Harrison Ford, his stock high following two stints as Han Solo in *Star Wars*, takes on the role of archaeologist-adventurer Indiana Jones in *Raiders of the Lost Ark* which opens in UK cinemas on 30th July. Armed with his fedora and bullwhip, Indy is on a quest to find the Lost Ark of the Covenant before the Nazis do and has to negotiate various obstacles on the way: a pit of vipers, unfriendly bandits and a rumbling boulder relentlessly pursuing him through a cavern.

Time Bandits
Terry Gilliam invites fellow Pythons, John Cleese and Michael Palin, to join him as he directs this time travel fantasy, in which a boy finds himself slipping through time and space in the company of a gang of dwarfs who are using a stolen map to steal treasures. They bump into Robin Hood, Agamemnon, and Napoleon along the way.

The Art of Darts
Darts game show Bullseye begins on ITV on 28th September, with Jim Bowen as host. With audiences of 20 million *Bullseye* serves up many a head-in-hands moment.

Postman Pat
Everyone's favourite postman makes his screen debut on 16th September. As well as delivering mail to the residents of Greendale, the community-minded *Postman Pat* helps to solve their daily dilemmas and problems, ably assisted by his faithful black and white cat, Jess.

Language, Timothy!
The BBC1 sitcom *Sorry!*, first broadcasts on 12th March, with diminutive Ronnie Corbett as Timothy Lumsden, a mild-mannered librarian in his forties, browbeaten by his domineering mother (Barbara Lott) into permanently living at home. Timothy's attempts to find a girlfriend and make a life for himself are repeatedly thwarted by mummy while his father, equally under the thumb, occasionally issues a stern, 'Language, Timothy!' from behind his newspaper, usually as a result of mis-hearing his son. *Sorry!* continues for seven series and by the final episode in 1988, when Timothy finally finds happiness with girlfriend Pippa, Corbett is fifty-seven years old!

Donkey Kong
Nintendo release the arcade game *Donkey Kong* in July. After Nintendo's *Radar Scope* (their answer to Space Invaders) failed, it is the firm's first global success and rescues them from financial ruin.

Chariots of Fire
'The British are coming' announces Colin Welland in his acceptance speech after winning the best screenplay Oscar for *Chariots of Fire*. The film wins four Academy Awards in total, including best picture and best soundtrack for Vangelis's unforgettable, swelling electronic theme song. A true story of two remarkable men and their rivalry at the 1924 Paris Olympics, this uplifting piece of period perfection is guaranteed to bring a lump to your throat.

Impulse buy
Impulse body spray, available in five different fragrances including 'Gipsy' and 'Hint of Musk', launches a memorable UK TV commercial this year, with a woman pursued through the streets by a man desperate to present her with a hastily purchased bunch of flowers, having caught a whiff of her magnetic scent, it's all because 'Men can't help acting on impulse.'

Ken and Deirdre get spliced
Jumping on the royal wedding bandwagon, Ken Barlow and Deirdre Langton say 'I do' on *Coronation Street*, on 27th July, two days before Charles and Di. Viewers, all 21 million of them, are amazed to see Deirdre without her trademark saucer-sized specs for once.

Cats opens in West End
Andrew Lloyd Webber's (photo) musical, *Cats*, based on T. S. Eliot's *Old Possum's Book of Practical Cats*, opens at the New London Theatre on 11th May. The musical is revolutionary; it's sung-through, and performed partly in the round with a hidden orchestra so the audience are part of an immersive experience. Lloyd Webber mortgages his house to help fund the venture, a risk worth taking as *Cats* runs for 8,949 performances until 2002; a benchmark for a new brand of blockbuster musical.

The Fizz come first at Eurovision
The Eurovision Song Contest takes place in Dublin on 4th April with a win for the United Kingdom thanks to Bucks Fizz, and the song *Making Your Mind Up*.

Noele reaches a career crossroads
Noele Gordon has played Meg Richardson in ITV's *Crossroads* since it first began in 1964. When Central TV take over the franchise from ATV, they plan a revamp which includes ridding the show of Meg. When the announcement is made in June there is public outrage; Gordon has been voted favourite female personality by *TV Times* readers no fewer than eight times. She makes her final appearance on 12th November.

Stately homes and teddy bears
The adaptation of Evelyn Waugh's 1945 novel, *Brideshead Revisited* on 12th October is one of the year's television events. Jeremy Irons is Charles Ryder who while at Oxford befriends Lord Sebastian Flyte played by Anthony Andrews. Invited to stay at Sebastian's palatial family pile, Brideshead Castle, Charles is dazzled and seduced by the Flyte family and finds his life interwoven with theirs over the coming years. Filming the seven two-hour episodes took forty-two weeks in total.

MUSIC

Collins goes solo
9th February 1981 Genesis singer-drummer and all-round workaholic Phil Collins releases his first album, *Face Value*, so beginning a phenomenal solo career running parallel with the band. Intensely personal and melancholic in tone, most of the album's songs concern his recent divorce from his wife Andrea.

Lennon tribute
7th February 1981 The shock waves from John Lennon's murder continue. Written by John for his *Imagine* album in 1971, *Jealous Guy* is the song that the re-formed Roxy Music choose when asked to honour Lennon on a German TV show. Liking the result, they release the track and achieve Roxy's first and only UK No. 1 during March.

Antmusic
9th May 1981 Adam and the Ants confirm their status as the pop sensations of the moment with *Stand and Deliver*, a No. 1 for five weeks. Adam is art student Stuart Goddard who dresses in pirate gear and Native American face paint and has a signature sound combining tribal drums and Gary Glitter-like hollers. It's a potent mix adored by the colour-rich teen pop magazines like *Smash Hits* now starting to appear in newsagents.

MTV opens

1st August 1981 A media revolution begins in the US with the launch of cable channel Music Television (MTV), devoted to playing music. It's a whole new marketing medium for the music industry but the channel is at first almost wholly reliant on UK record companies for material, as US labels aren't yet attuned to the potential of the promo video. The result is a new 'British invasion' of acts who break through in the US on the basis of their videos.

Ross sets a record

14th May 1981 After saying goodbye to Motown Records by duetting with Lionel Richie on the film theme *Endless Love*, Diana Ross ends her 21-year association with the label by signing for RCA in a deal worth twenty million dollars - an industry record. The move pays an immediate dividend with a No. 4 UK placing for a revival of Frankie Lymon's *Why Do Fools Fall in Love*.

Ghost Town

11th July 1981 Never has a record been more chillingly timed than the Specials' *Ghost Town*, which reaches No. 1 just as widespread rioting adds to the all-round malaise that pervades early 1980s Britain. It's the last record that the Specials will make in the band's current form: Neville Staples, Lynval Golding and Terry Hall are poised to form the Fun Boy Three. In the chart at the same time is another Midlands band with a Jamaican sound and a sharp political message: Birmingham's UB40 with *One in Ten*, about the ten per cent who now make up the unemployed in the UK.

Marley is dead

11th May 1981 Bob Marley, the great creative force in contemporary reggae and a peacemaker between warring factions in his native Jamaica, dies of cancer aged 36. After being diagnosed with a melanoma in his right foot he refused to have it amputated because of his Rastafarian beliefs. The cancer spread to his brain, lungs and liver. He is given a state funeral in Jamaica on 21st May.

Ballet spruce

16th August 1981 Out of the Blitz club in Covent Garden come Spandau Ballet, formed by brothers Gary and Martin Kemp. A feature on TV's *20th Century Box* launches them as a 'new romantic' band, as important for the styles they wear - anything from kilts to loin cloths - as the synth-led dance music they play. With Tony Hadley's trained voice giving them real distinction, the Spandaus reject punk gloom and embrace the lure of fantasy and dressing up. The funky *Chant No. 1* cements the band's rise.

Whole lotta Shakin' goin' on

28th March 1981 For many years Shakin' Stevens and his band the Sunsets were the hottest draw on the UK's rock'n'roll revival circuit playing Elvis. Now the Cardiff-born singer is at No. 1 with a brilliant rockabilly-style re-creation of the 1950s Rosemary Clooney hit *This Ole House.*

MY FIRST 18 YEARS TOP 10 — 1981

1. **Labelled with Love** *Squeeze*
2. **New Life** *Depeche Mode*
3. **Don't You Want Me** *Human League*
4. **In the Air Tonight** *Phil Collins*
5. **Being with You** *Smokey Robinson*
6. **Celebration** *Kool and the Gang*
7. **Bette Davis Eyes** *Kim Carnes*
8. **Kids in America** *Kim Wilde*
9. **I Go to Sleep** *The Pretenders*
10. **Once in a Lifetime** *Talking Heads*

Open | Search | Scan

Electro magnets

For a long time synthesisers were just a prog rock thing, but cheaper technology and the advent of the Roland drum machine in particular have changed the game. Allied to a showy 'new romantic' look, the electro sound is everywhere in the early 80s, whether in the hands of singer-plus-synth duos like Soft Cell (*Tainted Love*), Tears for Fears (*Mad World*) and Yazoo (*Only You*) or bands with a more art school bent like Sheffield's Heaven 17 and Human League. Some like ABC and Depeche Mode (photo) embrace the whole pop experience while others like Ultravox remain a bit aloof. The failure of the latter's somewhat pompous *Vienna* to shift Joe Dolce's novelty hit *Shaddup Your Face* from No. 1 is treated in some quarters like a national scandal.

Julio on the ball

5th December 1981 Once a promising young goalkeeper for Real Madrid, Julio Iglesias turned to singing when a car accident ended his football career. He now brings a whiff of old style tuxedo-and-bow-tie glamour to the UK chart with an ice-cream smooth chart-topping version of *Begin the Beguine*, written by Cole Porter in 1935.

League of their own

11th December 1981 Human League score the year's top-selling single and a Christmas No. 1 with *Don't You Want Me*, a really clever combination of a great pop break-up pop song, a synth-led soundtrack and a film noir-style video.

PHOTO CREDITS Copyright 2024, TDM Rights BV.

Photos: **A** Mirrorpix - Getty Images / **B** PA Images - Getty Images / **C** Central Press - Hulton Archive - Getty Images / **D** PA Images - Getty Images / **E** Avalon - Hulton Archive - Getty Images / **F** Tim Graham Photo Library - Getty Images / **G** Bettman - Getty Images / **H** Keystone - Hulton Archive - Getty Images / **I** Catie Falkenberg - Los Angeles Times - Getty Images / **J** Heritage Images - Hulton Archive - Getty Images / **K** Heritage Images - Hulton Archive - Getty Images / **L** Sunset Boulevard - Corbis Historical - Getty Images / **M** Studiocanal Films Ltd - Mary Evans / **N** Classic Media Rubicon Group Holding - Ronald Grant - Mary Evans / **O** Paramount Pictures - Moviepix - Getty Images / **P** Hilaria McCarthy - Hulton Archive - Getty Images / **Q** PA Images - Getty Images / **R** Fox Photos - Hulton Archive - Getty Images / **S** Ronald Grant Archive - Mary Evans / **T** AF Archive - Mary Evans / **U** Bill Marino - Sygma - Getty Images / **V** Michael Putland - Hulton Archive - Getty Images / **W** Paul Natkin - WireImage - Getty Images / **X** Chris Walter - WireImage - Getty Images / **Y** Michael Putland - Hulton Archive - Getty Images / **Z** Mirrorpix - Getty Images / **A2** Michael Putland - ulton Archive - Getty Images / **B2** Stills - Gamma-Rapho - Getty Images.

SPORT

Streaking for England

On 2nd January, during an international rugby match between England and Australia at Twickenham, Erika Roe runs onto the pitch and strips off her top and bra, much to the appreciation of the half-time crowd. Hustled off by police who cover her assets with a flag and helmet, the incident - described by the BBC as 'perhaps the most famous of all streaks' - makes front-page news.

Rebels suffer cricket ban

Fifteen English cricket players are banned from international cricket for three years, as a penalty for a 'rebel' tour of South Africa currently in progress.

Feel the burn

Jane Fonda's Workout video sparks a new craze for aerobics, women's fitness - and legwarmers - as Jane takes a rapidly growing fan base of keep fit devotees through routines to tone and hone, telling us to 'Feel the burn' and 'No pain, no gain'.

Disappearance of Mark Thatcher

12th January 1982 Mark Thatcher, son of Prime Minster Margaret Thatcher, is officially declared missing after a four-day loss of contact during the Paris-Dakar Rally. Missing somewhere in the Sahara alongside his driver and mechanic, a large search is launched by the Algerian military who finally locate him two days later, 31 miles off course.

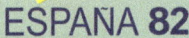

ESPAÑA 82

'The Best England Team That Never Won'?

England arrive at the World Cup in Spain with a line-up that includes Bryan Robson, Ray Wilkins, Kevin Keegan, Terry Butcher and Trevor Francis. England look like the team to watch during the group stages, beating France 3-1 in an inspired first match. They win the group but are next drawn against title holders West Germany and then Spain. Both matches are a draw; a missed header from Keegan against Spain is blamed on his perm softening the power of his attack. Despite scoring six goals in the tournament, conceding just one and not losing a match, England are knocked out and head home.

26 JAN 1982

UK unemployment figures reach 3,000,000 for the first time since the 1930s.

12 FEB 1982

George Davis opens the first Next clothing store. By the end of July, there are 70 branches around the country.

4 MAR 1982

The Barbican Centre is opened by the Queen after 11 years of construction and budget-blowing £153 million.

Watson wins Open double

American golfer Tom Watson becomes only the fifth man to win both the US and British Opens in the same year amongst the challenging bunkers at Royal Troon on 19th July.

A golden Commonwealth Games

The Commonwealth Games take place in Brisbane from 30th September to 9th October. Great Britain's gold medal tally is 38, one behind Australia.

First papal visit to UK

28th May 1982 Pope John Paul II becomes the first reigning Pope to visit the UK. Drawing crowds of thousands, his 'Pope-mobile' transports him around nine cities where he delivers speeches and open-air Masses.

DOMESTIC NEWS

DO YOU REMEMBER THIS?

VHS video recorder

Collapse of Laker Airways

5th February 1982 Laker Airways succumbs to increased competition and strategic behaviour in the aviation industry when it collapses leaving 6,000 passengers stranded. The airline's owner, Freddie Laker, sues 12 airlines for conspiracy, reaching an out of court settlement of $50 million.

Israeli ambassador shot

3rd June 1982 The 1982 Lebanon War breaks out after the attempted assassination of Israel's ambassador to the UK, Shlomo Argov. Attending a banquet at the Dorchester Hotel, Argov is seriously injured. He never fully recovers, remaining in hospital until his death in 2003.

Falklands War

2nd April 1982 War breaks out after the invasion of the Falkland Islands by Argentine forces. The British Falkland Islands government surrenders and the British surprise many from around the world by immediately dispatching a Royal Navy task force to recover the islands. Over the next the three months the public are gripped by events such as the sinking of the *General Belgrano*, HMS *Sheffield*, and HMS *Coventry*, and the *Battle of Goose Green*. The war lasts 74 days and ends with the surrender of Argentine forces at Port Stanley. 255 British and 649 Argentine lives are lost in the conflict.

2 APR 1982

Britain breaks off diplomatic relations with Argentina.

12 MAY 1982

The *QE2* leaves for the Falkland Islands

30 JUN 1982

Crimewatch begins on BBC1, aiming to highlight unsolved crimes and enlist the help of the public by asking for information.

20 pence coin introduced
9th June 1982
Further changes to the currency are made when the new 20 pence coin is introduced with 740 million

minted in the first issue. The new coin is a heptagon, and features a crowned Tudor rose on the reverse.

Hyde and Regent's Park bombs
20th July 1982 Two bombs planted by the Provisional IRA explode in central London. One bomb, in Hyde Park, targets mounted soldiers of the Household Cavalry regiment the 'Blues and Royals'. Four soldiers and seven horses are killed when a car bomb explodes as the soldiers ride past. Two hours later, a second bomb in Regent's Park explodes beneath a bandstand where the band of the Royal Green Jackets are performing to a large crowd. Seven bandsmen are killed, and across both attacks a further 51 people are injured.

Last telegrams sent
30th September 1982 The closure of the UK Inland Telegram Service means the UK says goodbye to

the telegram, a mode of communication in use for over 100 years.

Mary Rose raised
11th October 1982 The wreck of Henry VIII's flagship, the *Mary Rose*, is raised from the Solent after its discovery in 1971. The wreck is moved to a dry dock at the Portsmouth Historic Dockyard; a special museum opens to display the extraordinary artefacts discovered with it.

Droppin Well bombing
6th December 1982 A bomb planted by the Irish National Liberation Army explodes at a disco known as Droppin Well in Ballykelly. Many people are wounded and seventeen are killed, eleven of them British soldiers from the nearby barracks who were known to frequent the disco.

ROYALTY &
POLITICS

Riding with Reagan
The Queen invites US President Ronald Reagan and First Lady Nancy Reagan to stay at Windsor Castle. Reagan and Her Majesty go riding together in Windsor Home Park on the morning of 8th June; it is clear they have bonded over their shared love of horses.

Stranger danger
Early in the morning of 9th July, an unemployed North London labourer manages to break into Buckingham Palace and find his way to the Queen's bedroom undetected, where he appears with a bottle of wine found in the royal cellar. The Queen keeps calm and talks to the intruder until a maid and her page discover the situation and are able to raise the alarm.

19 JUL 1982
After admitting to a homosexual affair, the Queen's bodyguard, Michael Trestrail, resigns.

30 AUG 1982
St. David's Hall opens in the heart of Cardiff as a national concert hall for Wales.

22 SEP 1982
Prime Minister Margaret Thatcher arrives in China for talks over the future of Hong Kong.

1982

A midsummer prince is born

On 21st June, Prince Charles drives his wife to the Lindo Wing of St. Mary's Hospital where at 9:30pm she gives birth to a 7lb 1 ½ oz baby boy. Emerging from the hospital, Charles is greeted by chants of 'For He's a Jolly Good Fellow' and tells waiting reporters that he and Diana were still discussing names. Prince William Arthur Philip Louis, who is second in line to the throne, is christened at Buckingham Palace on 4th August.

Pope stabbed

12th May 1982 Less than a year since the last attempt on his life, Pope John Paul II is the intended victim of another attack. At the shrine at Fatima, a Spanish priest opposed to the Pope's reforms stabs him with a bayonet and is overcome by guards. The Pope is slightly injured but not in mortal danger. The priest is jailed for three years and excommunicated.

A new music medium

17th August 1982 Soon after the first commercially available compact disc player, the Sony CDP-101, is launched,  the first CD goes on sale. It is a 1979 recording of Chopin waltzes played by the Chilean pianist Claudio Arrau.

Commodore 64

With more than ten million copies sold, the Commodore 64 is the best-selling personal computer in history. The computer consists of a thick keyboard with 64 kilobytes of RAM underneath and a cassette port for loading games and professional software. It surpasses many more expensive competitors with its flexible hardware and great sound.

FOREIGN
NEWS

Climate change

1st January 1982 An alarming report by US researchers Atkins and Epstein shows that sea levels have risen by eleven centimetres since 1940. The reason: in the same time, 50,000 cubic kilometres of ice have melted at the North and South Poles. Sea level rise provides hard evidence that the Earth is warming.

Computer virus

30th January 1982 The first computer virus is found on a private PC. The Elk Cloner Virus is written during a winter vacation by fifteen-year-old student Richard Skrenta. It embeds itself via the floppy into the operating system, from where it copies itself onto every floppy inserted in the floppy drive.

2 OCT 1982

Popular Birmingham comic, Jasper Carrott, moves to the BBC with a new, live show called *Carrott's Lib*.

NOV 1982

The government announce that 400,000 houses have been purchased under its right-to-buy scheme.

15 DEC 1982

Gibraltar's border with Spain is opened after thirteen years.

Diet Coke

According to Coca-Cola, women drink too little of its brand, so the soft drink giant devises an attractive variant for those who are thinking about dieting: Diet Coke. The light version comes a full eighteen years after rival Pepsi launched Diet Pepsi and contains the sweetener aspartame instead of sugar, good for only thirteen instead of 142 kilocalories per can.

Princess Grace dies

13th September 1982 Princess Grace of Monaco, the former movie actress Grace Kelly, suffers a stroke while driving near her home. She dies in hospital the next day, aged 52. Over  400 dignitaries attend her funeral including Diana, Princess of Wales.

:-)

19th September 1982 At Carnegie Mellon University in Pittsburgh, a student prank prompts discussion about the limits of jokes. Computer scientist Scott Fahlman proposes labelling all messages on the digital notice board. If something is intended as a joke, you mark your message with :-). If the remark is meant to be serious, you add :-(to your message. The first emoticons are born.

Andropov replaces Brezhnev

10th November 1982 The death of Soviet leader Leonid Brezhnev is announced. His successor is KGB head Yuri Andropov who remains in post for fifteen months before his own death paves the way for Mikhail Gorbachev to take over.

ENTERTAINMENT

Bling *Dynasty*

Shoulder pads at the ready. *Dynasty* first airs on BBC1 on 1st May. The super-rich Carringtons of Denver, Colorado, headed by patriarch Blake Carrington (John Forsythe) have made their money in oil. Sound familiar? ABC creates the Aaron Spelling-produced *Dynasty* as a direct response to the success of CBS's *Dallas*, serving up supersize helpings of glitz, glamour, feuding, cat fights, bed hopping and preposterous storylines. The soap has moderate success in its first season, but the dramatic entrance of Joan Collins as Blake's first wife, Alexis, gives Dynasty a boost and by the mid-80s, it's a ratings winner. Despite the camp and melodrama, this is a show that puts older women centre stage, all while dressed to the nines by Nolan Miller. Quite simply, *Dynasty* is the show that defines the excess of the 1980s.

Bladerunner - beautiful dystopia

Widely recognised as a masterpiece of science-fiction cinema, *Blade Runner*, directed by Ridley Scott, is first shown in the UK at the Edinburgh International Film Festival in August. Set in a dystopian Los Angeles of 2019, Harrison Ford is detective Rick Deckard, searching out 'replicants' - androids masquerading as humans - while unwittingly falling for one (Sean Young). Scott's jaw-dropping sets show a future that is bleak but also beautiful.

1982

Dear Diary

The Secret Diary of Adrian Mole aged 13 and ¾ by Sue Townsend is published on 7th October. Adrian's daily ruminations not only reveal his innermost thoughts about his love for posh Pandora, his parents' marriage breakdown or the pain of trying to cover his Noddy wallpaper with black paint, but also act as an amusing guide to the early 1980s as he shares his views on the royal wedding, the Falklands War, Margaret Thatcher and Selina Scott.

Feeling blue

The Smurfs, the little blue people in Phyrgian caps created by Belgian artist Pierre 'Peyo' Culliford, have become a global phenomenon, with the film, *Smurfs and the Magic Flute* released in the UK in 1979, a hit song with Father Abraham in 1977 and 32 million collectible figures sold in 1981 alone.

Fame

'Fame costs, and right here's where you start paying - with sweat.' So goes the stern warning from Debbie Allan in the opening credits of *Fame*, the TV series based on the 1980 film in which Allan played dance teacher Lydia Grant. First broadcast on BBC1 on 17th June, for several years in the 1980s, thousands of UK teenagers wish they were students at the New York School of Performing Arts alongside Leroy, Doris, Bruno et al, where spontaneously breaking out into dance routines or belting out a heart-rending ballad at the piano seem a natural part of the daily timetable.

Rambo

Vietnam veteran John J. Rambo is on the run from the law and fighting his demons in *Rambo: First Blood*. Sylvester Stallone, pumped up and oiled, co-writes and stars in this box office smash, which inspires one of the easiest fancy dress outfits of the 1980s. Headband, check. Sweaty vest, check, A toy machine gun and round of ammo check. *Rambo* opens at UK cinemas on 16th December.

Gizza job

At the time *Boys from the Black Stuff* is shown on BBC2 between 10th October and 12th November, there are three million unemployed in Britain, making Alan Bleasdale's powerful drama a timely parable on the human cost of economic policy under Margaret Thatcher. A group of men, once part of a tarmac crew ('the black stuff') return to a Liverpool in the grip of industrial decline, to find the only jobs available are illegal and cash in hand.

Channel 4 launches

On 2nd November Channel 4 launches, with an ambitious menu of programmes. Quiz show *Countdown* (photo) has the honour of opening proceedings and continues as a mainstay of the channel for the next 40 years. A new soap, *Brookside*, set in a cul-de-sac of a modern housing estate in Liverpool, promises juicy, issue-led storylines considering it's the creation of Phil Redmond, best-known for *Grange Hill*, and on 5th November, a young bunch of comedians star in an Enid Blyton spoof, *Five Go Mad In Dorset*, under the name, *The Comic Strip Presents...*, among them Dawn French and Jennifer Saunders.

The Tube

Anarchic music programme *The Tube* broadcasts live from Tyne Tees studio in Newcastle for the first time on 5th November. Jools Holland, who is lead presenter with Paula Yates, later recalls of their audition, 'The TV people said we were hopeless but they couldn't stop watching us.' It's chaotic but cool, with an eclectic line-up every week from big names to new acts.

Scumbag students

Alternative comedy explodes onto screens on 9th November on BBC2 with *The Young Ones*. Written by Ben Elton, Rik Mayall and Lise Mayer, the action is set in the squalid flat of four Scumbag College students, violent punk Vyvyan, downtrodden hippy Neil, a self-important Rik (who worships Cliff Richard) and cool, calm Mike. It's a sitcom in the most anarchic, surreal and often puerile sense of the word.

Gandhi

Richard Attenborough's twenty-year quest to tell the on-screen story of Mohandas Kharamchand Gandhi finally comes to fruition with the release of *Gandhi* in cinemas on 3rd December. Ben Kingsley went full method in taking on the lead role; losing weight, and even learning to spin cotton. Attenborough too cut no corners in this epic, three-hour long film that uses authentic historical locations and hundreds of thousands of extras. *Gandhi* wins eight Academy Awards including Best Picture, Best Director for Attenborough and Best Actor for Kingsley.

The Sloane Ranger Handbook

The Official Sloane Ranger Handbook by Peter York and Ann Barr of *Harper's & Queen* magazine becomes a bestseller this year. Mildly self-deprecating but hugely amusing, the manual offers rules for wannabe and established Sloanes,

an upper-class species found roaming around Chelsea and Fulham or at home counties shooting parties. They're the types that wear pie crust collars, pearls, and Hunter wellies; who consider a crash in the Land Rover to be a mere prang, but the wrong shade of blue on a Tuesday to be an utter disaster. High priestess of this cult is Princess Diana, who features front and centre on the cover of this arch observation on a peculiarly British phenomenon.

Quatro

Fruity canned fizzy drink Quatro is launched this year claiming its place as a soft drink to define the decade with a TV advert where the tropical beverage is formulated in an arcade game-style vending machine, operated by a dude with a mullet. Quatro's fizz goes flat eventually, and it is discontinued in the UK in 1989.

A Touch of Glass

In the 2nd December episode of *Only Fools & Horses*, Delboy and Rodney take on a job in a country house cleaning chandeliers. Nothing ever goes smoothly where the Trotters are concerned, and this is no exception. The smashing climax becomes one of the sitcom's best-loved moments.

Walking in the Air

A Christmas tradition is born on Boxing Day this year when Raymond Briggs's 1978 illustrated book *The Snowman* is brought to life in an animation directed by Dianne Jackson for Channel 4. The

combination of Briggs' illustrations together with a score by Howard Blake (including *Walking in the Air* sung by St. Paul's Cathedral choir boy Peter Auty) makes *The Snowman* one of television's most timeless and magical festive treats. The following year, *The Snowman* has the added cachet of an introduction by none other than David Bowie.

E.T. phone home

E.T.'s strange but appealing appearance was apparently created by superimposing the eyes and forehead of Einstein onto a baby's face. Steven Spielberg's sweet extra-terrestrial proves not all aliens are out to get us in this charming film, released 13th August, which has the world repeating E.T.'s plaintive request, 'E.T. phone home.'

MUSIC

Ozzy's year
20th January 1982 Assuming it's made of rubber, Ozzy Osbourne bites into a live bat thrown from the audience at a gig in Des Moines, Iowa. But it's not the worst thing to happen to him this year: in March, a light aircraft in which his lead guitarist Randy Rhoads is a passenger, clips Ozzy's tour bus and crashes. Rhoads, his pilot and another passenger are killed. More happily, Ozzy marries Sharon Arden in Hawaii on 4th July.

Olivia gets *Physical*

23rd January 1982 Olivia Newton-John's *Physical* spends the last of ten weeks at No. 1 in the US - the longest chart-topping run since Elvis Presley's *Hound Dog* in 1956. It's a big switch of pace for the singer whose fame went up another level with the film *Grease* in 1978. A change of image sees her dressed in Jane Fonda-type aerobics gear (dig those legwarmers) in a curve-accentuating video and singing of, well, physical pleasures.

Goodbye to the Monk
17th February 1982 Jazz piano legend Thelonious Monk, known as the High Priest of Bebop, dies in New Jersey aged 64. His compositions included *Round Midnight* and *Straight, No Chaser*. His most famous saying was 'The piano ain't got no wrong notes.'

Doobies disband
31st March 1982 The Doobie Brothers, America's leading west coast band after the Eagles, announce their break-up. Formed in 1970, their *Listen to the Music* and *What a Fool Believes* remain all-time radio classics.

Rocking the Casbah
24th May 1982 One of the few original punk bands still espousing radical politics, the Clash release *Combat Rock* just as Topper Headon leaves the band and Joe Strummer returns from a mystery disappearance. It includes Clash classics *Rock the Casbah* and *Should I Stay or Should I Go*.

Get the Message
1st July 1982 Released today, *The Message* by Grandmaster Flash and the Furious Five is a genuine milestone. One of the first true hip hop records from a genius of the turntables, it breaks new ground with a portrait of inner-city life that's full of tension and fury.

Celtic soul
7th August 1982 Dexy's Midnight Runners lead man Kevin Rowland fashions a complete change of image - all dungarees and sandals - for the band to tie in with the release of new album *Too-Rye-Ay*. The single *Come On Eileen* harks back to Rowland's Belfast roots while the music is a hybrid that he calls 'Celtic soul', mixing blues rhythms and highly non-trendy folk instrumentation. Can anyone remember the last time an old-fashioned fiddle was heard on a No. 1 single?

Mad about the Boy

23rd September 1982
For UK parents, the sight of Boy George singing *Do You Really Want to Hurt Me* with Culture Club on *Top of the Pops* is one of those classic 'Is it a girl or a boy?' moments. Playing in a reggae-cum-soul style, Culture Club is another band to emerge from the Blitz club, the cradle of London's 'new romantic' scene. George explains that the band's name reflects its mixture of cultures - a gay Irishman on lead vocals, a black Londoner on bass, a white English-man on keyboards and a Jewish drummer.

MY FIRST 18 YEARS
TOP10   1982

1. **I Don't Wanna Dance** *Eddy Grant*
2. **Fame** *Irene Cara*
3. **House of Fun** *Madness*
4. **A Town Called Malice** *The Jam*
5. **Love Plus One** *Haircut 100*
6. **Planet Rock** *Afrika Bambaataa*
7. **Poison Arrow** *ABC*
8. **Centerfold** *J. Geils Band*
9. **Save a Prayer** *Duran Duran*
10. **The Model** *Kraftwerk*

Open 🟢 | Search 🔍 | Scan 📷

Pass the... what?

2nd October 1982 How did a song about passing round a marijuana joint make it to No. 1 - and in the hands of Musical Youth, a five-piece band from Birming-ham whose members are all under eight-een years old? The answer is that they changed the letter 'k' in *Pass the Kutchie* to 'd' and explained to the press that a 'dutchie' was a Jamaican serving dish.

Jackson heights

1st December 1982
Michael Jackson's *Thriller* hits the stores. Continuing his collaboration with producer Quincy Jones and songwriter Rod Temperton, it is set to top the chart in every country of the world and will become the biggest selling album of all time - 45 million copies and counting by 2024. No fewer than seven singles will be extracted from it including the title track, which is supported by a thirteen minute video directed by John Landis and featuring a red jacketed Michael dancing with a horde of zombies.

Marvin reborn

20th November 1982 After leaving Motown and moving to Belgium for tax reasons, Marvin Gaye emerges rejuvenated with *Sexual Healing* from the album *Midnight Love*. Returning to the erotic themes of his *Let's Get it On* period, he jump starts his career and wins his first Grammy award.

Weller splits the Jam

11th December 1982 The Jam play their final gig at Brighton Conference Centre, then disband. It is Paul Weller's decision and bassist Bruce Foxton will not speak to him for twenty years. The band bow out with a last No. 1, *Beat Surrender*.

SPORT

Dev digs deep
In the Cricket World Cup at the Nevill Ground, Tunbridge Wells, India's Kapil Dev gives an incredible individual performance during a group match against Zimbabwe. India have just 17 for 5 when Dev smashes a breathtaking 175 runs off 138 balls; an innings that includes sixteen boundaries and six sixes. Buoyed up by his brilliant performance, India proceed to defeat England and Australia, to reach the final at Lord's where they topple the mighty West Indies by 43 runs.

Jennings reaches 1,000 goal
Arsenal and Northern Ireland goalkeeper Pat Jennings becomes the first footballer in the English league to make one thousand senior appearances, at a match against West Bromwich Albion on 26th February, which, fortunately, is goalless!

Corbiere a winner
Corbiere wins the Grand National on 9th April, the first winner of the legendary steeplechase to be trained by a woman, Jenny Pitman.

World Championships in Helsinki
British athletes prove their worth on the world stage at the World Athletics Championship in Helsinki which has its final day on 14th August. Steve Cram emerges from the shadow of Ovett and Coe to take gold in the 1500m, while Daley Thompson seals victory in the decathlon. Elsewhere, American multi-discipline maestro Carl Lewis (photo) wins gold in the 100m, long jump and 4 x 100m relay.

England defeat the All Blacks
The All Blacks' rugby union tour of England and Scotland reaches its climax at Twickenham on 19th November, when a New Zealand team depleted of more experienced members, but still dangerous, meet England, who have not beaten them on home turf since 1936. In a rough match, beset by injury on both sides, England manage to hold off New Zealand to seal a 15-9 win, thanks in part to a try from Maurice Colclough.

8 JAN 1983
Margaret Thatcher arrives in the Falkland Islands for a four-day visit to British troops.

15 FEB 1983
The Austin Metro is Britain's best-selling car.

15 MAR 1983
The Budget raises tax thresholds, effectively cutting taxes by £2 billion.

DOMESTIC
NEWS

Police drown in Blackpool
5th January 1983 Tragedy strikes Black-pool as three members of the police force, two men and a woman, drown whilst attempting to rescue a man from the sea. The man had gone into the water after his Jack Russell terrier and cannot be saved despite best efforts.

Shooting of Stephen Waldorf
14th January 1983 26-year-old Stephen Waldorf is shot and seriously injured by armed policemen whilst travelling through London in the passenger seat of a friend's car. The police had mistaken Waldorf for an escaped prisoner, David Martin, who would be rearrested two weeks later.

DO YOU REMEMBER THIS?

Double deck cassette recorder

Seatbelts mandatory
31st January 1983 The wearing of seatbelts becomes mandatory across the UK. Seat belts have been essential safety components in cars since 1972, but compliance has been low. This next step of legislation leads to a 30% reduction in fatal injuries of front seat passengers.

Muswell Hill murderer
11th February 1983 Dennis Nielson is arrested and charged with murder after human remains are discovered at his Muswell Hill flat. As the investigation progresses, he is revealed to have mur-dered at least twelve young men and boys since 1978.

New £1 coin
21st April 1983 A new £1 coin is introduced to replace the £1 note, a feature of the British currency since 1797. The new coin features the Queen's portrait on the front, and a different reverse image is issued every year, starting with the royal coat of arms, and followed by emblems reflecting the different nations of the UK.

British Airways S-61 crash
16th July 1983 A British Airways helicopter flight is downed in heavy fog over the Celtic Sea. Twenty people on board are killed, while six are rescued by a lifeboat.

Maze Prison escape
25th September 1983 20 guards are injured, and one dies of a heart attack, when 38 IRA prisoners escape from HM Prison Maze in Northern Ireland. The prisoners escape using guns, smuggled into the prison, to hijack a lorry in what becomes the biggest prison break in British history.

23 APR 1983
The People's March for Jobs sets off from Glasgow, reaching London in early June.

11 MAY 1983
Aberdeen win the European Cup Winner's cup against Real Madrid 2-1.

23 JUN 1983
Monty Python's The Meaning of Life is released, the final film for the Python gang.

Thrust 2 land speed record
4th October 1983 Scottish entrepreneur Richard Noble breaks the land speed record in jet-powered car Thrust 2. Racing over a course in the Black Rock Desert in Nevada, he sets a speed of 634.051 miles per hour.

Brink's-Mat robbery
26th November 1983 A robbery at Heathrow International Trading Estate sees six thieves break into the Brink's-Mat warehouse. Described as the 'crime of the century', the men make away with 6,800 gold bars, diamonds, and cash, in total worth nearly £26 million. Whilst two men are arrested and convicted, most of the stolen goods are never recovered.

ROYALTY &
POLITICS

Thatcher wins second term in office
On June 10th, the Conservatives win a landslide victory in the General Election, with a 144 majority. The decisive victory leads to the resignation of Labour leader Michael Foot and the SDP's Roy Jenkins. On 2nd October, Labour elects 41-year-old Welsh left-winger Neil Kinnock as party leader, with the more moderate Roy Hattersley as deputy leader.

Tory scandal - Cecil Parkinson resigns
Cecil Parkinson, Secretary for Trade and Industry and mastermind of the Tory election campaign, admits to his long-term affair with his former secretary, who is pregnant with his child. Parkinson announces he will not be resigning, and has decided to stay with his wife. But Sara Keays gives an interview to *The Times*, and her revelations force Parkinson, Mrs Thatcher's golden boy (photo), to resign in disgrace. He is replaced by Norman Tebbit.

Harrods bombing
17th December 1983 A car bomb planted by the Provisional IRA explodes outside Harrods department store in London. Despite a warning being received, the area is not evacuated in time and six people are killed alongside 90 injured. Eight days later, on Christmas Day, another bomb explodes on Oxford Street with no casualties.

26 JUL 1983	**1 AUG** 1983	**5 SEP** 1983
Mother of 10, Victoria Gillick, loses a court case against the DHSS to prevent the distribution of contraceptives to under-16s.	Sales of new cars receive a boost as A-prefix car registration plates are introduced.	Adventure cartoon *He-Man and the Masters of the Universe* has its world premiere on Children's ITV.

Queen presents honour

The Queen presents the Order of Merit to Mother Teresa of Calcutta in a ceremony in the grounds of the Presidential Palace in New Delhi.

FOREIGN
NEWS

Switched on

1st January 1983 A switch is turned at the American Advanced Research Projects Agency. The switch marks the beginning of the internet as we know it.

Black holes

1st January 1983 Scientists discovered the first black hole - formed when a star implodes at the end of its existence - in 1971. Now an article appears about a second black hole, 170,000 light-years from Earth. It is smaller than Scotland, but weighs ten times as much as the Sun.

Fake Hitler diaries

30th January 1983 Fifty years after Adolf Hitler came to power, 62 of his diaries are found in Germany. The Führer describes his experiences from 1932 until the day before his death. Then master forger Konrad Kujau confesses that he wrote the diaries himself and that he received 2.5 million marks from the Der Stern journalist who supposedly 'discovered' them. The blunder marks a new low in European journalism.

Ice cold

21st July 1983 At the Vostok station in Antarctica, in the middle of the polar cap, the polar station measures a temperature of -89.2°C. It is the lowest reliably measured temperature ever recorded on Earth.

Korean Air Flight 007

1st September 1983 When Korean Air Flight 007 en route from New York to Seoul ends up in a restricted part of Soviet airspace due to a navigation error, the Boeing 747 is shot down 55 kilometres from Moneron Island. All 269 people on board are killed. It is another low point in the Cold War and sends a shiver across the world.

27 OCT 1983

A memorial service is held for much-loved actor and raconteur David Niven who had died on 30th July.

18 NOV 1983

Janet Walton from Liverpool gives birth to six baby girls after taking fertility drugs. The sextuplets become national celebrities.

3 DEC 1983

As part of an ongoing peace campaign, women protestors break into RAF Greenham Common in Berkshire.

Word and Lotus 1-2-3

1st October 1983 Microsoft releases the first version of the word processing programme Word, which allows computer users to format typed text with line breaks and bold and italic letters. Multi-Tool Word, as it is called, comes free with *PC World magazine*. Users find the interface strange and WordStar and WordPerfect prove more popular. How different things will be with Lotus 1-2-3, now ready for launch. Many businesses buy the IBM computer specifically for it, to create clear spreadsheets, graphs and databases.

US invades Grenada

25th October 1983 The Caribbean island of Grenada, a member of the British Commonweath, is invaded by US forces aiming to prevent communist rule there. For virtually the only time in Ronald Reagan's presidency, Margaret Thatcher expresses private

disapproval of US action, especially over the fact that the UK was not consulted.

Nuclear false alarms

As cruise missiles arrive in Europe for stationing in NATO countries, two major nuclear scares bring the world momentarily to the brink of catastrophe. On 26th September, Soviet officer Stanislav Petrov correctly identifies a warning of a US missle attack as a false alarm. On 7th November, a NATO exercise is misinterpreted by Soviet officials as cover for a nuclear attack and Warsaw Pact forces are placed on full alert. The danger passes with the conclusion of the exercise four days later.

ENTERTAINMENT

The Roly Polys

Dance troupe The Roly Polys, seven generously proportioned ladies, led by 4' 11" Mo Moreland, tap and shimmy their way onto screens for the first time on *The Les Dawson Show* on 15th January.

The Machine Gunners

The first episode of the TV adaptation of Robert Westall's 1975 Carnegie medal-winning children's novel, *The Machine Gunners*, is aired on 23rd February. The Second World War drama set in a north-east coastal town in February 1941 centres on Chas McGill and his friends who discover a crashed German plane, complete with machine gun and ammunition.

Home video surges

New figures show that 10% of UK households now own a video recorder - and that the vast majority of those prefer VHS to Betamax, its technically superior but more expensive rival format. Home video is a revolutionary new medium that enables recording and playback of television programmes, gives users the opportunity to make videos of their own, and makes movies old and new available for home viewing. By the end of the decade, more than half of households in the UK will own a VCR.

Let's act

Nagisa Oshima's *Merry Christmas, Mr. Lawrence* is released on 25th August. Based on Laurens van der Post's memoirs about his experiences in a Japanese POW camp in Java during the Second World War, Bowie is the rebellious Major Jack Culliers opposite Tom Conti and Ryuichi Sakamoto. Oshima cast Bowie in the role after seeing him perform in the play *The Elephant Man* on Broadway in 1980.

Wake up and smell… a rat?

Early risers can enjoy telly with their corn-flakes from 17th January, when *Breakfast Time* launches on BBC1. Hot on its heels is ITV's morning offering, *TV-am*, beginning on 1st February. *TV-am*'s early weeks are beset by problems and viewing figures flag but the introduction of puppet rodent Roland Rat on 1st April helps to revive its fortunes.

Corrie love triangle

Coronation Street fans are gripped during its 21st February episode when Ken Barlow discovers his wife Deirdre has been having an affair with Mike Baldwin who Ken describes as a 'spiv' and 'little creep'. It's an emotional scene full of high drama with the usually mild-mannered Ken losing his cool and almost throttling Deirdre when Mike arrives at their door.

Fan-dabi-dozee!

After years on the cabaret circuit, Wee Jimmy Krankie and his sensible, grown-up sidekick, Ian Krankie, have become TV favourites through appearances on *Crackerjack*. Their star has risen to such heights that they get their own show this year; *The Krankies Klub* begins on BBC1 on 10th September. Much loved by a generation of kids, who adore cheeky Jimmy Krankie's mischievous antics and his catchphrase, 'Fan-dabi-dozee', the eventual realisation that Jimmy is in real life Janette Krankie, a woman in her thirties who is married to Ian, comes as a shock, second only to finding out Father Christmas doesn't really exist.

DO YOU REMEMBER THIS?

Donkey Kong game

The Dark Crystal

Chief Muppeteer Jim Henson taps into the vogue for fantasy films, working with Frank Oz on *The Dark Crystal*, first shown in UK cinemas on 17th February. Five years in the making, it is essentially a tale of good versus evil, with the vulture-like Skeksis pitted against the gentle Mystics. In a plot that borrows liberally from Tolkein, two elfin Gelflings are tasked with spiriting the powerful Dark Crystal away from the Skeksis before the alignment of three suns.

Cabbage Patch craziness

Harrods is swamped with shoppers on 1st December, as they descend on the store to grab this festive season's must-have toy - a Cabbage Patch doll.
Despite their strange, pudgy faces, which everyone, even the buyers, agree are rather ugly, the Cabbage Patch phenomenon has caused violent riots among shoppers in the US.

Just Seventeen

On 20th October, comes the launch of *Just Seventeen* magazine, a fresh new title aimed at teenage girls, heavy on fashion, heartthrobs and pithy advice, and light on the soppy romance

photo-stories which magazines like *My Guy* peddle. *J-17* doesn't patronise its readers, has some great cover giveaways and feels like the ideal read for any sophisticated 1980s teen.

Tootsie

Tootsie steals the hearts of UK audiences when it opens on 28th April. Sydney Pollack's direction and Dustin Hoffman's entertaining turn as a difficult, out-of-work actor who lands a plum role in a primetime soap by becoming 'Dorothy Michaels', brings the screwball comedy of the 1930s bang up to date. There's an underlying message about gender and male privilege, but it's delivered without losing any of its sparkle. As she becomes an unlikely standard bearer for feminism, 'Dorothy' falls in love with his/her co-star played by Jessica Lange, who won an Oscar for Best Actress. A dragged-up delight.

I'll have a 'P' please, Bob

Blockbusters, a quiz game for sixth-formers hosted by Bob Holness, first airs on ITV on 29th August. More intellectually rigorous than the majority of teatime quiz shows, one solo player battles a team of two as they make their way across a board of interlocked hexagons by answering general knowledge questions linked to the letter on each hexagon. The winner goes on to try their luck at the Gold Run, with a chance to stay and defend their champion status each week.

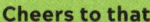

Cheers to that

Channel 4 builds a reputation for sniffing out great American sitcoms, beginning with *Cheers* which it presents for the first time on 4th February. Set in a Boston bar where 'everybody knows your name', the wisecracks flow as freely as the beer.

Tweenyboppers

Minipops airs for the first time on Channel 4 on 8th February. Featuring pre-teen children impersonating current pop stars and singing along to chart hits, the appearance of these mini-me popstrels with crimped hair and eyeliner is controversial to say the least and after one season, the ill-judged *Minipops* is dropped.

The A Team

On the run from the US government, 'for a crime they didn't commit', ex-commandos *The A-Team* become the action-adventure sensation of 1983. First screened on ITV on 22nd July, it's the de facto star, the muscular Mr T as B.A. Baracus, with his acres of gold chains, surly countenance and magical, mechanical know-how, who becomes a cult figure. Of course, nobody's perfect and B.A.'s Achilles heel is his fear of flying; 'I ain't getting on no plane' becomes one of the show's memorable catchphrases.

Tucker's Luck

The first episode of *Tucker's Luck*, a *Grange Hill* spin-off series, begins on BBC2 on 10th March. Featuring one of the most popular characters from *Grange Hill*'s original cast, it follows the teenage Peter 'Tucker' Jenkins (Todd Carty) as he negotiates life, work (or lack of it) and girls after leaving school.

Blue Peter's sunken garden vandalised

The decline of civilisation can perhaps be pinpointed to the moment in November 1983 when Blue Peter's Italian sunken garden is vandalised. Viewers are horrified as Janet Ellis confirms that the upturned sundial, ripped-up plants and oil on the pond are due to senseless vandalism. Percy Thrower finds it hard to hold back the tears and in a moment of political incorrectness, suggests the perpetrators are 'mentally ill'.

Thrills and chills

The golden age of the music video has truly arrived when Michael Jackson's *Thriller* is screened at the ungodly hour of 1:05am on Channel 4, introduced by Jools Holland of *The Tube*. Zombies, teen movie schtick and gobsmacking dance routines combine to make this a major multimedia event, at a time Jackson is reaching the peak of his solo success.

Swatch out

Swatch watches are launched on 1st March, Switzerland's riposte to the growing dominance of digital watches from Asia. Swatches are analogue, quartz time pieces, but they're also affordable and their colourful, simple design make them a classic 1980s accessory.

Caped crusaders

Early October sees the advent of two animated superheroes. On 3rd October, the lantern-jawed, fruit-fuelled *Bananaman*, who originated in the comic *Nutty*, comes to life on BBC1, voiced by members of The Goodies. *Superted* airs a day later, also on BBC1, almost a year after he had first been shown on Welsh TV channel, S4C. Originally created by Mike Young as a series of books, written to help cure his young son's fear of the dark, *Superted*, a toy factory reject, is brought to life by a visiting alien from the Planet Spot and given superpowers.

MUSIC

Blue Monday
19th March 1983 Breaking new ground musically, technically and commercially is *Blue Monday* by New Order. It uses a synth bassline, a sequencer and a drum machine. Sampling Kraftwerk's *Uranium* and echoing Donna Summer's *Our Love* and the soundtrack of *The Good, the Bad and the Ugly*, it's an extraordinary amalgam of sound and voice that is a hit twice during 1983, in twelve-inch and standard format versions.

Wizards of Oz
Men at Work lead a succession of Australasian bands to big success in the UK and US. With its ironic articulation of Antipodean clichés, their *Down Under* becomes almost a second Australian anthem, while 1983 sees Michael Hutchence's INXS (photo) debut in New York and Icehouse build their reputation by supporting David Bowie on tour. Nick Cave and the Bad Seeds emerge from the ashes of the much-admired Birthday Party, while Rick Springfield and the Little River Band each have a strong run of hits in more conventional soft rock mode in the US. Uncompromising and politically active, long-timers Midnight Oil are on the cusp of an international breakthrough as the year ends.

Pink Floyd on hiatus
21st March 1983 After releasing *The Final Cut*, which is largely the work of Roger Waters, Pink Floyd dissolve into acrimony. For the next four years the members will focus on solo work and dealing with legal action around the right to use the Pink Floyd name.

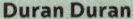

Duran Duran
26th March 1983 Hitting No. 1 for the first time - and doing so just one week after the single's release - are new romantic pin-up boys Duran Duran with *Is There Something I Should Know*. Thanks to their super-glamorous and very MTV-friendly videos, Simon Le Bon and friends are the hottest UK property in the US at the moment, where audience hysteria is likened to Beatlemania. They are named after a character in the 1964 sci-fi film *Barbarella* starring Jane Fonda.

Billy's innocent
The album of the year has to be Billy Joel's multi-platinum *An Innocent Man*, on which Long Island's finest pays homage to the singers and groups who influenced him. The songs brilliantly capture the styles, characteristics and qualities of the Drifters (the title track), Motown (*Tell Her About It*), doo wop (*The Longest Time*) and the Four Seasons (*Uptown Girl*). More than a tribute, it's a series of loving re-creations with nostalgically choreographed videos to match.

Bowie and Nile

9th April 1983 It's a marriage made in heaven - David Bowie teaming up with ex-Chic guitarist and producer Nile Rodgers for a chart-topping album and single, both called *Let's Dance*, that do not pretend to be anything more than solid slices of ultra-funky contemporary dance music. *China Girl* and *Modern Love* are also hits from the same album, the warm reception to which encourages Bowie to tour for the first time in five years.

MY FIRST 18 YEARS

TOP10 1983

1. **Billie Jean** *Michael Jackson*
2. **War Baby** *Tom Robinson*
3. **Lovecats** *The Cure*
4. **Karma Chameleon** *Culture Club*
5. **Every Breath You Take** *The Police*
6. **IOU** *Freeez*
7. **Islands in the Stream** *Dolly Parton, Kenny Rogers*
8. **Come Dancing** *The Kinks*
9. **Back on the Chain Gang** *The Pretenders*
10. **Heartache Avenue** *The Maisonettes*

Open | Search | Scan

Soul brothers

Young white soul boys are in their element in UK pop in the 1980s. Paul Weller launches the Style Council with Mick Talbot to create the Otis Redding/Curtis Mayfield style soul he adored as a teenager. Spandau Ballet swap outrageous new romantic get-ups for a smart-suited new look and storm the chart with *True*. And Paul Young (photo), has the temerity to cover a hallowed Marvin Gaye classic, *Wherever I Lay My Hat (That's My Home)*, and take it No. 1.

Pointed politics

Politics is part of the pop mix in 1983. Written in the wake of the Falklands War, two of the most pointed songs of the year both originate on Elvis Costello's *Punch the Clock* album - *Shipbuilding* and *Pills and Soap*. Beautifully covered in deadpan style by Robert Wyatt, once of Soft Machine, *Shipbuilding* is a swipe at the prospect of a closed-down British industry being revived for making battleships, told from the conflicted perspective of an unemployed man.

Thrashing it out

25th July 1983 The thrash metal genre arrives with a vengeance with *Kill ''Em All* by Metallica, a four-piece formed in 1981 by Lars Ulrich and influenced by the UK bands who comprised the 'new wave of heavy metal' at the time. Metallica combine speed and energy with a Zeppelin-esque density of sound and soon find themselves one of the big four of the metal scene alongside Anthrax, Slayer and a band formed by ex-member Dave Mustaine, Megadeth.

SPORT

A

Torvill and Dean's golden moment

One of the most iconic moments in sporting history takes place at the Winter Olympics in Sarajevo, appropriately on 14th February. The United Kingdom's Jane Torvill and Christopher Dean skate a risky routine of fluid grace and breath-taking romance to Ravel's Bolero in the free dance competition, earning them an unprecedented perfect score of 6.0 from every judge for artistic impression. The routine is watched by 23 million Britons at home.

The fall

South African athlete Zola Budd, who breaks American Mary Decker's 5000m world record in January, controversially gains a British passport on 6th April allowing her to compete at the Olympic Games in Los Angeles. When Budd (who runs barefoot) and Decker meet in the 3000m Olympic final more controversy follows. Budd makes her way to the front of the pack and Decker, pinned behind, trips over Budd's heel, and falls on her hip. Decker fails to finish the race and Budd comes seventh.

Lewis leads the way at the Olympics

Carl Lewis equals Jesse Owens' Olympic tally of 1936 by winning four gold medals, in the 100m, 200m, 4x100m relay and long jump. Seb Coe overcomes a period of injury and equals his own medal tally, by once again winning gold in the 1500m and silver in the 800m. Tessa Sanderson gains gold for Great Britain in the javelin, as does Daley Thompson in the decathlon. Steve Redgrave gets the first of his five rowing gold medals in the men's coxless fours. The LA Olympics has been a ritzy, glitzy affair, and one that shows hosting the Games can be a commercial success.

West Indies overwhelm England's cricketers

A majestic West Indies side under Clive Lloyd thrashes David Gower's England 5-0 in the summer Test series; the only instance where England have suffered such a resounding whitewash at home.

C

---

6 JAN 1984

The British turn their backs on cigarettes as anti-smoking group ASH say two million have given up in the last two years.

9 FEB 1984

As open civil war erupts in Beirut, 400 Britons are evacuated from the city.

28 MAR 1984

Nissan select the north-east town of Washington, near Sunderland, as the location for its new UK car plant.

Turnaround for the Toffees

Everton end a fourteen-year trophy drought and emerge from the shadow of their Merseyside sibling, Liverpool, by winning the FA Cup Final, beating Watford 2-0 on 19th May. It's a pivotal moment for manager Howard Kendall and his team signalling the beginning of purple patch of success.

Olympic boycott

8th May 1984 In retaliation for the decision of the US to boycott the Olympic Games in Moscow in 1980, the Soviet National Olympic Committee boycotts the Los Angeles Olympic Games. All Eastern Bloc countries with the exception of Romania also confirm their non-participation.

DOMESTIC
NEWS

Miners' strikes

12th March 1984 The National Union of Mineworkers go out on strike in protest at government plans that will see the closure of most of Britain's remaining coal pits. Clashes between police and miners in April and May continue into June, when the 'Battle of Orgreave' results in over 120 injuries and 95 arrests in one of the most violent incidents of the dispute. A mass lobby by miners at the Houses of Parliament ends in violence and 120 arrests, and in September the strike is ruled unlawful.

Chatham Dockyard closes

31st March 1984 The Medway in Kent witnesses an end to over 400 years of shipbuilding at the Chatham Dockyard, as it is closed for the final time. 84 acres of the Dockyard is preserved as a heritage attraction, telling the story of shipbuilding on the site since the reign of Elizabeth I.

Halfpenny withdrawn

1st February 1984 The government announces that the halfpenny is to be withdrawn from circulation at the end of the year. Whilst the new decimal version of the coin has only been in circulation since 1971, the country has had halfpennies since 1672.

WPC Yvonne Fletcher

17th April 1984 A gunman inside the Libyan Embassy shoots and kills WPC Yvonne Fletcher and wounds 11 others during peaceful protests outside. Following the shooting, armed police lay siege to the building, and Britain severs diplomatic ties with Libya.

21 APR 1984

Return of the groundbreaking US series *Cagney and Lacey* to BBC1.

19 MAY 1984

Poet and protector of Britain's building heritage, Sir John Betjamin dies at his Cornish home, aged 78.

22 JUN 1984

The first Virgin Atlantic flight to New York takes off from Gatwick, with fares costing £99.

Thames Barrier opened

8th May 1984 The Queen formally opens the Thames Barrier, a new system designed to protect London from flooding. High tides and storm surges have threatened the capital since the Roman period, and this new barrier will allow authorities to close the 520m width of the river when the city is in danger.

Abbeystead disaster

23rd May 1984 An explosion at a waterworks' valve house in Abbeystead, Lancashire, kills sixteen people. The explosion is caused by a build-up of methane gas that investigators determine has seeped into the pipes from nearby coal deposits, igniting when the valves were opened.

Hong Kong agreement

19th December 1984 After months of negotiations, Britain and China sign the Sino-British Joint Declaration, which agrees the return of the British Overseas Territory of Hong Kong to Chinese control.

Brighton hotel bombing

12th October 1984 The entire cabinet are the intended targets of a Provisional IRA bomb planted in the Grand Hotel in Brighton. The hotel is hosting the Conservative Party conference, and the explosion is intended to strike after Prime Minister Margaret Thatcher and her fellow ministers have arrived. Five people, including MP Anthony Berry, are killed and several more are seriously injured and trapped in the rubble.

BT privatised

20th November 1984 Shares in British Telecom go on sale after plans for the privatisation of the company were unveiled in 1982. The government retain 50% of the shares, whilst over two million members of the public choose to invest, amounting to approximately 5% of the population.

York Minster fire

9th July 1984 The country watches on in horror as a fire breaks out in the early hours of the morning at York Minster. Quick-thinking firefighters choose to collapse the roof of the South Transept, where the fire has started, in a successful attempt to prevent the fire from spreading, and the rest of the medieval building is saved.

12 JUL 1984

Robert Maxwell acquires Mirror Group newspapers and states his editors will be 'free to produce the news without interference'.

4 AUG 1984

The BBC continues its coverage of the Los Angeles Olympics until 4am each day, and supplements this with Ceefax Olympics AM.

29 SEP 1984

A huge IRA arms cache is discovered on board an Irish trawler sailing off the southwest coast of Britain.

1984

Gorbachev Visits UK

16th December 1984 The UK welcomes Soviet politburo member Mikhail Gorbachev on a week-long semi-official tour of the country. Gorbachev meets government ministers and politicians, and tours factories and cities, meeting with Prime Minister Margaret Thatcher at Chequers. Her verdict that 'we can do business together' proves prophetic as he shows himself to be a reformer seeking closer ties with the West.

ROYALTY & POLITICS

Birth of Prince Harry

The Princess of Wales gives birth to a second son on 15th September. The following day it is announced the new baby prince will be given the names Henry Charles Albert David, although he quickly becomes known as Prince Harry.

FOREIGN NEWS

First compact computer

24th January 1984 Apple launches the first compact computer with the Apple Macintosh 128k. The Macintosh has 128 kilobytes of RAM and its own operating system, Mac OS. The computer has no hard drive, and to keep the device as quiet as possible, Steve Jobs insists that no fan be built in.

CIA chief kidnapped

16th March 1984 The ongoing war in Lebanon claims another high-profile victim. The CIA's station chief in Beirut, Willliam Buckley, is kidnapped by the Islamic Jihad and dies in captivity.

Sony markets the Discman

19th November 1984 Just as its original Walkman design boosted sales of cassettes to unprecedented levels, so Sony's Discman is set to do exactly the same for the new compact disc format. More robust and user friendly than the Walkman, the Discman is the ultimate aid to personalised music listening.

1 OCT 1984

Dr. David Jenkins, the outspoken Bishop of Durham, makes a public attack on Margaret Thatcher's social policies.

20 NOV 1984

McDonald's makes its 50 billionth hamburger.

19 DEC 1984

Mrs. Thatcher signs the Sino-British Declaration handing Hong Kong to China, ending 155 years of British rule in the colony.

HIV positive

23rd April 1984 US Department of Health and Human Services Secretary Margaret Heckler announces that the cause of AIDS - the HIV virus - has been discovered by Dr Robert Gallo and colleagues at the National Cancer Institute. She reveals the development of a diagnostic blood test to identify infection and holds out the hope that a vaccine against AIDS will be produced within two years.

Reagan re-elected

6th November 1984 Ronald Reagan secures a second term as US President with a landslide win over his Democrat opponent Walter Mondale. Reagan achieves nearly 70 per cent of the popular vote and wins all the states except Washington DC and Mondale's home state of Minnesota.

Bhopal

3rd December 1984 Methyl isocyanate escapes from a Union Carbide factory in the Indian city of Bhopal. In a short time, this poisonous gas cloud kills more than 8,000 people outright and affects over half a million people. The final death toll is estimated at over 20,000. It is the worst industrial accident in history and results in criminal prosecutions against Union Carbide and individuals running the factory.

ENTERTAINMENT

Hartbeat

Tony Hart has been the go-to man for art on children's TV for twenty years, first with *Vision On*, and then *Take Hart. Hartbeat* is the latest iteration, airing for the first time on 14th September. It retains all the familiar aspects of previous programmes, including his plasticine sidekick, Morph, and The Gallery segment where viewers send in their own artwork. But there are updates too. The set is jazzier, Tony has female co-presenters and occasionally he invites a graphic designer onto the programme to show how to create designs on a computer.

DO YOU REMEMBER THIS?

Water ring game

Consumer trends

While McDonald's proclaims the consumption of its 50 billionth hamburger, new global business launches in 1984 include Papa John's Pizza, Dell Computers and LA Fitness. Wrist watch calculators are the must-have gadgets of the year. In the fast rising world of video games, Commodore International founder Jack Tramiel founds Tramel Technology, buys the consumer assets of Atari Inc from Warner Communications and renames the company Atari. The biggest selling toys on the planet are Hasbro's Transformers, cleverly promoted via a cartoon TV series. The Cambridge Diet is launched in Europe and Blue Nun white wine with its distinctive dark bottle and blue labelling enjoys its best year for sales since launching in the 1920s. It's also a peak year for Filofax sales and power dressing as yuppie culture takes hold.

The Box of Delights

The Box of Delights, BBC1's adaptation of the 1935 fantasy novel for children by John Masefield, broadcasts between 21st November and 24th December. At a cost of £1 million, it is the most expensive children's production the BBC has ever undertaken and wins several awards for its special effects. A landmark moment in children's television drama, *The Box of Delights* quite literally lives up to its name.

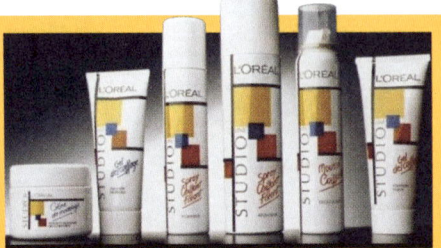

Mousse mania

First developed by L'Oréal in France, hair mousse becomes the favoured product to give your bonce the necessary 'bouff' as hair styles become progressively voluminous. L'Oréal's Studio Line range, with geometric, primary coloured packaging, is aimed at a younger customer; whereas its Freestyle product promises soft, sculpted waves for a sophisticated look.

Just like that

On 15th April, comedian and magician Tommy Cooper has a heart attack and collapses on stage at Her Majesty's Theatre during a live television broadcast to an audience of 12 million. He dies soon afterwards in Westminster Hospital. The following month, on 28th May, Eric Morecambe also dies after suffering a heart attack following a performance at a charity event at the Roses Theatre in Tewkesbury the day before.

Pranks a lot

Game for a Laugh first appeared on screens in 1981, dreamt up by ITV as a light entertainment rival to BBC1's *The Generation Game*. Hosted by a quartet of presenters perched on high stools, Henry Kelly, Matthew Kelly, Sarah Kennedy and Jeremy Beadle offer a mixed buffet of practical jokes, candid camera-style 'gotcha' moments and some of Britain's most bizarre eccentrics. The series continues until 1985 and on 25th August this year, a *GFAL* special 'Best of' programme is aired.

Tales of the River Bank

Following a successful film in 1983, a stop-animation TV series based on Kenneth Grahame's *Wind in the Willows* begins on ITV on 27th April. Produced by the Manchester-based Cosgrove Hall, already with well-established successes such as *Danger Mouse*, *Chorlton and the Wheelies* and *Jamie and the Magic Torch*, the *Wind in the Willows* characters are voiced by British acting's finest including Peter Sallis as Ratty, David Jason as Mr Toad and the recently knighted Sir Michael Hordern as Badger.

'Listen very carefully, I shall zay this only once'

René Artois is a French café owner, who simply wants a quiet life, but what with his nagging wife, complicated affairs with his waitresses, his involvement with the French resistance, the permanently suspicious occupying Nazis, a policeman prone to malapropisms ('Good moaning'), some stranded British airmen and the whereabouts of a painting of 'The Fallen Madonna with the Big Boobies', there is never a dull moment in 'Allo 'Allo, which begins on BBC1 on 7th September. 'Allo 'Allo is farcical fun, awash with exaggerated accents, national stereotypes and catchphrases. It runs for nine series and eighty-five episodes until 1992.

A new old Bill

The uniformed officers and detectives of Sun Hill police station make their debut on ITV on 16th October following a successful one-off 1983 drama called *Woodentop*. *The Bill* remains on screens for the next 26 years, the UK's longest-running police drama.

Spitting Image

British satire is alive and well and finds a new outlet in the form of puppetry when *Spitting Image* first broadcasts on ITV on 26th February. Lampooning politicians, the royal family and various public figures and celebrities, *Spitting Image* puppets includes Margaret Thatcher as a cigar-smoking tyrant in a pin-striped suit, a gin-swilling Queen Mother and a bumbling Ronald Reagan, the nuclear button unnervingly close to his bedside.

Body conscious

The Body Shop, originally a single shop founded by Anita Roddick in Brighton in 1976, has rolled out across the country by the mid-1980s, tempting shoppers with a whole new experience in beauty retail. The environmentally friendly products and the company's ethical practices are part of the appeal, but the shops are an Aladdin's Cave of novel smells and magical potions, with glass pipettes inviting us to sniff the various perfume oils and bottles bearing the brand's distinctive green labels. Fruit glycerine soaps, bath pearls, Japanese washing grains, cucumber cleansing milk, White Musk and Dewberry are just some of the tempting products concocted by this revolutionary retailer.

Gremlins and Ghosties

Comedy, horror, action, and special effects combine in two of this year's biggest movie blockbusters when *Gremlins* and *Ghostbusters* are both released on 7th December. *Gremlins* is given a 15 rating after American parents who had taken small children to see the film in the summer discovered that cute furry Gizmo actually spawns a marauding bunch of reptilian imps who go on a gruesome murder spree. *Ghostbusters* (given a PG rating) has the odd terrifying moment too but it's all very tongue-in-cheek and carried along by Ray Parker Jr.'s bouncing soundtrack. Who you gonna call?

This is Spinal Tap

Mocumentary rockumentary *This is Spinal Tap* follows the rise and rapid descent (mostly the latter) of the English metal band Spinal Tap, whose past members of whom have perished in the most ludicrous circumstances, as these rock losers try to tour their latest album, *Smell the Glove*, around the US to a rapidly diminishing fanbase. Treading a genius line between subtlety and stupidity, *This is Spinal Tap* sets the standard for all future on-screen spoofs, in time becomes nothing short of a cult sensation.

Mini-series addicts

British viewers can't get enough of American mini-series and this year sees a TV blockbuster based on a literary bonkbuster. Richard Chamberlain is sexy priest Father Ralph and Rachel Ward is Meggie in *The Thorn Birds*, based on Colleen Mc-Cullough's sprawling tale of forbidden love.

Nineteen-eighty-score

George Orwell's dystopian vision *1984* is ably transferred to the big screen by writer and director Michael Radford, with John Hurt as Winston Smith and Richard Burton playing O'Brien, his last screen role. The film is overshadowed by a row over the soundtrack. Radford wants a classical score. However, Virgin Films, who have provided finance for the movie, insist on a score of pop electronica by Eurythmics and release an album which includes the band's top 10 hit *Sex Crime* (1984).

Crackerjack the last broadcast

Crackerjack has been a stalwart of the BBC's children's programming since 1955, during which time it has been hosted by Eamonn Andrews, Leslie Crowther, Michael Aspel, Ed 'Stewpot' Stewart and Stu 'Crush a Grape' Francis. It blends comedy sketches and music acts with the long-running 'Double or Drop', a quiz where kids have to keep a grip on a mounting pile of prizes, as well as cabbages given for wrong answers.

United Colours of Benetton

Oliviero Toscani, creative director of Benetton, photographs the first multi-racial advertisement for the clothing brand, which is at the height of its desirability. As the decade progresses, the provocative nature of the Italian brand's campaigns continues to be a talking point.

MUSIC

The time is Now

17th January 1984 At No. 1 in the album chart is the very first compilation album in the hugely popular *Now That's What I Call Music* series. It comprises a whopping total of 30 current hits and is heavily promoted by television advertising. The series runs to 116 individual releases and lasts for four decades.

Elton marries
14th February 1984 Elton John bemuses friends, fans and the gay community by marrying recording engineer Renate Blauel. The couple divorce four years later.

Frankie say...
13th January 1984 Dominating 1984 are Liverpool club band Frankie Goes to Hollywood. They're a phenomenon through the brilliance of record label ZTT's promotion campaign, not to mention those iconic 'Frankie say' T-shirts. They court controversy from the start: *Relax*, backed by a video that is famously banned by the BBC yet still stays at No. 1 for nine weeks and on the chart for almost the whole year. The nuclear war-themed *Two Tribes* has a spoken section advising what to do in the event of an attack. From here, however, it is all downhill, as the US largely ignores them and MTV won't touch their videos.

All hail Madonna
27th January 1984 Is the UK ready for Madonna? A singer-dancer from Detroit with a brilliant grasp of look, fashion and choreography, she makes an arousing *Top of the Pops* debut with *Holiday*. Back in the US she films *Desperately Seeking Susan*, marries actor Sean Penn and closes the year with the image-defining *Like a Virgin*, produced by Nile Rodgers.

Marvin shot dead
1st April 1984 Now living at his parents' home in Los Angeles because they fear he is suicidal, Marvin Gaye is shot dead by his father during a violent family row. Marvin Gaye Sr receives five years for voluntary manslaughter.

Starlight Express
Starlight Express, the train engine musical with music by Andrew Lloyd Webber and lyrics by Richard Stilgoe, opens at the Victoria Palace Theatre on 27th March. Arlene Phillips choreographs the cast who perform entirely on roller skates.

George in a whisper
Youth unemployment is rising and, for some, now is the time to form a band and turn being on the dole to productive use. That's the idea behind Wham! - best pals George Michael and Andrew Ridgley - and it's the philosophy behind *Wham Rap* that launches the boys in 1982. Two years on, they're ruling the pop roost with such hymns to hedonism as *Wake Me Up Before You Go-Go* and *Club Tropicana*. But the ambitious George surprises all and sundry with *Careless Whisper*, a cutting, mature break-up ballad that's full of self-recrimination and regret. Released under his own name rather than Wham!, it's one of the records of the decade.

Tina is back

No comeback is more deserved than Tina Turner's. She left husband Ike in 1978 after over a decade of abuse and has spent much of her time since playing nostalgia shows. Asked to guest on records by Sheffield electro band Heaven 17 and boosted by David Bowie's verbal support, she re-launches her career in astonishing style with the UK-made *Private Dancer* album and singles *Let's Stay Together* and *What's Love Got to Do with It*.

MY FIRST 18 YEARS
TOP10   **1984**

1. **Careless Whisper** *George Michael*
2. **Radio Gaga** *Queen*
3. **Girls Just Wanna Have Fun** *Cyndi Lauper*
4. **White Lines** *Grandmaster Flash & Mel Melle*
5. **I Feel for You** *Chaka Khan*
6. **Smalltown Boy** *Bronski Beat*
7. **Nightshift** *The Commodores*
8. **Move Closer** *Phyllis Nelson*
9. **Last Christmas** *Wham!*
10. **Let's Stay Together** *Tina Turner*

Open ⓢ | Search 🔍 | Scan 📷

Prince of sales

7th July 1984 Prince Rogers Nelson, known to all as Prince, is an icon in the US but has been awaiting a UK breakthrough for years. Now it comes via the rock-soul hybrid *When Doves Cry* from his semi-autobiographical movie *Purple Rain*, the soundtrack of which sells over 20 million albums and sits atop the US chart for 24 weeks. He writes, produces and plays every instrument on the track but - curiously for a dance record, and in typically perverse Prince fashion - he omits a bassline.

Band Aid

25th November 1984 Following a distressing BBC TV news report about the famine in Ethiopia, Bob Geldof of the Boomtown Rats has an idea. He calls Midge Ure of Ultravox and together they write a song, *Do They Know It's Christmas*, to raise money for relief charities. They call on all the music stars they know to join them for the recording at Trevor Horn's studio - and dutifully, early on a Sunday morning, most of the biggest names in UK pop music turn up including George Michael, Paul Young, Sting, Status Quo, Spandau Ballet, Duran Duran, Bananarama, Bono and - hotfooting it late from New York on Concorde - Boy George. The record is pressed and on sale within ten days and by mid-December it's at No. 1. By the time Christmas 1985 rolls around, Band Aid's single will have raised £8 million and inspired a US counterpart, *We Are the World*, and the most famous concert in music history - Live Aid.

SPORT

Everton denied treble
18th May 1985 Manchester United beat Everton 1-0 at Wembley to win the FA Cup, denying Everton 'the Treble'. Having already secured victory in the Football League for the first time in fifteen years, Everton's hopes of a historic treble had been raised after their victory in the European Cup Winners' Cup just three days before the Wembley final.

Heysel Stadium disaster
29th May 1985 39 football fans are killed, and hundreds injured, as Juventus beat Liverpool in the European Cup. The victims are mostly Juventus fans who get crushed against a wall which then collapses, whilst fleeing a confrontation with Liverpool fans. An increasing culture of football hooliganism is blamed, and both the FA and UEFA impose bans on English teams playing in Europe. seventeen Liverpool fans are found guilty of manslaughter.

Becker wins Wimbledon
7th July 1985 Unseeded seventeen-year-old Boris Becker stuns the tennis world by beating Kevin Curren to become Wimbledon champion. It is the first time a player from Germany has won the championship, and Becker soon becomes an iconic figure in tennis, going on to win 64 titles. The women's event is won for the sixth time by Martina Navratilova in her fourth consecutive Wimbledon final.

Davis vs Taylor
27-28th April 1985 Steve Davis and Dennis Taylor meet in the World Snooker Championship Final, in what is considered by many to be the greatest snooker match of all time. With Davis having led for most of the sessions, the Championship comes down to the potting of the final black ball. Both players miss the shot several times before Taylor pulls off a surprise victory. The match is often credited with reviving the sport in the 80s and 90s.

JAN 1985

Vodafone launch the first UK mobile phone network.

9 FEB 1985

Madonna releases album *Like a Virgin*.

3 MAR 1985

UK Miner's Strike ends after a year of industrial action and violent clashes.

1985

England regain ashes

2nd September 1985 The Australian cricket team's six-Test tour of England is won by the hosts in the final Test. England are victorious after a more than 350-run batting partnership between Graham Gooch and David Gower, which sees them win the final Test by 94 runs and an innings.

Newry mortar attack

28 February 1985 A Royal Ulster Constabulary police station in Newry, County Down, is struck by mortar shells fired by the Provisional IRA; nine officers aged 19-41 are killed. Over 30 people are injured, including civilians, and the day is dubbed 'Bloody Thursday' by the British press.

DOMESTIC NEWS

E

Sinclair launches C5

10th January 1985 Sir Clive Sinclair launches his iconic but short-lived Sinclair C5, an electrified, one-person tricycle able to travel 20 miles before it needs a charge. Sinclair hopes the C5 will prove a popular mode of transport and replace petrol engines in the future, but sadly, despite proving a lot of fun, the product sells only 17,000 units and ceases production in August.

F

Bradford City Stadium fire

11th May 1985 Horror unfurls at a Third Division football match between Bradford City and Lincoln City when a fire starts in the main stand. Multiple fire hazards within the stadium, combined with windy weather, mean the whole stand is engulfed in less than four minutes, claiming the lives of 56 fans, and injuring over 260 more. Dramatic photos of the fire transfix a grieving nation, and calls are made for changes to safety regulations when it is revealed that exits were padlocked, barring escape routes.

TELEPHONE

Red telephone boxes

17th January 1985 The newly privatised British Telecom announce that they will phase out their iconic red telephone boxes. A huge campaign is launched to save them, but BT insist that they are rarely used and are expensive to clean and maintain. In response many local authorities give their phone boxes protected status, and over 2,000 are listed.

G

11 APR 1985

An eighteen-month-old baby becomes the youngest person in the UK to die in the AIDS epidemic.

22 MAY 1985

James Bond film, A *View to a Kill* permieres, it's the last to star Roger Moore.

23 JUN 1985

An Air India Boeing 747 disappears off the Irish coast after a bomb detonates killing all 325 people onboard.

Hole in the ozone
16th May 1985 Three scientists associated with the British Antarctic Survey, Joe Farman, Brian Gardiner and Jonathan Shanklin, discover a hole in the planet's ozone layer over Antarctica. Their research suggests that a group of chemicals known as chlorofluorocarbons are to blame.

White House Farm murders
7th August 1985 Grandparents Nevill and June Bamber, their daughter Sheila, and her six-year-old twin children are found shot dead in their home in a killing that horrifies the country. The investigation soon focuses on the Bambers' other child, Jeremy, who had claimed to be away from home at the time. Jeremy is found guilty of murder and sentenced to life in prison.

Manchester air disaster
22nd August 1985 55 people are killed when a British Airtours flight from Manchester to Corfu suffers damage to an engine and abandons take off. The accident causes a fire in one of the plane's underwing fuel tanks, and issues with the plane's emergency exits mean that only 80 of the 135 people on board make it off safely.

Broadwater Farm riot
6th October 1985 The death of a 49-year-old black woman, Cynthia Jarrett, who dies of heart failure during a police search, leads to a riot on the Broadwater Farm council estate in Tottenham. With tensions already enflamed following the Brixton riots a few days before, the violence leads to the murder of PC Keith Blakelock, who trips and falls whilst attempting to protect the London Fire Brigade from attack. He is set upon by a crowd armed with knives and other weapons.

Comic Relief launched
25th December 1985 Comedians Richard Curtis and Sir Lenny Henry found charity Comic Relief in response to the Ethiopian famine. Whilst Live Aid and Band Aid are the talk of the summer, Comic Relief proves to have much more longevity as it begins a biennial fundraising event, the first of which takes place in 1986. Becoming enormously popular for showing famous people doing silly things, the event becomes 'Red Nose Day' in 1988.

Titanic located
1st September 1985 The wreck of famous ocean liner the RMS *Titanic* is discovered by a joint French and American expedition, 3,700 metres below the surface of the North Atlantic. A few days later, the explorers take the very first photographs and footage of the wreck, showing it in two pieces rather than intact as had previously been believed.

6 JUL 1985
At Wimbledon, Martina Navratilova beats Chris Evert in 3 sets in the women's singles final.

22 AUG 1985
A terrible month for air travel sees three disasters across the globe claim the lives of 711 people.

19 SEP 1985
A magnitude 8 earthquake strikes Mexico City, killing over 5000 people.

1985

Queen tours Caribbean
9th October 1985 The Queen embarks on a royal tour of the Caribbean. Flying in to Belize, she will spend almost a month on board the Royal Yacht *Britannia* with Prince Philip, as they visit Belize, Bermuda, the Bahamas, St Kitts and Nevis, Dominica, St Lucia, St Vincent and the Grenadines, Grenada and Trinidad.

First black council leader
30th April 1985 The country gains its first black council leader, when Bernie Grant is elected leader of Haringey Council in London. Born in Guyana, he is a member of the Labour Party, and later becomes MP for Tottenham.

Anglo-Irish agreement signed
15th November 1985 Prime Minister Margaret Thatcher and Irish Taoiseach Garret FitzGerald sign the Anglo-Irish Agreement at Hillsborough Castle. The agreement gives the Irish government an advisory role in Northern Ireland in a move that it is hoped will lessen the violence of the Troubles.

Angel of Death
June 6 1985 The skeleton of Josef Mengele turns up in a grave near São Paulo in Brazil, proof that the 'Angel of Death' is no longer alive. Mengele is responsible for the deaths of hundreds of thousands of Jews in the Auschwitz concentration camp during World War II.

DO YOU REMEMBER THIS?

Kung Fu shoes

9 OCT 1985
Strawberry Fields memorial to John Lennon is revealed in Central Park, NYC.

21 NOV 1985
Soviet Leader Mikhail Gorbachev and US President Ronald Reagan hold productive meetings in Geneva in what Reagan calls a 'fresh start'.

9 DEC 1985
Argentinian Junta leaders Jorge Videla and Emilio Massera are sentenced to life imprisonment.

Apostle of peace

April 7 1985 The new leader of the Russian Communist Party, Mikhail Gorbachev, announces a unilateral moratorium on the deployment of the SS-20 medium-range missiles in Europe, valid until the end of November. Gorbachev indicates that he is looking for peace. With a five-year plan, he hopes to save the Soviet Union, which is in decline due to a very expensive war in Afghanistan and economic malaise. 'Uskorenie' (accelerated economic development), 'perestroika' (thorough reforms), and 'glasnost' (openness and transparency) are the main lines of his policy.

Schengen

June 14 1985 On a boat on the Moselle near the Luxembourg village of Schengen, the heads of government of the Benelux nations, West Germany and France agree that border controls between those countries will gradually disappear. This creates a 'Schengen area' without internal border controls on persons and goods.

Rainbow Warrior

The Greenpeace flagship, the Dutch *Rainbow Warrior*, sails to New Zealand for a demonstration against French nuclear tests. But things don't get that far, because in the port of Auckland, agents of the French intelligence service DGSE commit an attack on the ship with the blessing of French President Mitterrand. The *Rainbow Warrior* is sunk with mines secretly attached to the boat by divers. A Dutch photographer is killed in the attack. 'Opération Satanique' causes a major diplomatic row.

AIDS wave

October 2 1985 When American film star Rock Hudson dies of AIDS, his suffering and death make a deep impression. The masses now realize what AIDS is and the damage the disease causes. New statistics show that the number of AIDS patients in Europe has tripled in one year, to 1,126 registered cases.

ENTERTAINMENT

We are sailing

Howard's Way, a saga of yachts and yuppy types, begins on BBC1 on 1st September. It's a sort of British *Dynasty*, but set on the Hampshire coast instead of Colorado, and with deck shoes and jumpers casually tied round the shoulders instead of sequins and shoulder pads.

Victoria Wood As Seen on TV

The Beeb lures multi-talented comedian Victoria Wood away from ITV, and the result is *Victoria Wood As Seen on TV*, which first airs on BBC2 on 11th January. Wood, who writes all sketches, is given a decent budget, creative freedom and comes up with comedy gold. The show is bursting with what quickly become some of television's finest moments, from spoof soap *Acorn Antiques* to Julie Walters as a doddery waitress in the 'Two Soups' sketch; Wood as Ena Sharples in a 1960s episode of *Coronation Street* grimly predicting the endings of numerous characters, to musical numbers like the uproarious *Ballad of Barry and Freda - Let's Do It* where the line 'Beat me on the bottom with a *Woman's Weekly*' encapsulates her down-to-earth genius.

No Limits

A programme that combines pop music clips with young presenters roaming the country to share the best bits of the UK's different regions, *No Limits* is the brainchild of Jonathan King, who has been doing much the same thing with his own show *Entertainment USA*. *No Limits* begins on BBC2 on 30th July, presented by Jeremy Legg and Lisa Maxwell, who are later replaced with jokey pair Tony Baker and Jenny Powell.

The Broom Cupboard

As part of an overhaul of Children's BBC, Phillip Schofield appears from a control desk called 'The Broom Cupboard' on 9th September, where he provides links between programmes with the help of a furry friend called Gordon the Gopher. When Schofield begins presenting Saturday morning show *Going Live!*, Gordon goes with him, and The Broom Cupboard is occupied by Andy Crane and Edd the Duck. Andi Peters and Zoe Ball are two more who cut their presenting teeth in the country's best-known confined space.

Looking for love

Cilla Black plays cupid as host of ITV's new Saturday night fixture, Blind Date, which begins 30th November. With three possible dates hidden behind a screen, a contestant must decide which one they'd like to go on a date with according to how promising their answers are to three questions. After a round-up from 'Our Graham' (the voice of Graham Skidmore) the pair see each other for the first time as the screen falls back, and then learn whether they're going to the Caribbean or Clacton for their date.

I'll be back

Ex-body builder Arnold Schwarzenegger's wooden acting and deadpan delivery is just what director James Cameron needs for the cyborg assassin - *The Terminator* - sent from the future to destroy the mother of the boy who will grow up to lead a human resistance against Skynet's machines. Arnie's monotone promise 'I'll be back' proves propitious as *The Terminator* franchise goes on for five sequels.

Eastenders

13 million viewers tune in on 19th February to watch the first episode of BBC1's brand new soap, *Eastenders*. Set in the fictional borough of Walford in east London, the residents live in the characterful Albert Square, where, for some reason, London's soaring house prices are never discussed and local boozer the Queen Vic acts as a stage for feuds, punch-ups, scandals, revelations and even murder. The first episode sets the tone for a soap where trouble and strife are rarely far away. *Eastenders*, pitched to compete with ITV's *Coronation Street*, provides drama and characters to equal those of the Street, and soon its tropes and famous lines become part of soap opera lore, whether that's the inevitable black cab, hailed to spirit away departing characters, or Barbara Windsor's Peggy Mitchell screaming, 'Get outta my pub!'

Back to the Future

In *Back to the Future*, Michael J. Fox stars as Marty McFly, the high school kid who time travels back to 1955 in a bid to keep his parents together so that he can be born. Already a heartthrob thanks to his role in the US sitcom *Family Ties*, *Back to the Future* turns Fox into a movie megastar.

Girls on Top

Dawn French, Jennifer Saunders, Tracy Ullmann and Ruby Wax are four mismatched flat mates in *Girls on Top*, a female riff on *The Young Ones* format, first shown on ITV on 23rd October. Wax plays to type as a loud, brash American, French is a militant feminist who works at *Spare Cheek* (a skit on *Spare Rib*), Saunders is her doltish school friend, Ullmann a manipulative nymphomaniac, while veteran actress Joan Greenwood plays their eccentric landlady. Ullman departs after the first series to find stardom in the US, and after a second series in 1986, the cast are killed off allowing French and Saunders to tread their own paths, right to the top.

Levi's 5 'Oh!' 1

A new advertising campaign for Levi's 501, the 'original shrink-to-fit' jeans, has TV viewers looking as stunned as the ladies in the 1950s laundromat who watch in awe as Nick Kamen strips down to his boxers to wash his favourite jeans, to the strains of Marvin Gaye's hit, *I Heard it Through the Grapevine*. The commercial is a sensation; it leads to rocketing sales of 501 jeans. Gaye's song takes to the charts and Kamen, with his demi-god looks, has his own moment of pop stardom.

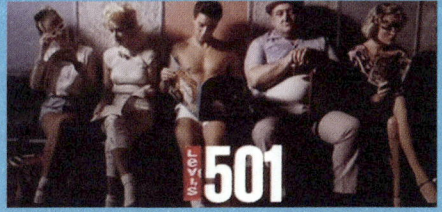

Cute + cuddly = cash

The cuddly Care Bears are first created by artist Elena Kucharik for American Greetings in 1981. Each one's tummy bears the insignia of a special emotion, and they live in the clouds in the faraway realm of Care-a-lot (aah). *A Care Bears* cartoon series for television and *The Care Bears Movie* this year guarantee the plush toy Care Bears are a money-spinner.

To the barricades

The Royal Shakespeare Company English-language production of Schönberg and Boublil's musical adaptation of Victor Hugo's novel, *Les Misérables*, opens at the Barbican Centre on 8th October and transfers to the Palace Theatre on 4th December. At the time of writing it is estimated that 132 million around the world have seen *Les Mis*, and it is the second-longest West End show after *The Mousetrap*.

Brat Pack's *Breakfast Club*

Arguably the ultimate teen flick. *The Breakfast Club* director and producer John Hughes assembles a group of young actors who become part of a set the media dub 'The Brat Pack'. Forced to endure a weekend detention at school in each other's company, a group of teenagers begin the morning as strangers but as they reveal their hopes, fears and frailties, depart united by their shared experience. The film relies largely on sharp dialogue rather than action, and with the talented cast and an 80s soundtrack led by Simple Minds' *Don't You Forget About Me*, it's a surprisingly emotive piece of cinema.

Rock me Amadeus

Tom Hulce brings some rock-star swagger to the role of the eighteenth century's musical prodigy in the film version of Peter Shaffer's play about Mozart which has its UK theatrical release on 17th January. F. Murray Abraham is the embittered court composer Salieri, whose consuming jealousy of the clownish Mozart's genius sours his entire career. *Amadeus* wins eight Academy Awards including Best Picture.

MUSIC

USA for Africa

28th January 1985 Prompted by the UK Band Aid charity single, dozens of US music stars pool their talents to record an American equivalent - *We Are the World*, written by Michael Jackson and Lionel Richie and released under the name USA for Africa. Performers include Ray Charles, Billy Joel, Bob Dylan, Smokey Robinson, Kenny Rogers, Diana Ross, Tina Turner and Bruce Springsteen. The record raises $50 million for famine relief.

Red Wedge

21st March 1985 A spine-tingling moment on *Top of the Pops* as Billy Bragg performs his unequivocally pro-miners and anti-Thatcher song, *Between the Wars*. Billy goes on to form the Labour Party-supporting musicians' collective Red Wedge with Paul Weller and Jimmy Somerville. Gigs and tours follow but, with as many critics on the left as on the right, it is wound up in 1990.

Going digital
13th May 1985 Led by guitarist brothers Mark and David Knopfler, Dire Straits are trailblazers for the new compact disc era with *Brothers in Arms*, one of the first to be recorded digitally rather than on analogue magnetic tape. It is the first album to sell more via the CD format than on vinyl and includes the self-deprecating *Money for Nothing*.

Springsteen fever
3rd July 1985 A month after his marriage to Julianne Phillips in Oregon and in the middle of an exhilarating 156-date world tour to promote his *Born in the USA* album, Bruce Springsteen plays three epic dates at Wembley Stadium. Such is the Springsteen fever overwhelming the UK this summer that his previous six albums all enter the chart on re-release.

Tipper's crusade
13th May 1985 Tipper Gore, wife of Senator Al Gore, forms the Parents Music Resource Center (PMRC) with three other 'Washington wives' to combat what they see as excessive reference to sex, violence, drugs and the occult in rock lyrics. Although much derided, they succeed in persuading the music industry to add 'parental advisory' stickers to products deemed likely to cause offence.

PARENTAL ADVISORY EXPLICIT CONTENT

Live Aid
13th July 1985 With wall-to-wall live television coverage, the momentous Live Aid concert takes place in Wembley Stadium and JFK Stadium in Philadelphia. Thanks to Concorde, Phil Collins performs at both. Status Quo open the London show with *Rockin' All Over the World*, with Queen, the Who, U2, Elton John and David Bowie all following. In Philadelphia, performers include the Beach Boys, the Pretenders, Santana, Neil Young, Duran Duran and a specially re-formed Led Zeppelin, who hate their performance so much they remove it from the official video. The total amount raised by both concerts is estimated at $150 million.

In Dublin's fair city
29th June 1985 Currently the top band on the planet thanks to their *The Unforgettable Fire* album, U2 come home to Dublin to play to a 55,000-strong audience at Croke Park. It is their biggest concert in their homeland to date.

Beatles publishing sold
6th September 1985 An unamused Paul McCartney discovers that the Northern Songs publishing catalogue containing most of the songs he composed with John Lennon has been sold to Michael Jackson.

1985

Angels and sisters

27th July 1985 Eurythmics - the oldest, canniest and most musically interesting of all the UK's many UK electro duos - miss out on Live Aid because of Annie Lennox's throat problems but top the UK chart with *There Must Be An Angel*, featuring Stevie Wonder on harmonica. Three months later they collaborate once more with soul music royalty - Queen of Soul Aretha Franklin - on the anthemic *Sisters Are Doin' It for Themselves*.

Norway's year

19th October 1985 Dedication pays off in the end. That's the lesson of Norwegian trio A-Ha's *Take On Me*, which has just been released for the third time in two years. Promoted this time by an award winning pencil-drawn animated video, it helps A-ha become the first Norwegian act ever to top the US chart.

MY FIRST 18 YEARS
TOP 10 — 1985

1. **Material Girl** *Madonna*
2. **Dancing in the Street** *Mick Jagger & David Bowie*
3. **Saving All My Love for You** *Whitney Houston*
4. **Between the Wars** *Billy Bragg*
5. **Would I Lie to You** *Eurythmics*
6. **Nightshift** *The Commodores*
7. **Frankie** *Sister Sledge*
8. **Running Up That Hill** *Kate Bush*
9. **A New England** *Kirsty MacColl*
10. **Glory Days** *Bruce Springsteen*

Open | Search | Scan

Lionel makes history

9th November 1985 Four years after leaving the Commodores (photo), Lionel Richie is now the leading solo act in the US. He moves on from steering the USA for Africa project to create history with *Say You Say Me* from the movie *White Nights*. He is the only composer ever to have written nine No. 1s in nine consecutive years. Now planning his next album and single, *Dancing on the Ceiling*.

SPORT

Chelsea win Full Members Cup
23rd March 1986 Chelsea become the first winners of the new 'Full Members Cup', a competition designed to fill the scheduling gap left by UEFA's ban on English clubs playing in European competitions. The final at Wembley sees an incredible fight back from Manchester City, who at one point are 5-1 down, to set the final score at 5-4 to Chelsea.

Argentina win World Cup
29th June 1986 Argentina secure victory in the 1986 FIFA world cup final in Mexico City, with a 3-2 win against West Germany. Argentinian captain Diego Maradona celebrates the win just a week after breaking English hearts with his famous 'hand of God' goal in their 2-1 defeat of England in the quarter-final.

Birmingham Superprix
24th August 1986 The inaugural Birmingham Superprix kicks off in the city centre, becoming the first motorsport street race to be held in mainland Britain. Part of the Formula 3000 Championship, the race is red flagged when bad weather leads to a crash, with Spanish driver Luis Pérez-Sala taking the win.

Liverpool victorious
5th May 1986 Liverpool beat Chelsea 1-0 to win the First Division title for the 16th time, a new record. Five days later they defeat local rivals Everton 3-1 to win the FA Cup in the first all-Merseyside final.

More hooliganism
8th August 1986 The future of English participation in European football is placed in further doubt when violence breaks out between Manchester United and West Ham fans onboard a ferry to Amsterdam. The clubs are both due to play friendlies in the city, whilst UEFA maintain their ban on English clubs in European competitions for a second season.

16 JAN 1986
Police arrest 2 IRA-terrorists in Amsterdam who had escaped from the Maze prison in 1983.

17 FEB 1986
Single European Act signed to establish the goal of a single market by 1992.

31 MAR 1986
Greater London Council abolished along with several other metropolitan county councils.

1986

Channel Tunnel planned
12th February 1986 France and the United Kingdom sign the Franco-British Channel Fixed Link Treaty to initiate the creation of a Channel Tunnel. The idea of a permanent tunnel connecting the two countries has been around since the early 1800s, but now the idea becomes a reality as the Eurotunnel Group is formed in August to finance and build the project.

John McCarthy kidnapped
17th April 1986 The Lebanon hostage crisis continues as British journalist John McCarthy (left) is kidnapped by Islamic jihadists in Beirut. In retaliation for US airstrikes in Libya, McCarthy is captured by gunmen on his way to the airport and held for over five years.

Northern Ireland Assembly dissolved
24th June 1986 Attempts to restore the devolution of power to Northern Ireland fall apart as the dissolution of the Assembly is ordered by the Secretary of State. Ian Paisley and his Democratic Unionist Party members refuse to leave their seats, leading to ugly scenes as they are dragged out by the Royal Ulster Constabulary.

New exams launched
September 1986 14-year-olds across Britain begin their new 'GCSE' courses, which replace the old GCE 'O' Levels and CSEs. The first exams will be sat in 1988.

Babes in the Wood murders
9th October 1986 Nine-year-old Nicola Fellows and her friend, ten-year-old Karen Hadaway, are reported missing near Brighton. The following day, their bodies are found in Wild Park. Russell Bishop, a twenty-year-old roofer, is soon arrested and charged, but thanks to errors in the investigation is acquitted, and will not be brought to justice until 2018.

M25 opens
29th October 1986 The London Orbital Motorway is finally completed 11 years after the first section opened in 1975. At almost 120 miles long, it opens as the longest ring road in Europe.

14 APR 1986
Desmond Tutu elected Archbishop of Cape Town, South Africa.

17 MAY 1986
Chicken Song by Spitting Image becomes number one in the UK Singles Chart.

8 JUN 1986
Alleged Nazi Kurt Waldheim elected President of Austria.

Childline opens

30th October 1986 A new telephone counselling service for children and young people launches in the UK. Childline is open 24 hours a day, 365 days a year, and is launched by Esther Rantzen at the BBC, who hopes it will help to intervene and save the lives of children in danger across the country.

Shetland Chinook crash

6th November 1986 A Chinook helicopter crashes into the ocean on the approach to Sumburgh Airport on the Shetland Islands. The helicopter is acting as a shuttle, carrying workers from the nearby Brent Oilfield back to the island, and comes down with 47 people on board, only two of whom survive.

AIDS crisis campaign

21st November 1986 Amid a rising death toll and estimates that as many as 30,000 people may be infected across the country, the government launches a £20 million campaign to raise awareness of the dangers of HIV, known as the 'Don't Die of Ignorance' campaign.

UNESCO designates UK sites

November 1986 The UK gains its first UNESCO World Heritage Sites, as places including Stonehenge, Durham Cathedral, Ironbridge Gorge and Giant's Causeway are officially recognised for their cultural significance.

British gas privatised

8th December 1986 Following the 'If you see Sid… tell him!' advertising campaign, 4 million people apply for shares of British Gas as it is floated on the stock exchange. The initial share offering gives the company a valuation of around £9 billion.

ROYALTY & POLITICS

The Westland affair

9th January 1986 Two cabinet ministers resign over the so-called 'Westland Affair' in a debacle that comes close to unseating the Prime Minister. In a cabinet disagreement over the future of Westland Helicopters, Secretary of State for Defence Michael Heseltine resigns after claiming Margaret Thatcher will not allow a full discussion of the issue at cabinet. Trade and Industry Secretary Leon Brittan follows when it is revealed he leaked confidential letters to the press.

Queen hit by eggs

February 1986 Queen Elizabeth is struck by an egg whilst touring in New Zealand. The Queen and Prince Philip are targeted by two assailants protesting an 1840 treaty made between the British Crown and New Zealand Maoris. The Queen is unharmed, and later jokes that she 'prefers her New Zealand eggs for breakfast'. She is clearly not deterred from public duty, as later in the year she becomes the first British monarch to tour China.

---

1 JUL 1986

Unemployment hits a post-war high of 3,280,106 meaning almost 15% of the workforce are affected.

19 AUG 1986

National Bus Company privatised as Devon General bought out by management.

8 SEP 1986

The Oprah Winfrey Show is first broadcast in the US.

1986

Prince Andrew marries
23th July 1986 The Queen's third child, Prince Andrew, marries Sarah Ferguson at Westminster Abbey. In honour of the event, the Queen makes the new couple the Duke and Duchess of York.

Archer resigns
26th October 1986 Deputy Chairman of the Conservative Party Jeffrey Archer resigns over a *News of the World* story that claims he paid a prostitute £2,000 to leave the country.

DO YOU REMEMBER THIS?

Pogo Ball

FOREIGN
NEWS

Challenger disaster
28th January 1986 Immediately after the launch of the Challenger space shuttle, things go horribly wrong. A sealing ring on a thruster malfunctions and gas and fuel begin to leak. After 73 seconds, the Challenger turns into a huge fireball. One of the seven-person crew is 37-year-old teacher Christa McAuliffe, who Americans had already taken to their hearts. The launch is recorded and broadcast on television with a delay. The crew compartment, human remains and other fragments from the shuttle are recovered during a three-month recovery operation. The space shuttle programme is suspended for three years.

People power
25th February 1986 The twenty-year dictatorship of President Ferdinand Marcos of the Philippines ends when he is forced into exile by what is described as a 'people power' revolution and, crucially, the removal of US support. Corazon Aquino, widow of the murdered opposition leader, becomes President.

1 OCT 1986
'Big Bang' Day in London Stock Exchange as computerisation is introduced and foreign companies are welcomed.

22 NOV 1986
Mike Tyson becomes youngest heavyweight champion of the world at 20 years old.

9 DEC 1986
First case of bovine spongiform encephalopathy is diagnosed i British cattle as the BSE crisis unfolds.

Iran-Contra affair

21st November 1986 On this day, as investigations into the Iran-Contra affair continue, Lieutenant Colonel Oliver North and his secretary begin shredding documents implicating them in selling weapons to Iran and using the proceeds to fund the Contra rebels in Nicaragua. Although Iran was and remains under an arms embargo, it emerges that a secret deal to sell arms was made to try to facilitate the release of US hostages then held in Lebanon. President Reagan denies all knowledge.

Chernobyl burns

26th April 1986 The worst nuclear disaster in history unfolds. Due to human error during a safety test, explosions occur in nuclear reactor 4 of the Chernobyl nuclear power plant in Ukraine, then part of the Soviet Union. The first explosion blows away the 2,000-ton lid of the reactor vessel. The graphite blocks catch fire and the power plant continues to burn for ten days. The fire releases enormous amounts of radioactive materials into the atmosphere. Communication about the catastrophe from the Soviet authorities is slow. More than 100,000 residents from the immediate area are evacuated. Chernobyl and the larger Pripyat turn into ghost towns. The radioactive cloud spreads rapidly across Europe and Asia. Thousands of kilometres away, radioactive particles flutter down. To prevent further spread of radioactive materials, a gigantic concrete sarcophagus is built around the nuclear reactor in Chernobyl. Although the first explosion kills just 31, thousands to tens of thousands of people die due to the effects of radioactive radiation, mainly from cancer.

Olof Palme

28th February 1986 Swedish Prime Minister Olof Palme and his wife are shot dead in the street in central Stockholm after a visit to the cinema. The murder of a democratically elected head of government is a huge shock in normally peaceful Sweden and far beyond.

ENTERTAINMENT

The Color Purple

Stephen Spielberg takes a step away from fantasy and sci-fi to direct the film version of Alice Walker's book *The Color Purple*, with newcomer Whoopi Goldberg revelatory as a wonderfully expressive Celie, and Oprah Winfrey making her screen debut as Sofia. UK audiences get to see it on 11th July.

Neighbours

The inhabitants of Ramsay Street, Erinsborough are introduced to British viewers at 1:25pm on 27th October, as part of its new daytime scheduling. *Neighbours* tackles the same themes as other soaps but it has the exotic appeal of being Down Under in houses and with weather less familiar to British viewers. It's also populated by a clutch of teenage characters who soon gain thousands of British fans. The burgeoning romance of Scott and Charlene, played by Jason Donovan and Kylie Minogue, sees the show enjoy peak viewing figures when their wedding takes place in 1988, with both actors using their characters' relationship as a platform for their music career. Australia seems to be having a moment with the Poms, as film comedy *Crocodile Dundee*, starring Paul Hogan, is also released this year, on 12th December.

Out of Africa

'I had a farm in Africa'. So begin Karen Blixen's memoirs, translated to the screen by Sydney Pollack in a sweeping romance in which the majestic Kenyan countryside shares top billing with Meryl Streep as Blixen, and Robert Redford as the dashing adventurer, Denys Finch-Hatton, into whose arms she falls. *Out of Africa* is one of those stately, heart-swelling, mustsee movies. Not only does it scoop eight Academy Awards but it leaves many wishing they too could have their hair washed by Robert Redford!

Top Gun

'I feel the need, the need for speed!' Thrilling fighter jet sequences, Harley Davidsons, jukebox crooning, beach volleyball and a locker room bristling with testosterone: Tony Scott's *Top Gun* delivers a glossy, action-packed adrenalin rush which catapults Tom Cruise as 'Maverick' into Hollywood's super-league. A thundering soundtrack which includes Kenny Loggins' *Danger Zone* keeps up the pace and Berlin's *Take My Breath Away* spends four weeks at No.1 after the film's UK release on 3rd October.

Bobby Ewing's soapy return

The makers of *Dallas* like nothing better than leaving its viewers teetering on the edge of a cliffhanger at the end of each season, and season 9 is no exception when Pam finds husband Bobby lathering himself in the shower. Barely cliffhanger material you might think, except Bobby was killed off at the end of season 8. The entirely logical explanation for Bobby's resurrection, revealed in season 10, is that Pam had dreamt the entire past 31 episodes.

Merchant Ivory - a very British film partnership

Released in the UK on 18th April, *A Room with a View* cements the reputation of producer-director team Ismail Merchant and James Ivory for gorgeous, literary period films. It also thrusts Helena Bonham-Carter into the spotlight as she plays Lucy Honeychurch, the young woman whose romantic awakening takes place against picturesque Tuscan scenery. A sterling British cast including Maggie Smith, Denholm Elliott, Julian Sands and Daniel Day-Lewis lend admirable support.

Racy *Riders*

Riders by Jilly Cooper, is published this year, the first book in the author's steamy Rutshire Chronicles; a racy page-turner about the rivalries and love affairs in the world of competitive showjumping.

Bread

The first episode of *Bread* airs on BBC1 on 1st May and introduces viewers to the Boswells, a close-knit, working-class family presided over by matriarch and staunch Catholic Nelly 'Ma' Boswell, whose disgust at her husband's mistress 'Lilo' Lill leads to her frequently spitting the line, 'She is a tart!'. Nelly's brood of four sons and a daughter, through back handers, dodgy deals and dole diddling keep the family finances afloat with the day's 'bread' (money) donated to a chicken-shaped pot every episode under the watchful eye of their indomitable mother.

Lovejoy

Ian McShane is lovable rogue *Lovejoy*, an antiques dealer and part-time detective with an eye for a bargain as he tootles around the pretty Essex and Suffolk countryside wheeling and dealing. The first series begins on 10th January.

I have a cunning plan

The first series of *Blackadder*, set in the fifteenth century, had enjoyed modest success but the arrival of his descendant, Edmund Blackadder, a suave and shrewd Elizabethan courtier, in *Blackadder II* on 9th January, makes this historical comedy, a nationwide favourite. Rowan Atkinson's wily Edmund is both supported and hampered by his loyal, turnip-eating servant Baldrick whose cunning plans to get his master out of his latest scrape are invariably rejected. The rest of the cast provide brilliant Tudor caricatures.

The Singing Detective

Dennis Potter's *The Singing Detective* starring Michael Gambon as the hospitalised detective Philip Marlow, reminiscing about his childhood and unravelling mysteries in his head, airs on BBC1 on 16th November. Potter suffered from the same painful skin disease as his character and was sometimes forced to write with his pen tied to his wrist, as Philip does in the final episode.

Casualty rates

Casualty begins on BBC1 on 6th September, a hospital drama set in the accident and emergency department of Holby City Hospital, in a fictional area of Bristol. Written by Jeremy Brock and Paul Unwin, who based the storylines on observations they had personally made in NHS hospitals, the show is initially planned to run for fifteen episodes. Instead, its popularity leads to it becoming a more permanent fixture and *Casualty* goes on to become the longest-running medical drama in the world.

Fashion fix

Style mavens get a weekly fashion fix with the launch of BBC1's *The Clothes Show* on 13th October. Presented by designer Jeff Banks, who developed the idea out of the fashion slot he had on *Pebble Mill at One*, his co-host is Selina Scott, and they are later joined by fashion journalist and cool cat Caryn Franklin. Together they bring news from the catwalks, show viewers how to create budget looks at home, investigate great arbiters of style, and run a nationwide model competition.

Trouble and strife

Tensions are high in the Queen Vic on 16th October as two of *Eastenders'* most popular characters, Den and Angie Watts (Leslie Grantham and Anita Dobson) have an entire half hour devoted to their marriage breakdown and a surprising denouement. Den wants a divorce, and to leave Walford behind to make a new life with his mistress Jan. Angie tries to distract him and reveals to Den that she has only six months to live, obliging him to promise to stay with her.

The video age

The Chart Show begins on Channel 4 on 11th April, launching its first episode with the music video *What You Need* by INXS. Created to rival *Top of the Pops*, but without any cheesy DJ presenters, *The Chart Show* has in fact no presenters at all.

The Golden Girls

The Golden Girls comes to Britain this year, with the first episode broadcast on Channel 4 on 1st August. The chemistry between Bea Arthur as Dorothy, Betty White as Rose, Rue McClanahan's Southern belle Blanche and Estelle Getty as Dorothy's feisty, wise-cracking mother is irresistible as the four characters rub along together in the Florida house they share.

MUSIC

West End boys

11th January 1986 Just as the electro pop era appear to be passing, another solemn-looking pair of Brits in long coats appears. The Pet Shop Boys offer a new slant, however. A former journalist with *Smash Hits*, Neil Tennant and synth-playing partner Chris Lowe write smartly rhymed lyrics to disco rhythms and deliver them in a passionless, almost bored style. With its echoes of Grandmaster Flash and T. S. Eliot's *The Waste Land*, *West End Girls* is the first No. 1 of 1986 and announces a duo who will still be having hits nearly 40 years later.

Europe rocks
6th December 1986 With an apocalyptic lyric partly inspired by David Bowie's *Space Oddity, The Final Countdown* tops the UK chart for two weeks for Swedish hard rock band Europe.

Sister in control
4th February 1986 Working with producer-writers Jimmy Jam and Terry Lewis, Janet Jackson emerges from brother Michael's shadow with break-

through album *Control* and single *What Have You Done for Me Lately*. In a year when Michael releases no new material, Janet fills the vacuum with her own pot-pourri of funk, soul and Paula Abdul-directed choreography.

Running the world
June 1986 Having had to turn down an invitation to play Live Aid, UK synth duo Tears for Fears back the next Ethiopian relief fund raiser, Sport Aid, by re-recording their BRIT Award-winning *Everybody Wants to Rule the World* as *Everybody Wants to Run the World*. The song was originally featured on the album *Songs from the Big Chair*, which achieved ten million sales in 1985 and established the band as a major force in the US.

Chain Reaction
8th March 1986 After Barbra Streisand and Dionne Warwick, newly married Diana Ross is the latest music diva to benefit from the hit writing skills of Barry, Robin and Maurice Gibb. A homage to her Motown past, *Chain Reaction* tops the UK and most overseas charts but flops completely in the US.

Arise, Sir Bob
10th June 1986 Dublin-born Bob Geldof receives an honorary British knighthood for his work raising money for famine relief in Ethiopia.

Last gigs
9th August 1986 At the end of a tour promoting the *A Kind of Magic* album and single, Queen play what will turn out to be their last concert with Freddie Mercury as lead singer, at Knebworth Park in Hertfordshire. A number of other leading bands play their last concerts this year - pending reunions, of course - including Madness, Boomtown Rats, Weather Report, Wham! and the Clash, while the Smiths drift inexorably towards disbandment.

Graceland controversy
25th August 1986 Paul Simon's *Graceland* album is released to a barrage of criticism over his decision to record in apartheid-gripped South Africa. Simon counters by pointing out his employment of and close collaboration with black musicians who wouldn't otherwise be heard anywhere in the West.

1986

Hip hop hybrid
New York hip hop kings Run-DMC didn't plan to smash genre boundaries with their take on a 1975 Aerosmith track, *Walk This Way*. With the latter's Steve Perry repeating the original's irresistible guitar riff, they create an eye-opening hybrid of rap and metal that defies US radio conventions and leads rock music into a whole new direction.

Bangles go manic
California's all-female Bangles become the UK's favourite American band of 1986 with the 1960s-styled guitar-and-harmonies hits *Manic Monday* (written by Prince), *Going Down to Liverpool* and *Walk Like an Egyptian*.

Blue collar rock
Maybe it's the Springsteen influence but 'blue collar rock' - rugged no-nonsense rock'n'roll aimed at a working-class audience - is in many ways the sound of 1986. Setting the standard is New Jersey boy Jon Bon Jovi and his band, whose *Slippery When Wet* album tops the US listings. The highlight is a blue collar anthem to cap them all - *Livin' on a Prayer*.

MY FIRST 18 YEARS
TOP10   1986

1. **The Way it Is** *Bruce Hornsby and the Range*
2. **Sledgehammer** *Peter Gabriel*
3. **Caravan of Love** *The Housemartins*
4. **Addicted to Love** *Robert Palmer*
5. **Holding Back the Years** *Simply Red*
6. **Papa Don't Preach** *Madonna*
7. **Take My Breath Away** *Berlin*
8. **White Wedding** *Billy Idol*
9. **Kiss** *Prince*
10. **Word Up** *Cameo*

Open | Search | Scan

Hull of a band
20th December 1986 They look gawky, dance like dads at a disco and play up their roots in unfashionable Hull. But for all the Housemartins' comic veneer, *Happy Hour* delivers a strong pro-union and anti-Murdoch message. During the year-long miners' strike, Paul Heaton and friends played more gigs for miners' families than any other band in the country. A captivating album cheekily titled *London O Hull 4* is followed by an unexpected Christmas No. 1 - a lovely acapella version of the Isley Brothers' *Caravan of Love*.

SPORT

Football firsts

1987 sees some footballing firsts, as Aldershot FC become the first team to win promotion through the new playoff system, Arsenal win the League Cup for the first time, and Coventry become first-time winners of the FA Cup.

First Rugby World Cup

22nd May 1987 The very first Rugby World Cup kicks off in New Zealand with a home side victory over Italy. 16 nations battle it out, with Wales proving the best performing home nation, securing third place over joint-hosts Australia. Favourites New Zealand go on to win the tournament with a 29-9 victory over France as the Webb Ellis Cup is lifted for the first time.

Great year for British golf

19th July 1987 Nick Faldo wins the Open Championship by just one stroke, becoming the first Englishman to claim the title since Tony Jacklin in 1969. One week later, Laura Davies, just 23 years old, wins the US Women's Open, having won the British Open the previous year.

Whitbread gold

6th September 1987 British athlete Fatima Whitbread puts in a wonderful performance at the World Athletics Championships to win the country's only gold medal with an incredible 76.64 metre throw in the javelin.

Cricket Cup and controversy

8th November 1987 England are defeated by Australia in the final of the Cricket World Cup in Calcutta, a disappointment that is followed in December by fractious scenes on the English tour of Pakistan. During the second test, Captain Mike Gatting and umpire Shakoor Rana engage in a foul-mouthed shouting match that is broadcast worldwide. Gatting issues Rana with a written apology.

DOMESTIC NEWS

Naji al-Ali shot in London

22nd July 1987 Shots ring out in London as Palestinian cartoonist Naji al-Ali is attacked outside the offices of Kuwaiti newspaper *al-Qabas*. Famed for his satirical cartoons lampooning politicians across the Middle East, his sharply critical commentaries earned him many enemies, including Yasser Arafat. His murder is still unsolved.

B

1 JAN 1987

British Airways is floated on the stock market ahead of its privatisation in February.

27 FEB 1987

The General Synod of the Church of England votes for legislation to allow the ordination of women priests.

24 MAR 1987

Soul Train Music Awards winners are Janet Jackson and Luther Vandross.

MS *Herald of Free Enterprise*

6th March 1987 Tragedy strikes as car and passenger ferry the MS *Herald of Free Enterprise* gets into difficulty leaving the harbour of Zeebrugge in Belgium. The bow door of the ship is left open, allowing the ferry to flood with water and capsize, coming to rest on its side. Many stories of bravery emerge following the rescue attempts, but despite most of the 539 passengers and crew on board being rescued safely, 193 passengers lose their lives in the worst British maritime disaster in over 150 years.

Knightsbridge robbery

12th July 1987 Two men hold up the Knightsbridge Safe Deposit Centre and steal £60 million in what would prove to be one of the largest robberies in history. The mastermind, Valerio Viccei, is identified by a fingerprint at the scene and, despite having fled the country, is later arrested when he returns to pick up his Ferrari Testarossa.

Spycatcher causes trouble

31st July 1987 Trouble erupts over the publication of the book *Spycatcher,* an autobiography written by former MI5 officer Peter Wright. The book, which contains many embarrassing details about the activities of the secret services, is banned from publication in the UK. Gag orders are served to several newspapers who attempt to publish details of some of the allegations made, leading many to mock and ridicule the Law Lords. The book is eventually cleared for publication in 1988.

Archer wins libel case

25th July 1987 Former Conservative deputy chairman Jeffrey Archer wins a libel case against the *Daily Star*, and the tabloid is forced to pay him £500,000 in damages. Despite this, he is found guilty of perjury in 2001 after providing a false alibi during the trial.

The Troubles

The Provisional IRA conduct a number of attacks in 1987, including a bomb at a British Army barracks in Rheindahlen, West Germany, which injures 31. In November, the Enniskillen bombing claims the lives of 12 people at a Remembrance Day service and injures over 60 who had gathered to commemorate the war dead. The IRA themselves suffer their biggest loss of the Troubles in May, when eight members are killed by the SAS in an ambush at Loughgall, County Antrim, in which a civilian is also killed.

Hungerford massacre

19th August 1987 Gunman Michael Ryan goes on a rampage armed with handguns and a semi-automatic rifle in the town of Hungerford, Berkshire. He kills sixteen people, including his own mother, and injures sixteen more before turning the gun on himself.

3 APR 1987

Gorbachev offers to remove all Soviet short-range weapons from Eastern Europe.

11 MAY 1987

British Rail rebrands its second class as 'standard class' travel.

12 JUN 1987

Ronald Reagan challenges Mikhail Gorbachev to 'tear down' the Berlin wall.

The Great Storm
15th - 16th October 1987 England is struck overnight by the 'Great Storm', hurricane force winds which cause extensive damage and claim the lives of 22 people in the UK and Normandy. An estimated 15 million trees are felled, several ships are wrecked and the whole of the National Grid South East power system is shut down. Initial weather predictions had assumed the storm would be limited to coastal areas, and BBC weatherman Michael Fish receives much criticism for appearing to downplay the severity of the approaching winds.

No sign of Nessie!
11th October 1987 A million-pound project to scan the entirety of Loch Ness in search of the Loch Ness Monster fails to get a glimpse of the legendary beast. Operation Deepscan deploys 24 boats with echo-sounding equipment to scan the waters, and despite encountering several unidentified objects, the results are written off as debris on the loch bottom and seals at play.

IKEA arrives in the UK
1st October 1987 The first IKEA store in the UK opens in Warrington, Cheshire. The Swedish store, founded in 1943, has been popular across the continent for decades and now for the first time Brits can get their hands on the reasonably priced flatpack furniture that makes the store famous.

King's Cross fire
18th November 1987 A terrible tragedy strikes the London Underground as a fire takes hold on an escalator at King's Cross Underground Station. The fire quickly burns out of control, filling the tunnels with noxious gases and claiming the lives of 31 people.

ROYALTY & POLITICS

1987 General Election
11th June 1987 Margaret Thatcher wins a third term in office as the Conservatives secure another landslide victory. Despite losing 21 seats Thatcher is still comfortable with 376, a majority of 102.

SDP merges with Liberals
6th August 1987 The Social Democratic Party votes to merge with the Liberal party in a move that sees leader Dr David Owen resign. He is replaced as leader by Robert Maclennan but founds a breakaway faction of the party to continue outside the proposed merger.

7 JUL 1987
Chessington Zoo reopens as a theme park, Chessington World of Adventures.

1 AUG 1987
MTV Europe launches; *Money For Nothing* by Dire Straits is the first video played.

1 SEP 1987
The Montreal Conference sees over 70 nations agree on measures to protect the ozone layer.

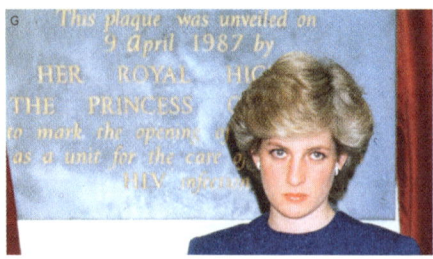

Diana opens AIDS ward

9th April 1987 Princess Diana opens the Broderip Ward at the Middlesex Hospital, the first ward in the UK exclusively for the treatment of HIV and AIDS. The princess makes a stir when she shakes the hands of patients without wearing gloves, directly challenging the fear many people had of the disease.

FOREIGN
NEWS

Political suicide

22nd January 1987 A bizarre scene on television in the US. R. Budd Dwyer, Pennsylvania's state treasurer, has been taking millions of dollars in kickbacks from a computer company and faces 55 years in prison. The day before the prison sentence starts, Dwyer holds a press conference. Everyone expects him to announce his resignation. But Dwyer takes a revolver from an envelope and shoots himself in the head.

Terry Waite kidnapped

20th January 1987 Terry Waite, the Archbishop of Canterbury's special envoy, is in Lebanon to attempt to negotiate the release of UK hostages held there when he himself becomes a victim of kidnapping. He will remain captive until 1991.

Andy Warhol dies

22nd February 1987 Pop art godfather, film maker and entrepreneur Andy Warhol dies in New York, aged 58. In his time he has elevated such everyday things such as Campbell's soup cans to art. Out of his New York City studio The Factory came a revolution that swept the art world, while Warhol also made a huge contribution to the history of rock music through sponsoring and producing the Velvet Underground.

Waldheim banned

27th April 1987 The US Department of Justice declares Kurt Waldheim, former Secretary General of the UN and now the elected President of Austria, 'an undesirable alien' over his recently discovered role in Nazi persecution during the Second World War.

Black Monday

19th October 1987 The global stock exchanges are turning into battlefields. After five years in which stock prices rose by an average of 350 per cent, the bubble has suddenly burst. It's Black Monday: 600 billion dollars on the Dow Jones evaporates in one day. The exact cause of the sudden stock market crash is unclear.

30 OCT 1987
George Michael's debut album *Faith* is released.

18 NOV 1987
King's Cross fire kills 31 people on the London Underground.

1 DEC 1987
Construction begins on the Channel Tunnel.

Very expensive Van Goghs
30th March 1987 Vincent van Gogh sets the record twice for the most expensive painting ever. A Japanese insurance company pays $39.7 million for *Vase of Fifteen Sunflowers* (1889) at an auction at Christie's in London. On 11th November, the controversial Australian businessman Alan Bond buys Van Gogh's *Irises* (1889) at Sotheby's for 49 million dollars.

Five billion
11th July 1987 UN figures reveal that the world's population now stands at five billion.

Rudolf Hess dies
17th August 1987 Rudolf Hess, Adolf Hitler's deputy, commits suicide at Spandau prison in West Berlin aged 93. He had been imprisoned since his conviction for crimes against peace in 1947.

INF Treaty
8th December 1987 In the White House, American President Ronald Reagan and Soviet leader Mikhail Gorbachev conclude a historic agreement. The superpowers agree that both sides will no longer possess, make or test ground-launched missiles with a range of 500 to 5,000 kilometres.

Flying stunt
28th May 1987 German teenager Mathias Rust performs a stunt that makes world news. The eighteen-year-old boy from Wedel rents a Cessna plane in Hamburg and flies to the Russian border via Iceland and Scandinavia. He flies on to Moscow and circles his plane a few times above the Kremlin, before landing the plane next to Red Square. He is arrested and sent to a labour camp. After fourteen months, Rust is pardoned.

ENTERTAINMENT

Through the Keyhole
Nosy types tune in to *Through the Keyhole* on 3rd April, as Lloyd Grossman snoops around celebrity homes while the panellists back in the studio, guided by David Frost, try to guess 'who might live in a house like this?' It's a perfect opportunity to see how the other half live and reminds us that money doesn't necessarily buy good taste.

Going for Gold

Quiz show *Going for Gold*, presented by Henry Kelly, begins on BBC1 on 12th October. Seven contestants from different European countries battle it out through several rounds in a bid to make it to the grand final.

Prime Minister's questions

Prime Minister Margaret Thatcher appears on *Saturday Superstore* on 10th January, taking part in their Pop Panel, and burying the hatchet in the career of indie band Thrashing Doves by praising their latest hit. When teenager Alison Standfast rings in and persists in asking Thatcher where she will be in the event of nuclear war, asking bluntly, 'Haven't you got a bunker or something?', things suddenly feel rather awkward. *Saturday Superstore's* final episode is on 18th April and a new Saturday morning show, *Going Live!*, presented by Philip Schofield, begins in the autumn this year.

It's a Royal Knockout

The Royal Family appear on the small screen this year when they take part in *The Grand Knockout Tournament* on 15th June, with a medieval tournament theme. Organised by Prince Edward, there are four teams led by himself, the Princess Royal, and the Duke and Duchess of York, each aiming to raise funds for their individual charities. In support is an eclectic mix of celebrities from Meatloaf to John Mills participating in what some see as an undignified display of royal buffoonery (apparently the Queen disapproves). Nevertheless, *It's a Royal Knockout* raises £1.5 million and has an estimated global audience of 400 million.

Coffee?

The first TV commercial for Nescafé Gold Blend airs this year, featuring yuppy neighbours Sharon Maughan and Anthony Head who begin a flirtation over coffee. Their on-screen chemistry leads to a series of adverts over the next six years in an ongoing will they/won't they soap opera. 30 million viewers tune in to see the finale where he finally professes his love. Meanwhile, Nescafé Gold Blend sales increase by 70%.

Bring me the finest wines

Richard E. Grant is the Withnail in *Withnail and I*, playing the hungover, loquacious libertine with boundless gusto. Withnail and Marwood (Paul McGann) are out-of-work actors who leave their squalid Camden flat for a holiday in the Lake District where they stay in a rundown cottage owned by Withnail's Uncle Monty. Full of memorable moments including the scene when Withnail strides into a Penrith tearoom and demands, 'We want the finest wines available to humanity. We want them *here*. And we want them *now*!', never has a miserable existence been quite so hilarious.

The Untouchables

Released 18th September, the violent underworld of Prohibition-era Chicago is the backdrop to Brian de Palma's thrilling, *The Untouchables*, with Kevin Costner as Treasury agent Eliot Ness, who assembles a team of uncorruptible law men to dismantle the power base of mob boss Al Capone and bring him to justice. As Capone, Robert de Niro takes on another role requiring him to pile on the pounds, while Sean Connery wins Best Supporting Actor Oscar for playing heroic cop Jimmy Malone.

Thundercats - Innocence under siege

Lion-O, Cheetara, Panthro, Tygra et al thunder onto the small screen on 2nd January, a team of handsome cat-human heroes determined to save the Eye of Thundera from the Mutants of Plum-Darr and evil sorcerer, mummified Mumm-Raa. Along with other American imports like *Transformers* and *He-Man*, *Thundercats* is criticised not only for the level for violence, but also how commercially driven it is.

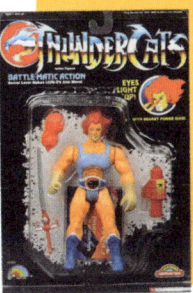

Chucklevision

Paul and Barry Chuckle bring a finely-tuned blend of slapstick, jokes and vivid characters to CBBC on 26th September in *Chucklevision*. They travel around on the Chuckmobile, mess up every job they take on and coin a series of catchphrases that infiltrate the subconscious of adults as well as children. Through a staggering 293 episodes over 22 years, 'From Me...To You' and 'No slacking' become part of the national lexicon.

Blackadder the Third

Beginning on BBC1 on 17th September, *Blackadder the Third* transports Edmund Blackadder to the eighteenth century this time, where he is courtier and friend to Hugh Laurie's frightfully dim Prince of Wales, while Baldrick is still filthy, still stupid and still existing on a diet of turnips. Ben Elton and Richard Curtis have great fun with the Georgian references from Mrs. Miggins's Pie Shop to the episode where Baldrick accidentally burns Samuel Johnson's dictionary, obliging Edmund to re-write it in a weekend.

Logan's Eurovision Run

Following on from his 1980 success with *What's Another Year?* on 9th May, Irish crooner Johnny Logan returns to the Eurovision Song Contest, this time held in Brussels, for another stab at glory with *Hold Me Now*. He brings the title back home to the Emerald Isle and passes into Eurovision legend as one of only two double winners in the history of the competition. He also pens Ireland's 1992 winning entry, *Why Me?*, sung by Linda Martin.

DO YOU REMEMBER THIS?

Treets now M&M's

Morse code

A cerebral detective inspector who drives a Jaguar Mark 2 and has a fondness for real ale, opera and cryptic crosswords, *Inspector Morse*, first shown on ITV on 6th January, is a different animal to the traditional TV cop. In fact, Morse, who first appeared in a series of books by Colin Dexter, couldn't be more different than Jack Regan, the police character previously played by John Thaw in *The Sweeney*. The crimes are somehow more elevated too, being carried out among the dreaming spires of Oxford and surrounding countryside. Accompanied by the down-to-earth Geordie Sergeant Lewis (Kevin Whateley), Morse runs until 1993; at its peak drawing audiences of 18 million.

Top toys

Among this year's best-selling toys are Hasbro's My Little Pony, colourful equine figures with delicious names like Apple-jack and Peachy, with toy sales boosted by *My Little Pony - The Movie*. And firmly entrenched as a family favourite is Trivial Pursuit, the game of general knowledge based on the famous quotation from Pope's *Rape of the Lock* - '*What mighty contests rise from trivial things.*'

Jailbirds

Prisoner Cell Block H, the Australian soap opera set in a women's prison, first airs on Central TV on 25th April (although Yorkshire TV has been showing it since 1984). It soon becomes a surprise, late-night ratings success.

MUSIC

House on fire

24th January 1987 Jack Your Body by Steve 'Silk' Hurley is the first record in the 'house' genre to top the UK chart. Originating in Chicago, house is a form of electronic dance music ruled by producer deejays such as Frankie Knuckles and Farley 'Jackmaster' Funk. In the UK, Beatmasters, Bomb the Bass and others are fuelling the Manchester-centred acid house boom to come.

Smiths to split

14th June 1987 The headline in *New Musical Express* reads 'Smiths to split'. It's premature, but it's correct: singer Morrissey and guitarist Johnny Marr are no longer talking. Marr is having much more fun working with Billy Bragg, Bryan Ferry and Talking Heads, while the opinionated, talented but difficult to like Morrissey is plotting a solo career.

'Nobody puts Baby in the corner'

When Frances 'Baby' spends her summer at a holiday resort in upstate New York with her parents in 1963, she falls in love with Johnny, a dance instructor from the wrong side of the tracks whose moves and grooves are anything but polite. *Dirty Dancing's* multi-million selling soundtrack includes the hit song, *I've Had The Time of My Life* - played during the film's climax when Baby and Johnny dance the routine they've practised and finally smash THAT lift. *Dirty Dancing* is a global sensation; UK audiences flock to see it when it opens on 16th October.

Def Jam

10th February 1987 Founded in 1985, producer Rick Rubin's New York-based Def Jam label is the epicentre of east coast hip hop with LL Cool J, the Beastie Boys and Public Enemy on its books. The latter's debut album *Yo! Bum Rush the Show*, released today, mixes in-your-face lyrics with radical political messaging.

Flower of Scotland

Just as the Pogues' *Fairytale of New York* is part of a venerable tradition of Irish diaspora songs, so the Proclaimers' *Letter from America* does the same for the Scottish emigration story. Twin brothers Craig and Charlie Reid are just the latest flowering of talent from Scotland.

Beasties in Britain

30th May 1987 Every couple of years, the UK press and publicity-seeking MPs create a media panic about some new band or style. This year their target is white hip hop trio the Beastie Boys, whose reputation follows them from the US. Tonight sees a particularly infamous gig in Liverpool including fights, missiles, a mini-riot and the arrest of Beastie Adam Horovitz, but did they really 'sneer at dying kids' as the *Daily Mirror* claims? Of course not.

D'Arby debut

13th July 1987 Attracting huge media attention is the debut album by Terence Trent D'Arby, R&B singer-songwriter whose rebel attitude saw him court martialled out of the Army in 1983. Entitled *Introducing the Hardline According to Terence Trent D'Arby*, it features four major hit singles including *Wishing Well*.

Blockbusters

Three blockbuster albums dominate the sales charts in 1987. Now the world's mightiest stadium band, U2 (photo) sell fourteen million with *The Joshua Tree*, which also wins the Grammy for best album and produces two US No. 1s. Michael Jackson's *Bad*, despite uneven reviews, produces five US No. 1s - a new record for any album. Then comes the biggest selling debut album ever: *Appetite for Destruction* from new hard rock icons Guns N' Roses.

1987

Family matters
Five Star seem to have it all: a solid disco-funk sound, cross-generation appeal, great choreography and TV-friendly looks. From Romford, Deniece Pearson and her four siblings are the missing link between the Jacksons and Sister Sledge.

Hit factory
The studio owned by production/writing team Mike Stock, Matt Aitken and Pete Waterman is called 'the hit factory' - and no wonder. Two No. 1s - *Respectable* by Mel and Kim (photo) and *Never Gonna Give You Up* by the boyish but big-voiced Rick Astley - follow hits for Dead or Alive and Bananarama, plus a dance track called *Roadblock* that they release anonymously to fool their critics. And all this is before a certain actress arrives from Australia to discuss making a record.

A Christmas fairytale
23rd November 1987 Irish punk folk band the Pogues record *Fairytale of New York* with Kirsty MacColl. Inspired by J. P. Donleavy's novel, it's a bruising but touching account of an Irish couple down on their luck in post-war Manhattan. Although a No. 2 hit, no one guesses how the song will keep coming back every Christmas and earn classic status - even if colourful language like 'scumbag', 'slut' and 'faggot' causes airplay issues in later years.

SPORT

Eddie the Eagle wins hearts

28th February 1988
The XV Winter Olympics in Alberta, Canada, draws to a close having made a star of one British athlete. Despite the representatives from Great Britain winning not a single medal across the games, the charm of Michael 'Eddie the Eagle' Edwards, Britain's first ever entry into the ski jumping event, captures the world's hearts. Edwards comes last in both the 70m and 90m events, despite setting a British record, but his enthusiasm is contagious, and wins him a legion of fans.

Seoul Summer Olympics

2nd October 1988 The British team return with five golds, ten silvers and nine bronzes from a games marred with controversy over drug taking. Canadian Ben Johnson (photo) is stripped of his 100m gold medal and world record when he tests positive for a banned substance, bumping Brit Linford Christie up to silver, and he is joined by nine other athletes across several disciplines who are all disqualified. Highlights of the games include US sprinter Florence 'Flo-Jo' Griffith-Joyner who secures gold in both 100 and 200m finals, and British gold for Steve Redgrave and Andy Holmes in the coxless Pairs.

Sandy Lyle wins US Masters

10th April 1988 The prestigious US Masters golf tournament falls to a Brit for the first time, as Scotsman Sandy Lyle takes the victory following an incredible fairway bunker shot and birdie putt that lives long in the memory.

European Championships

18th June 1988 England are knocked out of the Euros after losing all three group games and finishing bottom, a devastating result that is made even more sour by the arrest of over 100 fans for incidents of hooliganism. The tournament is eventually won by the Netherlands who beat the Soviet Union 2-0 in the final.

Exciting finishes in Cups

24th April 1988 A goal in the 92nd minute sees Luton Town FC secure a 3-2 victory over Arsenal in the final of the Littlewoods Football League Cup. The FA Cup also witnesses a fairytale result as Wimbledon FC beat league champions Liverpool 1-0 in the final after only two seasons in the first division, and Celtic do the double, coming from behind in the Scottish Cup Final to beat Dundee United with two late goals.

22 JAN 1988

Colin Pitchfork becomes first person convicted of murder based on DNA fingerprinting.

8 FEB 1988

Comic Relief's inaugural BBC 'Red Nose Day' raises over £15,000,000 for charity.

9 MAR 1988

Audrey Hepburn is appointed a UNICEF Special Ambassador.

1988

DOMESTIC NEWS

Railway killer sentenced
26th February 1988 One of the infamous 'Railway Killers', John Duffy, is sentenced to life imprisonment following a trial at the Old Bailey. He is convicted of two murders and four rapes, although he later admits to a further 17, conducted in dark places near railway stations. His accomplice in many of the attacks, David Mulcahy, is arrested in 1999.

Operation Flavius
6th March 1988 The deaths of three provisional IRA members at the hands of the SAS during 'Operation Flavius' in Gibraltar mark the beginning of a chain of violence, as the funerals of the three men are attacked by a loyalist paramilitary in the Milltown Cemetery attack. Three days later, during the funeral of a victim of the second attack, two British soldiers drive into the funeral procession, are dragged from their cars and shot, in what becomes known as the 'corporal killings'.

£1 note discontinued
11th March 1988 The £1 note, in circulation in one form or another since 1797, is no longer legal tender having been replaced with the £1 coin in 1983.

Piper Alpha disaster
6th July 1988 An explosion on board the Piper Alpha oil rig in the North Sea leads to its collapse and the deaths of 167 workers on board. Two would-be rescuers are also killed by the 200m-high flames. Only 61 of the 226 people on board are rescued and the disaster leaves behind enormous economic and ecological damage.

Pope heckled by Paisley
12th October 1988 During an address at the European Parliament, Pope John Paul II is heckled by Democratic Unionist Party leader and MEP Ian Paisley, who calls him the Antichrist. Paisley holds up a sign reading 'Pope John Paul II ANTICHRIST' and is forcibly removed from the chamber having been pelted with objects thrown by his fellow politicians.

IRA interviews banned
19th October 1988 The British government bans interviews with members of certain republican and loyalist organisations from being broadcast on radio or television, with the ban including the IRA and the Ulster Defence Association, among others. The move proves controversial as many in the media speak out against censorship, with multiple news outlets using professional actors to dub interviews instead.

5 APR 1988
A Kuwaiti airliner carrying members of the Kuwaiti royal family is hijacked in Iran.

1 MAY 1988
The first GCSE exams are sat by sixteen-year-olds across the country.

27 JUN 1988
Mike Tyson KOs Michael Spinks in 91 seconds.

Clapham Junction crash
12th December 1988 A signal failure leads to a collision between two busy commuter trains just outside of Clapham Junction station. 35 people are killed, 69 seriously injured and over 400 people suffer minor injuries. The first people on the scene are students and staff from a nearby school, who are later commended by the Prime Minister for their assistance.

Lockerbie bombing
21st December 1988 A bomb on board Pan Am Flight 103 to New York detonates at 7pm over the town of Lockerbie, killing all 259 people on board and 11 people on the ground. The nation grieves as news channels capture shocking images of the wreckage-strewn town. In 2001 a Libyan intelligence officer, Abdelbaset al-Megrahi, is convicted of the bombing, and Libyan leader Muammar Gaddafi pays compensation to the victims.

Ashdown new leader
28th July 1988 Following the merger of the Social Democratic and Liberal parties, a new leader, Paddy Ashdown, MP for Yeovil, is elected to take the new Social and Liberal Democratic Party forward. He will remain their leader for 11 years.

Birth of Princess Beatrice
8th August 1988 The country is delighted with the news of the birth of Princess Beatrice, the first child of the new Duke and Duchess of York.

ROYALTY & POLITICS

Prince Charles avoids avalanche
10th March 1988 Prince Charles comes face to face with death on a skiing holiday in Klosters, Switzerland, when an avalanche claims the life of his companion Major Hugh Lindsey, a former equerry to the Queen.

Currie causes outrage
3rd December 1988 Under-Secretary for Health Edwina Currie is forced to resign after she inspires widespread outrage by stating that most British eggs are infected with salmonella. The resulting 60% plummet in egg sales angers farmers, leads to the slaughter of four million hens, and earns her the nickname 'Eggwina'.

1 JUL 1988
The Young British Artists display their work at Surrey Docks, London, in Damien Hirst's 'Freeze' exhibition.

21 AUG 1988
New licensing laws allow pubs to open between 11am and 11pm outside of Sundays.

11 SEP 1988
Steffi Graf completes a record four Grand Slams and an Olympic gold in one year with victory in the US Open.

1988

Hole in the ozone layer
15th March 1988 A disturbing report from NASA shows that the ozone layer, which protects the Earth against UV radiation, is breaking down faster than thought.

Bush is President
8th November 1988 George Bush, who was Vice President during the Reagan administration and before that was one-time chief of the CIA, wins the US Presidential election. He defeats his Democrat challenger Michael Dukakis with over 53 per cent of the popular vote, despite having a somewhat gaffe-prone running mate in Dan Quayle.

Soviets pull out
15th May 1988 As promised by Mikhail Gorbachev, the Soviet Union begins pulling out its forces from Afghanistan after more than eight years. Often referred to as 'Russia's Vietnam', the Afghan conflict revealed the ineffectiveness of Russian military tactics against a committed guerrilla army.

Airliner shot down
3rd July 1988 During rising Iranian-US tension in the Gulf a civilian Iranian airliner is mistakenly shot down by USS *Vincennes*, killing all 290 passengers and crew.

Mitterand re-elected
8th May 1988 Francois Mitterand is re-elected President of France, defeating former Mayor of Paris Jacques Chirac.

Zia is killed
17th August 1988 President Muhammad Zia-ul-Haq of Pakistan is killed alongside several of his military commanders and US ambassador Arnold Raphel when their plane crashes near Bahawalpur.

CDs outsell LPs
29th December 1988 Year-end figures show that compact discs are outselling vinyl records for the first time in the US, fuelled by major releases such as George Michael's *Faith* and Van Halen's *OU812*. Total CD sales for 1988 are 150 million compared to vinyl album sales of 72 million.

Air show deaths
28th August 1988 An air show disaster in Germany claims the lives of 70 people, the majority of them spectators, when three jets of an Italian demonstration team collide.

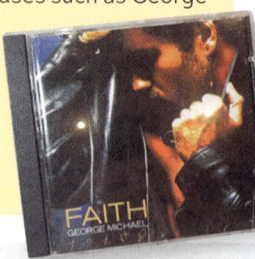

30 OCT 1988
Prince Charles speaks out against works of architecture, such as the National Theatre, that he feels are destroying the country's cities.

13 NOV 1988
Legandary McLaren driver Ayrton Senna wins his first Formula 1 World Drivers, Championship.

15 DEC 1988
Unemployment reaches an eight-year low at just over 2,100,000.

 # ENTERTAINMENT

Bunny boiler

A one-night stand with a work colleague has serious repercussions for happily married Michael Douglas in *Fatal Attraction*, a thriller that turns out to be one of this year's biggest movie successes. Glenn Close plays the increasingly unhinged Alex, who takes rejection rather badly. *Fatal Attraction* opens at UK cinemas on 15th January.

Good Morning, Vietnam

Robin Williams' rapid-fire stand-up style finds a perfect outlet as he takes on the role of real-life U.S. Armed Forces DJ Adrian Cronauer in *Good Morning, Vietnam* released in the UK on 30th September. Director Barry Levinson decided to let Williams's natural knack for ad-libbing take centre stage and simply let the cameras roll during the broadcast scenes, with many of the manic monologues done off the cuff.

Film love

It's an excellent year for arthouse cinema. *Distant Voices, Still Lives*, Terence Davies' elegiac film about his Liverpool childhood is released; Spanish auteur Pedro Almodovar wows with his *Women on the Verge of a Nervous Breakdown* (released in Spain this year), and then there is Guiseppe Tornatore's *Cinema Paradiso*, a film about the love of film. Its climactic ending, consisting of a cascade of censored film clips showing couples kissing, must surely be one of the greatest film finales ever.

DO YOU REMEMBER THIS?

Levi's 501

What a Relief

The first *Night of Comic Relief* takes place on 5th February - Red Nose Day - an eight-hour telethon featuring the best of British comic talent performing specially written sketches and skits to raise money for the Comic Relief charity.

There's a special *Spitting Image* version of *Question of Sport*, a one-off *Blackadder* special called *The Cavalier Years*, a classic episode of *Dad's Army*, and much more, all presented by Lenny Henry and Griff Rhys Jones. *The Night of Comic Relief* raises £15 million.

Fire! Fire!

London's Burning follows the lives and loves of the members of Blue Watch, a London Fire Brigade unit based in Blackwall, east London. Based on Jack Rosenthal's 1986 TV movie, the series begins on 20th February and continues until 2002, one of ITV's longest-running programmes after *Coronation Street* and *Emmerdale Farm*.

Morning from Merseyside

Liverpool's recently restored Albert Dock is the setting for ITV's new show *This Morning* with husband-and-wife team Richard Madeley and Judy Finnegan. The two-hour show, beginning on 3rd October, brings together health and family topics, cooking, fashion, hair and beauty and celebrity interviews.

Red Dwarf

Red Dwarf, a sci-fi comedy, touches down on BBC2 on 15th February. Craig Charles is Dave Lister, an astronaut who has been in stasis for three million years and wakes to find he is drifting around space alone except for a hologram of former crew member, Rimmer (Chris Barrie), and The Cat (Danny John-Jules), a feline humanoid who has evolved from the cat he originally smuggled onto the ship. By series III, this raggle-taggle trio is joined by Kryten, a robot with self-confidence issues. They are steered around the universe under the deadpan guidance of the ship's computer, 'Holly'.

Cartoon capers

Seamlessly blending live action and animation, *Who Framed Roger Rabbit* is released on 2nd December, starring Bob Hoskins as private eye Eddie Valiant, with Kathleen Turner providing the husky voice of the iconic cartoon screen siren and sex symbol, Jessica Rabbit.

A Fish Called Wanda

Farcical comedy *A Fish Called Wanda*, starring Kevin Kline, Jamie Lee Curtis, Michael Palin and John Cleese (who is also co-writer), is released on 14th October. The ensemble cast gel brilliantly but it is Kline who wins an Academy Award for best supporting actor.

Through the wardrobe

BBC1's adaptation of *The Lion, the Witch and the Wardrobe* by C. S. Lewis begins in its early Sunday evening slot on 13th November. It has taken the BBC several years to acquire the rights to the book, during which time technology has advanced enough to make a convincing production using animation and special effects to successfully recreate the magic of Narnia. This includes a huge Aslan, operated with two people inside the lion's body and a series of complex electronics.

Armchair shopping

Classy high street store Next launches the Next Directory this year, a mail order catalogue that is a cut above the rest. With a glossy magazine layout, fashion 'stories', exclusive designs and even fabric swatches, the Next Directory provides a luxe retail experience from the comfort of home.

Blood Brothers

Willy Russell's musical, *Blood Brothers*, about twin brothers separated at birth, originally makes its debut with a short run in Liverpool and the West End in 1983. But it is this year's revival at the Albery Theatre (later renamed the Noel Coward Theatre), beginning on 28th July, which goes on to become one of theatre's most successful musicals, running for 24 years and 10,000 performances.

Bough's off

Frank Bough has been a lynchpin of the BBC since 1963, a reliable presenter of breakfast news and sport with a smooth manner and penchant for sensible knitwear. Given Bough's squeaky-clean image, when the *News of the World* breaks a story alleging his involvement with cocaine and prostitutes, it's a scandal of epic proportions. Bough leaves the BBC in June.

Masquerade charade

When Kit Williams's exquisitely illustrated book *Masquerade* was published in 1979, it triggered a nationwide treasure hunt, as many tried to solve the book's fiendish, cryptic riddles to find a golden hare jewel buried somewhere in Britain. But on 11th December this year, the *Sunday Times* publishes a story about *Masquerade*'s winner who had managed to find the location of the jewel through insider links.

Die Hard

Bruce Willis and Alan Rickman fully commit to their respective roles of tough, vest-wearing hero cop John McClane and saturnine bad guy Hans Gruber in *Die Hard*, a tightly plotted, compelling action flick, which goes on to become a winning formula followed by four more sequels.

Whose Line Is It Anyway?

Channel 4 launches *Whose Line Is It Anyway?* on 23rd September, presented by Clive Anderson where four quick-witted performers are given a series of improvisational challenges. Based on the original radio programme also aired this year, *Whose Line Is It Anyway?* is huge fun and makes stars of a number of rising British and American stand-ups and comic actors including John Sessions, Tony Slattery, Josie Lawrence, Mike McShane, Greg Proops, Paul Merton and Rory Bremner.

That's Life - A moving moment

In February 1988, Nicholas Winton appears on *That's Life*, as presenter Esther Rantzen goes through his scrapbook from the time he had helped organise the rescue, transport and care of 669 mainly Jewish children from Nazi-occupied Czechoslovakia in 1939. During the programme, Rantzen tells Winton that the woman sitting next to him is Vera Gissen, who, as a little girl, was among those in his 'Kindertransport'. Three more of Winton's rescued children are also seated nearby. Winton is invited back on the show on 3rd July when Rantzen asks, 'Is there anyone who owes their life to Nicholas Winton?' When several rows of the audience stand up around him, it's one of the most moving and powerful moments in television history. Winton is knighted in 2003 and dies in 2015 at the age of 106.

MUSIC

Holly victory

19th February 1988 In an important test case, Holly Johnson of Frankie Goes to Hollywood wins the court action brought against him by record label ZTT, which sought to prevent him from signing with MCA as a solo artist.

Kylie's so lucky

20th February 1988 With one Australian No. 1 behind her - *The Locomotion* - Kylie Minogue starts recording *I Should Be So Lucky* with the hottest UK producers around, the team of Stock, Aitken and Waterman. Spending five weeks at No. 1, it begins one of the most enduring recording careers of the post-Beatle era. Kylie's success attracts a host of other soap opera stars to take a stab at the charts.

Tracy's triumph

11th June 1988 Stevie Wonder was to be the unannounced superstar of the Mandela concert at Wembley until a technical malfunction made it impossible for him to perform. In his place, with 45 minutes to fill, the little-known Tracy Chapman plays an impromptu acoustic set that turns her into an overnight star.

Girl power 80s style

Never has there been a year when the charts have been so dominated by female voices. Formerly of US all-girl band the Runaways, Belinda Carlisle kicks off 1988 at No. 1 with *Heaven is a Place on Earth*, to be followed by sixteen-year-old Tiffany with *I Think We're Alone Now* and Kylie's *I Should Be So Lucky*. Another teen star is the emerging Debbie Gibson, who writes her own material, while Robin Beck, Enya and Whitney Houston all have UK chart-toppers. And the most perfect pop record of the year? A tie between Yazz's (photo) *The Only Way is Up* and Fairground Attraction's *Perfect*, featuring the glorious voice of Glasgow folk and blues singer Eddi Reader.

P

Celine's a winner
30th April 1988 Ne parlez pas sans moi wins the Eurovision Song Contest for Switzerland, performed by a little-known French-Canadian singer with a voice as big as her future - Celine Dion.

The Big 'O' departs
6th December 1988 The sudden death of Roy Orbison throws the future of the Traveling Wilburys into doubt. The Wilburys are the ultimate rock super-group - a part-time fun project for Roy and fellow veterans Bob Dylan, George Harrison, Tom Petty and Jeff Lynne, who elect to continue as a foursome.

Concert for Mandela
11th June 1988 Concert of the year is at Wembley Stadium - a multi-act 70th birthday tribute to anti-apartheid leader Nelson Mandela, who has been incarcerated on Robben Island for 25 years. Musically, the line-up is even more impressive than Live Aid, bringing together Sting, George Michael, Eurythmics, Al Green, Natalie Cole, the Bee Gees, Simple Minds, Whitney Houston, UB40, Dire Straits and South African music stars Miriam Makeba and Hugh Masekela.

Gangsta rap
8th May 1988 As rap's reputation for confrontation continues to close off many UK venues to visiting hip hop artists, Wembley Arena bars Run DMC. Rap's image is further dented - or enhanced, depending on your point of view - by the release of *Straight Outta Compton* by NWA in August, its advocacy of violence denying it airplay and incurring a warning from the FBI. As if NWA care: the album is certified platinum within a year and 'gangsta rap' is the new buzzword.

Elton wins his case
11th December 1988 The day before his libel case against The *Sun* is due to be heard, Elton John receives a million pounds in damages. He was suing the paper over drug and rent boy allegations that were wholly untrue.

Motown is sold

6th July 1988 MCA Records buys Motown for $61 million, ending the latter's 30 years as an independent company.

Brosmania

For proof that the old-fashioned pop attributes of pretty faces, catchy tunes and ephemeral fame are re-asserting themselves, look no further than Bros, two twin brothers (Matt and Luke Goss) and their best mate Craig Logan, who debut with an anthem for the age of celebrity – *When Will I Be Famous*. The trio's eighteen months in the spotlight eventually dissolve into courtroom acrimony.

MY FIRST 18 YEARS
TOP10   1988

1. **Fast Car** *Tracy Chapman*
2. **Orinoco Flow** *Enya*
3. **When I Fall I Love** *Rick Astley*
4. **Rush Hour** *Jane Wiedlin*
5. **Don't Worry Be Happy** *Bobby McFerrin*
6. **Don't Be Cruel** *Cheap Trick*
7. **I Don't Want to Talk ...** *Everything but the Girl*
8. **A Little Respect** *Erasure*
9. **Girlfriend** *Pebbles*
10. **Sweet Jane** *The Cowboy Junkies*

Open | Search | Scan

In memoriam

Among the music greats leaving us this year are jazz trumpeter Chet Baker, aged 58, and singer and bandleader Brook Benton, 56. In March, Barry, Robin and Maurice Gibb mourn younger brother Andy who had three US No. 1s in 1977-78. David Prater, one half of soul duo Sam and Dave, dies in a car accident in April aged 50, and German singer Nico of Velvet Underground fame dies aged 49 in Ibiza from an untreated head injury.

Jackson v. Prince

14th July 1988 There's a clear hint of rivalry behind the respective touring plans of Michael Jackson and Prince. Jackson begins a UK visit with seven dates at Wembley Stadium. By the time of his last concert in September at Aintree Racecourse, he will have played in front of three quarters of a million Brits. Just two days after Jackson's last stadium date, Prince opens his European *Lovesexy* tour with seven nights at Wembley Arena and arrives onstage in a pink Cadillac.

SPORT

Faldo wins Masters

10th April 1989 Nick Faldo wins the Masters Tournament, becoming the first English player to take the trophy. Despite going into the fourth round five shots off the lead, Faldo makes it into a playoff with Scott Hoch and takes victory with a 25-foot putt on the second hole.

Desert Orchid

16th March 1989 Fan favourite Desert Orchid wins the Cheltenham Gold Cup in an exciting finish. Despite setting off an 11-4 favourite, 'Dessie', as he became known, hated the mud and the left-handed track and was being tried over a far longer distance than he had run before. After the race his jockey, Simon Sherwood, stated that he had 'never known a horse so brave'.

Hillsborough disaster

15th April 1989 Tragedy strikes the FA Cup semi-final between Nottingham Forest and Liverpool at Hillsborough, Sheffield, when a crush kills 97 fans and seriously injures 300 more. *Sun* prompts outrage by falsely claiming that survivors robbed the dying and attacked emergency services. Stadiums around the country move to remove perimeter fences and standing sections. A month later, Liverpool win the FA Cup final 3-2 over Everton, but Liverpool fans have to wait years for justice, with a second inquest finally finding that the victims were unlawfully killed in 1996.

Mansell wins Grand Prix

26th March 1989 British racing driver Nigel Mansell shocks fans in his first season with Ferrari by winning an unlikely Grand Prix in Brazil. The race is at the home track of his rival, Nelson Piquet, who many expect to dominate, but despite prior issues with the car's new semi-automatic gearbox, Mansell powers to victory.

First UK WWF event

10th October 1989 The London Arena plays host to the very first World Wrestling Federation event held in the UK. Known as the 'UK Rampage', it is broadcast live on the new Sky One channel and features top performers such as Hulk Hogan and Randy Savage, who battle it out for the Heavyweight Championship.

---

20 JAN 1989

George Bush Senior is sworn in as the 41st President of the United States.

2 FEB 1989

F. W. de Klerk replaces P. W. Botha as South Africa's National Party leader.

20 MAR 1989

Two superintendents of the Royal Ulster Constabulary are shot dead by the IRA.

DOMESTIC
NEWS

Kegworth air disaster
8th January 1989 Just weeks after the Lockerbie bombing, the country is brought to a standstill again as 44 people are killed when British Midland Airways Flight 092 crashes into an embankment on the M1.

Satanic Verses protests
14th January 1989 Protests in Bradford erupt over the publication in September 1988 of Salman Rushdie's *The Satanic Verses*, which some Muslims find offensive. Books are burned in the streets, and the following month the Iranian Ayatollah Ruhollah

Khomeini issues a fatwa calling for Rushdie's death. In March diplomatic relations between Iran and the UK are broken over the book, and Rushdie is forced to go into hiding.

Sky Television launches
5th February 1989 Sky Television, the world's first commercial direct broadcast satellite system, launches. The system carries three new channels, Sky

News, Sky Movies and Eurosport, alongside the already existing Sky Channel.

Lawyer murdered
12th February 1989 The murder of lawyer Pat Finucane by the Ulster Defence Association sends shockwaves across Northern Ireland when he is shot fourteen times whilst eating a meal at home with his wife and children. The British security services later admit collusion in the killing and issue an apology in 2011.

Serious Crime Squad disbanded
14th August 1989 Following repeated allegations of wrongdoing, the Serious Crime Squad of the West Midlands Police is broken up. Many detectives are suspended when stories of abuse and incompetence hit the news, most famously involving the wrongful convictions of the 'Birmingham Six' who alleged that they were beaten and deprived of food and sleep.

Marchioness disaster
20th August 1989 In the early hours of the morning the *Marchioness*, a pleasure boat, is struck twice by a dredger, the *Bowbelle*. The *Marchioness*, which had been hired for a birthday party, is forced onto her side, and sinks quickly, trapping many of the young partygoers inside. 51 of the 130 on board are killed.

5 APR 1989
Channel Tunnel workers strike for two weeks, over pay and working conditions.

2 MAY 1989
Prisoners at Risley Detention Centre riot, protesting on the roof for three days.

3 JUN 1989
Ayatollah Khomeini, who founded the Islamic Revolution in Iran, dies.

Deal bombing

22nd September 1989 The Royal Marines School of Music at the Royal Marine Depot in Deal is bombed by the Provisional IRA. Eleven Royal Marine bandsmen are killed when the building collapses after the bomb explodes in the changing room.

Ashdown throws gauntlet

15th September 1989 Paddy Ashdown makes a rousing speech at the annual conference of the Social and Liberal Democratic Party, in which he calls for an 'end to Thatcherism'. A month later, the party is rebranded as the 'Liberal Democrats'.

ROYALTY &
POLITICS

FOREIGN
NEWS

Diana visits New York

February 1989 Princess Diana makes her first solo trip to New York, with a brief to promote British industries abroad. She surprises many by visiting social projects in the more deprived areas of New York. This famously includes a visit to an AIDS ward in Harlem Hospital, where she hugs a young patient.

Princess Diana opens AIDS centre

25th July 1989 Diana, Princess of Wales, officially opens a new day centre for people with AIDS in Tulse Hill, London.

Exxon Valdez oil spill

24th March 1989 The supertanker *Exxon Valdez* spills over 10 million gallons of crude oil into Prince William Sound after striking Bligh Reef off Alaska. It creates one of the worst environmental disasters in memory and affects 1,300 miles of coastline, killing wildlife, savaging the local economy and blighting Prince William Sound for years to come.

Communism falls

It is the year of the greatest upheaval in Europe since the French Revolution. Revolutions are overthrowing communism in almost all Eastern Bloc countries. People are also turning against communism in the Baltic states. On 23rd August two million people from the three different countries form a 600-kilometre-long chain between the capitals of Tallinn, Riga and Vilnius. In Czechoslovakia, hundreds of thousands of people jingle their keys in Prague in November, as a sign that they want to be freed from communism.

European elections

19th June 1989 The Labour Party secure big wins in the European Elections, earning 45 of the 78 constituencies up for grabs. This shows a big shift in fortunes for Labour, who have been out of power in the UK for over a decade.

9 JUL 1989

Boris Becker beats Stefan Edberg and wins his 3rd and last Wimbledon title.

1 AUG 1989

The last colliery in Kent closes, ending almost 100 years of mining in the Kent Coalfield.

7 SEP 1989

Heidi Hazell, wife of a British soldier, is killed by the IRA in West Germany.

Perestroika too slow

26th March 1989 That major changes are afoot in the Soviet Union becomes crystal clear during the elections for the Congress of People's Deputies. For the first time, Russians are allowed to vote anonymously and candidates from outside the Communist Party are allowed to stand as candidates. The popular Boris Yeltsin (photo left), who has just been expelled from the party due to his criticism of Mikhail Gorbachev's too-slow *perestroika* (restructuring), wins in Moscow with an overwhelming score of 92 percent of the votes.

Tank Man

5th June 1989 A protest begins in Beijing's Tiananmen Square. Encouraged by developments in the Soviet Union and the Eastern Bloc, students and workers demand far-reaching reforms. The crowd in Tiananmen Square grows to more than a million demonstrators. Deng Xiaoping decides to put a rigorous end to the protest and sends tanks to the square. Between 3,000 and 10,000 people die during the action to clear the square. The most famous image is that of a man stepping in front of a column of tanks to block their way. Film and photo images of the unknown 'Tank Man' are going around the world.

The Wall falls

9th November 1989 Developments in the Eastern Bloc have a huge impact in East Germany, which is still trying to resist *glasnost* and *perestroika*. Tens of thousands of East Germans flee to the West. The socialist utopia is practically bankrupt and demonstrations against the regime are swelling in all major cities. On 7th November, the government collapses and the Politburo resigns a day later. Completely unexpectedly, East Berlin party secretary Günter Schabowski gives a press conference on 9th November and announces that East German citizens will now be allowed to travel freely. To a question from an Italian journalist when exactly these rules will come into effect, Schabowski answers: *'Sofort, unverzüglich'*. (Immediately, immediately.) Immediately, tens of thousands of East Berliners gather at various border crossings in Berlin. The border guards, the Stasi and the army are completely overwhelmed. The Berlin Wall has fallen after 28 years. Before the end of the year, US President Bush and Russian leader Gorbachev will shake hands in Malta to mark the end of the Cold War.

17 OCT 1989
A large earthquake in San Francisco kills 63.

21 NOV 1989
Cameras are permitted in the House of Commons.

2 DEC 1989
Margaret Thatcher joins Mikhail Gorbachev and George Bush to declare the Cold War over.

The next domino

16th December 1989 Following relatively bloodless revolutions in East Germany, Hungary and Czechoslovakia and the installation of new governments, Romania is the next domino to fall. It begins with demonstrations and ends on 22nd December when the army deserts President Nicolae Ceausescu and he is forced to flee. He and his wife are captured and executed on Christmas Day.

US invades Panama

20th December 1989 The US launches an invasion of Panama to oust President Manuel Noriega. He is captured on 3rd January and taken to the US for trial.

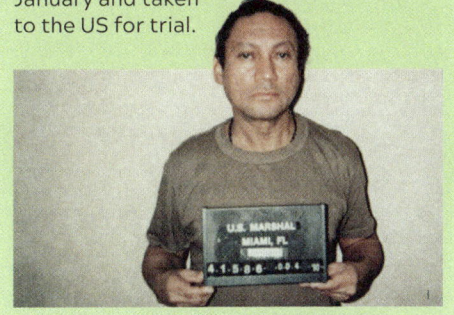

Gaming on the go

Nintendo brings out the Gameboy console this year, offering complete portability and games on the go. The Nintendo Gameboy costs £59.99 and comes with a variety of games such as *Super Mario Land* and *Tetris*. Adverts target cool, older gamers as well as kids, showing the Nintendo in use anytime, anywhere with the slogan, 'There's nowhere you can't play it'.

Dramatic beginnings

Three popular children's television dramas begin this year. First up is *Press Gang*, ITV's comedy drama about a junior newspaper run by kids from the local comprehensive school which first airs on 16th January. *Children's Ward* begins on ITV on 15th March, and on 8th November, *Byker Grove*, the gritty drama about the Geordie scamps at a Newcastle youth club, is first broadcast on BBC1. All three are seedbeds for some of television's best talent.

Kiss the boys

In 1987, *Eastenders* causes controversy when its gay character Colin Russell gives his boyfriend Barry a peck on the forehead. But that's nothing compared to the scene in this year's 24th January episode when Colin has a full-on snog with Guido Smith. It is the first mouth-to-mouth gay kiss on British television and sparks a torrent of complaints and abuse.

ENTERTAINMENT

Desmond's

Channel 4's comedy about a barber shop run by the Guyanese Ambrose family, *Desmond's* is less about haircuts (which are generally bad) and more about friendship and community. Episode one, the first of s71, airs on 5th January. Thirty years on from that date, writer Trix Morrell tells the *Guardian*, 'I didn't write *Desmond's* for black people. I wrote it for white people so they could see how black people really are.'

Action Anneka

Anneka Rice has made a name for herself on Channel 4's *Treasure Hunt* where viewers are used to seeing her zipped into a boilersuit, hopping in and out of helicopters as contestants direct her next move

by solving a series of puzzles. *Challenge Anneka*, which begins on BBC1 on 8th September, makes use of Rice's can-do attitude and action girl reputation as she takes on a series of tasks each episode, usually with a charitable focus.

Blackadder Goes Forth

In Blackadder's fourth and final outing, first broadcast on 28th September, Edmund finds himself an officer in the trenches on the Western Front, more world weary and cynical than ever, which is no surprise when he's surrounded by imbeciles; a subaltern twit, George (Hugh Laurie), batman Baldrick and, safely in his chateau HQ, General Melchett (Stephen Fry) who is intent on sending his men to certain death. The last episode, *Goodbyee,* is disarmingly poignant as Blackadder assembles, ready to go 'over the top' in the 'big push', with the characters we've grown to know and love over the years. But this time, it really is goodbyee.

When Harry Met Sally

A timely confluence of great writing from Nora Ephron, director Rob Reiner's comic touch, and Billy Crystal and Meg Ryan at the top of their game, *When Harry Met Sally* explores the truth in Harry's belief that, 'men and women can't be friends because the sex part always gets in the way'. The film goes on general release in the UK on 1st December and is remembered above all for the scene in a busy deli when Ryan demonstrates how easy it is to fake an orgasm. The follow-up line from a fellow diner, 'I'll have what she's having', is actually delivered by Reiner's mother, Estelle.

Maid Marian and her Merry Men

Tony Robinson (*Blackadder's* Baldrick) writes and stars in *Maid Marian and Her Merry Men*, starting on BBC1 on 16th November. It's partly a broad comedy with physical jokes but also a sophisticated, cleverly scripted parody of the traditional Robin Hood story. The programme flips gender roles, with Maid Marian the idealistic and passionate leader of the forest-dwelling gang, and Robin an ex-tailor and all-round wet drip who insists everyone wears green 'to coordinate with the trees'. For those too young to watch *Blackadder, Maid Marian and her Merry Men* is a more than worthy substitute.

DO YOU REMEMBER THIS?

Acid house smiley

Birds of Feather

Birds of a feather, flock together. That's what Sharon (Linda Robson) and Tracey (Pauline Quirke) do in this hit comedy, which first airs on BBC1 on 16th October. After their husbands are jointly sent down for armed robbery, Tracey moves from her grotty Edmonton flat to her sister Sharon's deluxe Essex home in Chigwell, where their neighbour, middle-aged man-eater Dorien Green (Lesley Joseph, upstaging everyone and wearing the hell out of leopard print) is a regular uninvited guest. Together they are the older, wiser and funnier flag bearers for the 'Essex Girl' of the 1990s.

The Cook, The Thief, His Wife and Her Lover

Peter Greenaway's stylish, opulent, unsettling film, released 13th October, is his damning indictment of Thatcher's government, metaphorically at least. Michael Gambon perfectly expresses the greed and excess of Tory Britain as the sadistic, violent Albert Spica, surrounded by henchmen and sycophants as they devour an ostentatious banquet each evening at his restaurant. Helen Mirren, exquisitely dressed in Jean Paul Gaultier, is his wife who begins an affair with a bookish diner under her husband's nose, while the cook provides cover for their passionate liaisons.

Bodacious!

Time-travelling twerps Bill (Alex Winter) and Ted (Keanu Reeves) enlist the help of Napoleon, Joan of Arc and 'So-crays' to write their history paper (and avoid Ted being banished to military school) in *Bill and Ted's Excellent Adventure* released 10th August. Bill and Ted introduce audiences to phrases like, 'Bodacious' and 'Party on, dudes!' but above all, remind everyone to 'Be excellent to each other.'

A new era for *Batman*

Batman, released 11th August, goes from the kitsch, comic character of the past to a brooding, conflicted superhero of the present in a Tim Burton makeover which lays the foundation stone for comic-based blockbusters of the future. Michael Keaton is a darker Batman altogether, saving Gotham City while wrestling with the memories of his murdered parents. Jack Nicholson in daubed makeup as the Joker is a captivating baddie, his purple suit echoing various tracks throughout the film, provided by His Royal Purpleness, Prince.

My Left Foot

Daniel Day-Lewis deservedly wins Best Actor Oscar at the 1990 Academy Awards for his performance as Christy Brown in *My Left Foot*, while Brenda Fricker, playing his careworn mother, takes home the award for Best Actress in a supporting role, dedicating it to Bridget by saying, 'anyone who gives birth 22 times deserves one of these'. The story of Brown's remarkable life, where he overcame crippling cerebral palsy and prejudice to become a respected writer and artist, is unflinching but also uplifting.

Nielsen gets naked

It's easy to forget Leslie Nielsen has spent decades as a serious actor, so easily does he slip into characters such as the incompetent detective Lieutenant Frank Drebin in *The Naked Gun: From the Files of Police Squad!*, which has its UK release on 10th February.

Based on the comedy television series *Police Squad!* the film, and its two sequels, cement Neilsen's reputation as 'the Olivier of spoofs', a title suggested by American film critic Roger Ebert.

Rain Man

Rain Man, which UK audiences can see from 3rd March, wins four Oscars at the 61st Academy Awards. Tom Cruise and Dustin Hoffman are perfectly cast; Cruise as arrogant and shallow car salesman Charlie who learns his late father has left everything to a brother he never knew he had: autistic savant, Raymond (Hoffman). Their road trip across the country is a journey of understanding and self-discovery, as Charlie emerges from the experience a better and more decent man.

MUSIC

BRIT Awards chaos

13th February 1989 The annual showpiece BRIT Awards are televised live from the Royal Albert Hall. Everything that could go wrong does. The hosts, Samantha Fox and Mick Fleetwood, are completely mismatched and can't manage the autocue. Government minister Kenneth Baker is roundly booed, causing Cliff Richard to castigate the audience for their lack of respect. Boy George appears when the Four Tops are announced. Transatlantic links fail, some live performances are out of tune and some awards are not presented at all. From now on, the BRITs will be recorded the night before to ensure that the bad bits are edited out before broadcast.

Madonna v. the Vatican

2nd March 1989 Madonna is no stranger to controversy; she pushes the boundaries further with *Like a Prayer*, the video for which plays provocatively with Catholic iconography.

The Vatican expresses outrage and a planned world tour is cancelled. Is she bothered? Not at all. The *Like a Prayer* album is the top selling record of 1989 at 15 million, beating Janet Jackson's *Rhythm Nation*, Phil Collins' *But Seriously* and a resurgent Cher's *Heart of Stone*.

Mike and the Mechanics
25th March 1989 Phil Collins plays Great Train Robber Buster Edwards in *Buster* but his solo work has put his band, Genesis, on hiatus for a while. Fellow members Tony Banks and Mike Rutherford start other projects, the latter topping the US chart with *The Living Years* as leader of Mike and the Mechanics.

Boy band on the block
26th April 1989 Now undertaking their first UK tour, New Kids on the Block were formed in 1985 as a white answer to black teenage quintet New Edition. New Kids have tightly choreographed stage moves, carefully developed individual personas, sweet harmonies, all-round good looks and just a touch of bad-boy menace. With six US Top Ten records during 1989 including three No. 1s, they create the template for the Backstreet Boys, Take That, Boyzone and all the boy bands who follow in their wake.

Soul II Soul
24th June 1989 That British-made black music is now a real force is clear from the rise of Soul II Soul, a collective founded by north Londoner Jazzie B (photo) and Bristol-based Nellee Hooper of Massive Attack. Caron Wheeler joins for *Back to Life*, now at No. 1 for four weeks.

Monkees reunite
9th July 1989 Following a successful tour featuring three of the original Monkees, Mike Nesmith joins Mickey Dolenz, Peter Tork and Davy Jones to receive their own stars on the Hollywood Walk of Fame.

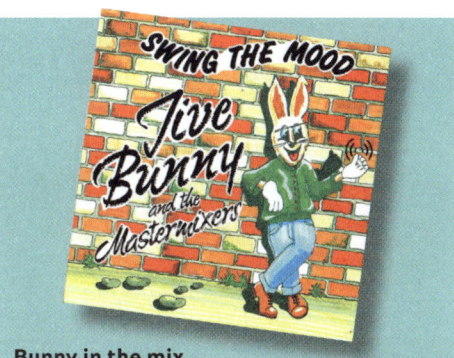

Bunny in the mix
5th August 1989 Every mobile DJ in the country envies John and Andy Pickles, who have hit on the simple idea of putting their megamix medleys on record. Taking the name Jive Bunny, they are now at No. 1 with *Swing the Mood* which combines nine 1950s rock'n'roll tracks with Glenn Miller's *In the Mood* and Chubby Checker's *Let's Twist Again*. The Jive Bunny formula will be good for two more No. 1s.

1989

Bangles break
21st September 1988 The Bangles split up just months after *Eternal Flame* - inspired by the flame burning on Elvis Presley's grave - is a transatlantic No. 1.

Death of Ewan MacColl
22nd October 1989 Ewan MacColl, father of Kirsty and the prime mover behind the UK's post-war folk music revival, dies aged 74. His songs include *Dirty Old Town* and *The First Time Ever I Saw Your Face*.

MY FIRST 18 YEARS
TOP10 — 1989

1. **Ride on Time** *Black Box*
2. **Wind Beneath My Wings** *Bette Midler*
3. **All Around the World** *Lisa Stansfield*
4. **When Love Comes to Town** *U2 with B. B. King*
5. **Love and Regret** *Deacon Blue*
6. **The Second Summer of Love** *Danny Wilson*
7. **Sowing the Seeds of Love** *Tears for Fears*
8. **If I Could Turn Back Time** *Cher*
9. **You Keep it All In** *The Beautiful South*
10. **Sweet Child of Mine** *Guns N' Roses*

Open | Search | Scan

Hello, Madchester
2nd December 1989 The appearance of Happy Mondays and the Stone Roses (photo) on the same edition of *Top of the Pops* awakens the world to the fast blossoming Manchester scene and rave culture in general. The peculiarly Mancunian mix of loopy electronic dance rhythms, chiming guitars, acid-laced bonhomie and baggy trousers, fused in clubs like the Hacienda, is going national. 'Madchester' has arrived.

Ice Cube goes solo
23rd December 1989 Ice Cube departs the most controversial rap band of all, NWA from Compton in Los Angeles. He is already recording his first solo album.

Housemartins go south
Following the end of the Housemartins, Paul Heaton and Dave Hemmingway retain their base in Hull and form a new five-piece, the ironically named Beautiful South. Beginning with a song about the cynical side of songwriting, *Song for Whoever*, they specialise in barbed wire lyrics couched in the sweetest of soul-influenced melodies.

SPORT

1990 Commonwealth Games
3rd February 1990 At the 14th Commonwealth Games, hosted by New Zealand, the medal table is topped by Australia, with England coming in second with an impressive tally of 128 medals, 46 of which are gold.

Shock Tyson defeat
11th February 1990 One of the biggest upsets in boxing history occurs when undefeated, undisputed heavyweight Champion of the World, Mike Tyson, is knocked out in the tenth round by the 42 to 1 opponent, Buster Douglas.

Hendry youngest champ
29th April 1990 Twenty-one-year-old Stephen Hendry secures victory over Jimmy White at the Crucible to become the youngest ever World Snooker Champion. Leading from the start, he wins the match 18-12 in a tournament that sees 18 century breaks.

World Cup heartbreak
4th July 1990 England make it through to the semi-finals of the FIFA World Cup before losing in heartbreaking fashion to West Germany following a penalty shootout. West Germany go on to take the tournament in a 1-0 victory over Argentina, with England losing to tournament hosts Italy in the third place playoffs.

UEFA lifts ban
10th July 1990 Five years after it was implemented following the Heysel Stadium disaster, UEFA finally lifts its ban on English football clubs participating in European competitions. Incidents of football hooliganism have reduced over the previous year, and Manchester United celebrate a return to European football by winning the Cup Winners' Cup in the 1990-1991 season.

21 JAN 1990
The first MTV Unplugged is aired, featuring the band Squeeze.

13 FEB 1990
Britain and France give Germany the OK to reunify.

2 MAR 1990
Gorbachev is elected President of the USSR.

Stormy weather

1990 proves a year of extremes in weather as a series of storms, including the Burns Day Storm which kills 39 people, batter the country in January and February. August sees a formidable heatwave reach a high of 37.1°C, before heavy snow blankets the country in December leading to power cuts lasting several days.

Poll tax riots

9th March 1990 The new Community Charge introduced by the government prompts rioting across the capital. Protesters object to the fixed rate tax, which would see all residents contribute the same amount to their local authority, regardless of income. The tax is introduced despite protests but is replaced just three years later with a new 'Council Tax' system.

The Year of budget brands

1990 proves the year of discount shopping as three low-cost supermarket chains launch in Britain for the first time. German supermarket Aldi, Danish chain Netto, and British store Poundland all open their first UK branches in 1990, catering to customers looking for better value deals.

Strangeways Prison riot

1st April 1990 Rioting breaks out at Strangeways Prison in Manchester, leading to 25 days of violence. Following several smaller protests, and growing frustrations at conditions in the compound, hundreds of prisoners riot following a service in the prison's chapel. One prisoner is killed, and 194 people, both prisoners and guards, are injured.

MP killed by IRA

30th July 1990 Ian Gow, Member of Parliament for Eastbourne, is killed by the IRA after a bomb is planted under his car at home. His death comes just days after a bomb had targeted the Stock Exchange Tower in London, and weeks after a bombing at the Carlton Club which killed one and injured twenty. Later in the year, Air Chief Marshal Sir Peter Terry narrowly survives after being shot nine times by the IRA at home.

Brian Keenan released

24th August 1990 Northern Irish writer Brian Keenan is released from captivity in Beirut, Lebanon, having spent over four years as a hostage. His release leads to hope that his fellow hostages, including John McCarthy and Terry Waite, will soon be released as well.

---

27 APR 1990

Axl Rose of *Guns N' Roses* marries Erin Everly, daughter of Don Everly of the Everly Brothers.

1 MAY 1990

Imports of British beef banned by several European countries over BSE.

21 JUN 1990

Large earthquake in Iran kills 35-50,000.

Channel Tunnel connected

1st December 1990 A major milestone is celebrated by workers on the Channel Tunnel as labourers on the French and British sides meet in the middle 40 metres below the seabed. The two countries are now connected by land for the first time in 8,000 years. Sadly, a more sombre milestone had been reached in May, when Billy Cartman became the sixth Briton to die during the tunnel's construction.

Contaminated blood scandal

11th December 1990 The British government announces that it will make available £42 million to be used as compensation for those affected by the 'contaminated blood' scandal in an out of court settlement. Over 1,200 haemophiliacs are known to have been infected with the HIV virus through transfusions which had been collected from unsafe sources, predominantly prisoners in the US. The true scale of the scandal does not become apparent for many years, as deaths from Hepatitis C are added to the equation and it emerges that over 30,000 people were affected. As of 2023 at least 3,000 people have died as a result.

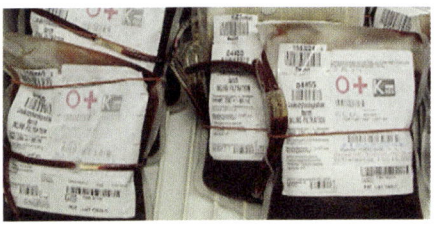

ROYALTY & POLITICS

New princess born

23rd March 1990 Prince Andrew and his wife Sarah, the Duchess of York, welcome their second child, a baby girl. In December she is christened Princess Eugenie Victoria Helena of York at St Mary Magdalene Church, Sandringham. She is the first royal baby to have a public christening.

Deputy PM resigns

1st November 1990 Divisions in the Conservative Party widen as Deputy Prime Minister Geoffrey Howe resigns over European policy and the Community Charge. Twelve days later he delivers a blistering attack on Thatcher in his resignation speech during Prime Minister's Questions, accusing her of risking the country's future and undermining her cabinet colleagues.

BBC Radio 5 launched

27th August 1990 The BBC launch their first new radio station in over 20 years as Radio 5 hits the airways for the first time. Providing a mix of sport and educational programming, it also features children's shows, and will run until 1994 before being replaced by BBC Radio 5 Live.

3 JUL 1990

Members of 2 Live Crew formally charged with obscenity in Florida for performing the song *Me So Horny*.

27 AUG 1990

The BBC launch their first new radio station in over 20 years as Radio 5.

13 SEP 1990

The first episode of *'Law and Order'* created by Dick Wolf premieres.

1990

Thatcher falls

14th November 1990 Michael Heseltine announces a challenge to the leadership of Prime Minister Margaret Thatcher in what would prove to be the beginning of the end for her tenure as leader. Six days later, she falls short of an outright victory in the leadership contest and on the 22nd announces her resignation as leader. After eleven years as Prime Minister, she is replaced by her Chancellor, John Major.

FOREIGN NEWS

Big Mac Soviet style

31st January 1990 The symbol of Western consumer society lands in the former epicentre of communism. The Berlin Wall is barely down before the very first McDonald's in the Soviet Union opens on Pushkin Square in Moscow. Thousands of Muscovites queue for a Big Mac. On the first day, 34,000 units are sold.

Goodbye Charlie

1st January 1990 More than 200,000 West and East Germans celebrate New Year at the Brandenburg Gate in Berlin. Soon thousands of former East Germans storm the Stasi headquarters to view their files. On 29th January former leader Erich Honecker is arrested on suspicion of high treason. On 19th February at midnight, border guards begin demolishing the Berlin Wall in the heart of Berlin, near the Reichstag. The well-known guard post, Checkpoint Charlie, disappears and the original guardhouse is moved to a museum.

Not a mental illness

17th May 1990 At the start of the year, homosexuality is still on the list of mental diseases of the World Health Organisation (WHO) alongside schizophrenia, dementia and depression. Today it disappears from that list and the date is declared International Day against Homophobia, Biphobia, Transphobia and Intersexphobia.

We will rock you

3rd January 1990 Panamanian President Manuel Noriega is finally captured by US invasion forces. The dictator, controller of a large drug and money laundering network, has been hiding in the Vatican embassy. He surrenders after the Americans play loud hard rock music for days to break him mentally.

18 OCT 1988	**14 NOV** 1988	**2 DEC** 1988
Britain joins the European Exchange Rate Mechanism.	Britain performs nuclear test at Nevada Test Site.	Helmut Kohl becomes Chancellor of a united Germany.

A wider web

13th November 1990 The Internet already has more than 300,000 hosts but Tim Berners-Lee wants to connect computers in an even smoother way. The UK software developer envisions a huge digital library that stores all information and human knowledge and is available to every computer user. Together with Robert Cailliau, he designs the system that forms the basis of the World Wide Web.

Hubble Space Telescope

24th April 1990 NASA and ESA launch the Hubble Space Telescope. The Hubble reveals spectacular secrets of the universe with its infrared camera and spectroscope, including the fact that the universe is expanding faster than thought. Its sensational and razor-sharp images stun the world.

Digital camera

15th November 1990 The new Dycam Model 1 - also known as Logitech Fotoman - is a revolutionary step in photography but is not a commercial success. As the first fully digital camera for consumers, it is easy to operate with just one shutter button. The days of taking a film roll to the chemist and waiting a week for your prints are over.

Mandela released

11th February 1990 After 27 years of incarceration, Nelson Mandela is released. South African President Frederik Willem de Klerk realizes that apartheid can no longer be maintained due to enormous internal and international pressure. The whole world watches as Mandela leaves prison near Cape Town, hand in hand with his wife Winnie. After his release, Mandela speaks to 100,000 people in the Johannesburg football stadium. Mandela becomes political leader of the ANC, and in May he begins negotiations with de Klerk. The end of apartheid is in sight.

Saddam invades Kuwait

2nd August 1990 Treated with kid gloves for years by western powers anxious to have a bulwark against Iran, Iraqi President Saddam Hussein becomes the world's bogeyman as he launches an invasion of neighbouring Kuwait. The UN condemns the invasion and an international community united since the end of the Cold War imposes a boycott and an ultimatum on Iraq: withdraw from Kuwait by 15th January or the UN will end the occupation by force.

Iraqi TV Taped Broadcast

Herman the bull

16th December 1990 Herman is the first transgenic bull in the world. The outcome of genetic modification, he is the first bull to carry the human gene. The theory is that his female offspring will produce milk that contains anti-inflammatory protein but the milk of his 55 descendants proves unsuitable as medicine because there is too little of the protein in it.

1990

Mr Bean
Airing on the first day of a new decade, rubber-faced Rowan Atkinson is the gawky, gauche, tweed-jacketed *Mr. Bean*, whose daily life is littered with misadventure and mishaps as he attempts to achieve apparently simple tasks in increasingly convoluted ways. Bean is largely non-verbal, communicating purely through physicality and unintelligible mumbling. Mr. Bean becomes one of Britain's best-loved and most exportable characters.

Pretty Woman
The basic premise of *Pretty Woman* may be questionable but it's hard not to fall in love with the romcom that revives Richard Gere's career and makes a star of Julia Roberts and her megawatt smile. Roberts plays Vivian, a streetwalker who by chance walks into millionaire businessman Edward's life. Their relationship, at first a business transaction, blossoms into romance. A feel-good fairy tale for modern times.

Teenage Mutant Hero must-haves
Leonardo, Raphael, Michaelangelo and Donatello, the pizza-loving, crime-fighting, sewer-dwelling *Teenage Mutant Hero (Ninja) Turtles* make their UK debut on 3rd January and by Christmas, their play figures are the UK's number one Christmas toy as Britain goes turtle crazy.

Baywatch
The show that launches a million posters, and inhabits the dreams of countless teenage boys, *Baywatch* comes to British TV screens on 6th January. Baywatch follows a lifesaving team in Los Angeles County, California, populated by various demi-gods and goddesses, including ex-Playboy model Pamela Anderson as P. J. Parker, and David 'The Hoff' Hasselhoff as Mitch Buchannon. In between rescuing weak swimmers or fending off shark attacks, the *Baywatch* lifeguards mainly run up and down the beach in slow-motion and conduct most of their business wearing the iconic *Baywatch* red swimsuit.

Keeping Up Appearances
The fact that Hyacinth Bucket insists her surname is pronounced 'Bouquet' tells you all you need to know about her. Patricia Routledge excels in the role as the overbearing and occasionally monstrous Hyacinth whose curtain twitching, candlelit dinner parties and 'RP' phone manner are all part of her drive to mix with the right crowd. If only her social aspirations weren't continually thwarted by her common as muck sisters, Daisy and Rose.

Tip Top Tippety Top

Harry Enfield's Television Programme begins on 8th November where Enfield, along with pals Kathy Burke and Paul Whitehouse, introduces us to characters like Tim Nice-But-Dim, Mr. Cholmonde-ley-Warner (who presents everything in the style of a flickering 1940s newsreel), Wayne and Waynetta Slob (and baby Spudlika), The Scousers, and not forgetting over-the-hill radio DJs Smashie and Nicey. The show is rebirthed in 1994 as *Harry Enfield and Chums*.

Supermodels

The supermodel phenomenon goes mainstream this year when George Michael features some of the world's most famous faces (and bodies) in his *Freedom: '90* music video. Soon, everyone knows the names of Cindy Crawford, Naomi Campbell, Linda Evangelista, Christy Turlington, Claudia Schiffer and the other Amazonian beauties who dominate catwalks and glossy magazine covers through the decade.

The Little Mermaid

12th October 1990 After an extended fallow period, Disney adapts a well-loved fairy tale and finds its mojo again, casting its spell over Hans Christian Anderson's story, *The Little Mermaid*. Flame-haired Ariel makes a deal with the Ursula the sea-witch in order to become human and find true love with Prince Eric.

Masterchef

Masterchef, a competition for amateur cooks, begins on BBC1 on Sunday afternoon on 2nd July. Carried out in a hushed studio, it's presented by Loyd Grossman who goes off to 'cogitate' with a different chef and celebrity each week as they decide who goes through to the next round.

Twin Peaks

23rd October 1990 Co-created by Mark Frost and David Lynch, *Twin Peaks* subverts the traditional detective series with elements of the surreal and supernatural, and emerges as something much more original. Kyle McLachlan is FBI Special Agent Dale Cooper who arrives in the Pacific North West town of Twin Peaks to investigate the murder of prom queen Laura Palmer. So far, so typical, but *Twin Peaks'* dream-like weirdness and cast of eccentric characters wins it a cult-like following.

Beverley Hills 90210

90210 is the postcode of the exclusive Los Angeles enclave for the wealthy and well-heeled and when the Midwest-raised Walsh twins, Brandon and Brenda, touch down in the area after their father gets a job as accountant to the filthy rich, they take a while to fit in with their new, sophisticated school mates. Created by Aaron Spelling (whose daughter Tori is one of the stars), the series begins on 30th December. UK teenagers go mad for *Beverley Hills 90210* and especially its two dreamboat male leads, Jason Priestley and Luke Perry. Grange Hill was never like this.

Married to the Mob

Martin Scorsese's *Goodfellas*, his operatic tale of an uneasy brotherhood of New York mobsters, hits cinemas on 26th October. Ray Liotta plays the central character and narrator, Henry Hill, whose entanglement with Jimmy (Robert de Niro), Tommy (Joe Pesci) and other neighbourhood crooks, brings a lavish lifestyle but at a cost. As Henry becomes increasingly mired in a life of crime and adultery, trust between the gang begins to crumble. With virtuoso performances from all cast members, it's Pesci, as the foul-mouthed psychopathic Tommy, who personifies the violent, bloody world of what the *Telegraph* review calls, 'Scorsese's explosive Mafia cocktail'.

Big Night Out

Surreal comedy reaches new heights as Vic Reeves and Bob Mortimer invite everyone along to *Vic Reeves Big Night Out* on 25th May, the most bizarre variety show ever created. Germinated as a comedy club night at the Goldsmith's Tavern in south-east London and with characters like bickering brothers Donald and Davy Stott, Wavey Davey and the Man with the Stick ('What's on the end of the stick, Vic?'), *Big Night Out* is bemusing, bonkers and utterly brilliant.

Home Alone

7th December 1990 John Hughes is the writer behind *Home Alone*, the box-office monster that makes a huge star of ten-year-old Macaulay Culkin. The film centres on Kevin McAllister, a kid accidentally left 'home alone' when his family travel to Paris for Christmas. Kevin defends the family home from two bungling burglars (Joe Pesci and Daniel Stern) by setting up a series of booby traps.

I don't *BELIEVE* it!

Everyone's favourite misanthrope, Victor Meldrew, is introduced to viewers on 4th January, with the first episode of new sitcom *One Foot in the Grave*. Richard Wilson plays Victor, whose enforced early retirement as a security guard has left him bitter, frustrated and at war with the world, causing him to voice his contempt with a variety of phrases, most famously uttering, 'I don't believe it!!' at the latest humiliating development. With Annette Crosbie as his long-suffering wife and Angus Deayton the neighbour who is convinced Victor is mad, *One Foot in the Grave* is darker than your average sitcom and is all the better for it.

Ghostly encounters

Ghost has its UK release on 5th October, and becomes 1990's highest-grossing film. Patrick Swayze is Sam, a ghost trapped in limbo after being mugged and murdered, who must find a way to protect his girlfriend Molly (Demi Moore) from those who killed him. Help comes in the unlikely form of Oda Mae Brown, a charlatan psychic played by Whoopi Goldberg. The film's iconic potter's wheel scene goes on to be much-parodied, even featuring in *Naked Gun 2 ½*.

MUSIC

Hip hop lite

Representing a lighter, far less controversial stream of hip hop than society-defying NWA and Public Enemy are MC Hammer and Vanilla Ice. Hammer announces himself with *U Can't Touch This* and eye-poppingly baggy trousers. The much ridiculed Vanilla Ice (real name Robert Van Winkle) is the first solo white performer to embrace rap with UK No. 1 *Ice Ice Baby*, on which he makes liberal use of the bassline from the Queen-David Bowie track *Under Pressure*.

Nothing compares

3rd February 1990 Well known in new wave circles since the mid-80s, Irish singer Sinead O'Connor catapults to No. 1 in the US and UK with a stark, emotional version of a little-heard Prince song, *Nothing Compares 2 U*. The stripped back arrangement is the work of Nellee Hooper of Soul II Soul.

Solo Sting

12th February 1990 Seven years on from the break-up of the Police, Sting's support for environmental causes is unwavering. Tonight he joins Paul Simon, Bruce Springsteen, Jackson Browne and Herbie Hancock at a fundraiser in Beverly Hills for the Rainforest Foundation. His big solo hit this year is a remix of an earlier release, *An Englishman in New York*, a tribute to expatriate writer Quentin Crisp.

Concert for Mandela

16th April 1990 A packed Wembley Stadium hosts a televised tribute concert in honour of the recently freed Nelson Mandela. Artists performing include Peter Gabriel, Tracy Chapman, Simple Minds, Lou Reed and Neil Young.

Spike Island

27th May 1990 Manchester band the Stone Roses headline a concert at Spike Island in Widnes that becomes the stuff of legend. More than 30,000 attend 'the baggy Woodstock', but the Roses' seemingly inexorable rise is disrupted by disputes with their record label Silvertone, which delays the release of what should have been their breakout album - *Second Coming* - by four years.

Elton at No. 1 - at last

23rd June 1990 Nineteen years on from his first UK chart entry, Elton John finally achieves a solo No. 1 with *Sacrifice*. He divides all his royalties from the record between four nominated AIDS charities.

1990

World Cup fever

7th July 1990 Luciano Pavarotti, Placido Domingo and Jose Carreras join forces as 'the Three Tenors' at a televised concert in Rome to celebrate Italy's hosting of the FIFA World Cup. Back in England, a rare run to the semi-finals lifts *World in Motion* by the England World Cup Squad and New Order to No. 1 for two weeks.

Judas Priest verdict

24th August 1990 A six-million-dollar law suit against UK heavy metal band Judas Priest ends, brought by the parents of a teenage boy who shot himself after listening to one of their albums. The case rests on subliminal messages supposedly hidden on the record. A judge in Reno, Nevada, rules that the band was not responsible for the boy's actions.

The great deception

14th November 1990 The truth is out. After a malfunction on a live MTV show revealed that German duo Milli Vanilli were miming, producer Frank Farian admits that session singers had sung their parts on their records. The pair - Fab Morvan and Rob Pilatus - hit back by calling Farian 'a maniac'. The name of Milli Vanilli, who have sold over eight million records to unsuspecting fans, is now a byword for deception and fakery in the music business.

Marital matters

21st November 1990 The day before Bill Wyman confirms his split from wife Mandy Smith (photo), Mick Jagger and model Jerry Hall tie the knot in Bali. Ronnie Wood can't attend as he is in hospital with two broken legs after a motorway accident.

SPORT

A

Season's best
15th May 1991 Manchester United win the European Cup Winners' Cup, beating Barcelona 2-1 in Rotterdam. It is the first European success enjoyed by an English club since the lifting of the five-year ban on participation that followed the Heysel disaster in 1985. In domestic competition, Arsenal are league champions while North London rivals Tottenham win the FA Cup for a record eighth time, beating Nottingham Forest 2-1 in a game that sees a career-impacting injury to England midfielder Paul Gascoigne.

A new elite league
8th April 1991 The Football Association announces controversial plans to create a new 'super league' creaming off the top eighteen clubs in the current First Division. Agreement is reached during the autumn between the FA, the Football League and the clubs involved for the Premier League.

Sumo
9th October 1991 An official sumo wrestling tournament is mounted over five days at the Royal Albert Hall in London (photo) - the first outside Japan. Forty of Japan's leading wrestlers compete for the Hitachi Cup and the honour of winning the first foreign *basho*.

UK first in Tokyo
30th August 1991 Scottish 10,000 metre runner Liz McColgan wins the UK's first ever gold medal at the World Athletics Championships in Tokyo. In November she wins the New York City marathon, her first competitive attempt at the marathon distance.

Magic retires
7th November 1991 US basketball legend Magic Johnson of the Los Angeles Lakers announces his immediate retirement after revealing that he is HIV positive.

Australian victory
2nd November 1991 Australia wins the Rugby Union World Cup at Twickenham, beating England 12-6. It is the first World Cup to be held in the northern hemisphere, with matches spread across England, Wales, Scotland, Ireland and France.

B

3 JAN 1991
Iraqi embassy officials are expelled from the UK.

21 FEB 1991
British ballerina Dame Margot Fonteyn dies in Panama aged 71.

15 MAR 1991
Stansted Airport's new terminal building is opened by the Queen.

1991

M40 completed
16th January 1991 The M40 motorway between London and Birmingham is completed as the final section through Oxfordshire is opened to traffic.

Introducing TESSA
1st January 1991 A new acronym enters the financial lexicon - TESSA. The initials stand for 'tax exempt special savings account' and it is the brainchild of former Chancellor of the Exchequer John Major, now Prime Minister. Anyone over 18 can apply and save up to £9,000 free of UK income tax over a five-year period.

Mortar attack on No. 10
7th February 1991 With war in the Gulf in its third week and London on high alert, the Provisional IRA chooses this moment to launch what could have been a deadly mortar attack against 10 Downing Street. No one is hurt in the attack but all the windows of the Cabinet room are blown out. Eleven days later one person is killed by a bomb left at Victoria Station in London. In November, two IRA members are killed when the bomb they are planting explodes prematurely in St Albans, Hertfordshire.

Birmingham Six go free
14th March 1991 Following revelations that police fabricated evidence, the six men found guilty of the Birmingham pub bombings in 1974 that killed 21 people are freed by the Court of Appeal. Their convictions are declared unsafe and unsatisfactory, and they subsequently receive compensation of between £840,000 and £1.2 million.

Two million unemployed
15th March 1991 Unemployment figures reach two million in the UK - the highest in over two years.

Hillsborough inquest
28th March 1991 The inquest closes into the deaths of 96 fans in severe overcrowding at the FA Cup semi-final match at Hillsborough, Sheffield, in 1989. The coroner returns verdicts of 'accidental death' instead of the 'unlawful killing' verdicts which many of the fans' families had hoped for. The full truth about the police handling of the disaster emerges much later and the verdicts are finally overturned in April 2016 after many years of campaigning by supporters' groups.

20 APR 1991
Small Faces and Humble Pie singer-guitarist Steve Marriott is killed in a house fire.

4 MAY 1991
Death of comedian Bernie Winters of Mike and Bernie Winters fame.

23 JUN 1991
Sega launches a new video game - *Sonic the Hedgehog*.

First Brit in space

18th May 1991 Sheffield-born scientist Helen Sharman makes history as the first UK citizen to go into space, as a member of the Soyuz TM-12 mission. She spends eight days in space, much of it on the Mir space station.

McCarthy and Waite freed

8th August 1991 In Lebanon, British hostage John McCarthy is freed by his captors after five years. The Archbishop of Canterbury's special envoy Terry Waite is finally freed on 18th November.

Hitting the heights

26th August 1991 One Canada Square is officially opened for business in the Docklands area of East London. It is the tallest building to date in the UK at 770 feet.

Riots across UK

August - September 1991 Rioting breaks out in Cardiff, Leeds, Birmingham, Dudley, Oxford and Tyneside.

TV-am to close

16th October 1991 Several of the best known ITV companies lose their franchises in the biggest shake-up of broadcasting since the 1960s. Among them are London's weekday service provider Thames Television and TV-am, the breakfast television service that has only been operating since 1983.

PC World arrives

18th November 1991 Indicating the huge growth in personal computing, computer retailer PC World opens its first store in Purley Way, Croydon.

Maxwell drowns

5th November 1991 Media magnate, *Daily Mirror* owner and former MP Robert Maxwell disappears from his yacht off the coast of Tenerife and is later found drowned. Suggestions of suicide are given credence when it emerges that he had removed £350 million from the *Daily Mirror* pension fund before his death. The Maxwell empire goes into receivership one month later with debts exceeding £1 billion.

Head of MI5

16th December 1991 The appointment of Stella Rimington is announced as the first female Director General of MI5, the UK's internal security service.

ROYALTY & POLITICS

Poll tax poleaxed

23rd March 1991 Prime Minister John Major tells the House of Commons that the contentious and unpopular Community Charge - disparagingly known as the 'poll tax' - is to be scrapped. It will be replaced by a more equitable Council Tax in 1993.

---

31 JUL 1991

125,000 pack into rain-soaked Hyde Park for a Luciano Pavarotti concert.

16 AUG 1991

Terminator 2: Judgement Day opens in UK cinemas.

19 SEP 1991

German tourists discover a mummy. Ötzi, as he is nicknamed, who lived more than 5,000 years ago.

1991

Major's charter

22nd July 1991 John Major unveils his government's White Paper detailing proposals for a 'Citizen's Charter'. Aimed at raising standards in public services, its measures guarantee redress when the service fails to reach established benchmarks. The announcement comes on the same day that the Bank of England closes down the Bank of Credit and Commerce International due to allegations of fraud. Numerous local authorities across the UK stand to lose millions from their investments in the bank.

Heading for separation

17th August 1991 Prince Charles and Princess Diana take a yachting holiday in Italy that is described in the press as a 'second honeymoon'. Royal watchers note an increasing distance between the couple. Diana is making her feelings known about the marriage in a series of secret tapes that author Andrew Morton is using as the basis for his forthcoming book, *Diana: Her True Story*.

By-election blues

7th November 1991 Two by-election results point to the likelihood of defeat for the Conservatives in the General Election due next year. Labour wins the safe Tory seat of Langbaurgh in north east England while the Liberal Democrats take Kincardine and Deeside in Scotland from the Conservatives.

FOREIGN NEWS

WWW launched

6th August 1991 Tim Berners-Lee introduces the World Wide Web project and software on the alt.hypertext newsgroup. What is effectively the world's first website, 'info.cern.ch', is now publicly available.

Operation Desert Storm

15th January 1991 The international coalition's ultimatum to Iraq to leave Kuwait expires. A military offensive to liberate Kuwait is inevitable. The international coalition led by the US and backed politically by the Soviet Union launches the largest air offensive in history: Operation Desert Storm. Iraqi radar stations are disabled and military positions destroyed. Saddam, who has raised a huge and relatively modern army, presents himself as the great leader of the Arab world and tries to get other Arab countries on his side with Scud attacks on Israel. The coalition is superior in the air and defeats almost the entire Iraqi air force and navy to prepare for the ground offensive that starts on 24th February. After seven weeks of bombing, the Iraqi army offers little resistance. On 27th February, French troops reach Kuwait City. That evening, Iraq surrenders and accepts all UN resolutions regarding the withdrawal from Kuwait. As they retreat, Iraqi troops set fire to Kuwait's oil fields.

6 OCT 1991
The final episode of *Dallas* is transmitted in the UK.

3 NOV 1991
Ayrton Senna wins his third and last World Drivers' Championship.

1 DEC 1991
Ukrainian people vote for independence.

Mobile phone revolution
1st July 1991 The Global System for Mobile Communications (GSM) is the new standard for mobile telephony. The second generation of mobile phones (2G) use a digital system for the first time, have much better sound, are ready for the introduction of SMS and come equipped with a SIM card, which allows you to make calls abroad and exchange phones without any problems. By the end of the millennium, more than 500 million people worldwide have a mobile phone.

Yugoslavia breaks up
May - June 1991 After the fall of East Germany, almost all communist regimes in the Eastern Bloc have collapsed. The federation of states that is Yugoslavia also falters, with Slovenia the first to declare its independence in June. The conflict explodes when Croatia holds a referendum in May and breaks away. It is the start of a bloody civil war which will also spread to Bosnia-Herzegovina.

A coup in Moscow
19th August 1991 Communist hardliners stage a coup in Moscow. Soviet Union President Gorbachev is placed under house arrest at his dacha in the Crimea. But the President of the Russian republic, Boris Yeltsin, elected only in July, sides with Gorbachev. He climbs on a tank in front of the parliament building and addresses the crowd, after which the army rallies behind him. One by one, the Soviet republics secede, beginning with Estonia. After 72 hours the coup leaders are captured and Gorbachev returns, but the days of the Soviet Union - and Gorbachev's presidency - are numbered. The white-blue-red flag of Russia is hoisted, with Yeltsin an unassailable leader with the backing of the Russian parliament. On Christmas morning, Gorbachev resigns. There is no Soviet Union left to govern.

ENTERTAINMENT

Dances with Wolves
8th February 1991 Kevin Costner turns to directing with *Dances With Wolves*, an epic three-hour Western in which he also takes the leading role as the Civil War veteran who becomes fascinated with the Native American Lakota Sioux. Costner's ambitious film is spectacular to look at; romantic, heartbreaking, often humorous, and portrays the Lakota tribe with respect and admiration. Costner proves himself as a director when *Dances With Wolves* gallops away with seven Oscars this year, including Best Picture.

Band tragedy
16th March 1991 The country music community is no stranger to tragic events but today's news is off the scale. Seven members of Reba McEntire's backing band are killed together with her road manager when their plane crashes in California. Reba dedicates her next album to them, *For My Broken Heart*.

You've Been Framed

With video camera ownership on the rise, TV prankster Jeremy Beadle presents *You've Been Framed* from 16th April on ITV, a show with a simple formula. Members of the public send in their funny home videos and receive a payment of £100 (later rising to £250) if their film features. Each week we laugh out loud at babies falling asleep face first in their porridge, kids being tipped out of swings or crashing a sledge, and deckchairs collapsing under stout aunties.

The Commitments

The Commitments is released on 4th October. Jimmy Rabbitte wants to bring the sound of soul to the world and Dublin is the place to start because, as Jimmy says, 'we're the blacks of Europe'. Audition flyers bring forth a dubious set of hopefuls before he discovers some musical diamonds in rough including the obnoxious Deco whose Joe Cocker-esque voice and swagger make him a shoo-in as lead singer. The band enjoys local success until personal grievances and rivalries cause its short-lived harmony to fracture. But while it lasts, *The Commitments* is foot-tappingly good for the 'soul'.

The Darling Buds of May

David Jason and Pam Ferris star as Pa and Ma Larkin which begins on 7th April on ITV. The Larkins and their sunny Kentish idyll enchant the nation. We fall for Pa's charm and his cheeky wheeling and dealing ways; and swoon at Ma's gargantuan plates of food and her infectious laughter. *The Darling Buds of May* celebrates the sheer joy of living. It also makes a star of Catherine Zeta Jones, in her breakout role as eldest of the Larkin brood, the ravishing Mariette.

Cue *Big Break*

BBC's *Big Break* begins on 30th April, hosted by Jim Davidson, with ex-player John Virgo as referee. Contestants team up with well-known snooker stars including Stephen Hendry, Jimmy White and Ray Reardon, combining their general knowledge and potting skills to win prizes. Each week, Virgo sets up a trick shot for the losers to attempt in order to win a consolation prize.

Robin Hood: Prince of Thieves
Robin has an American accent, Alan Rick-man hams it up as the dastardly Sherriff of Nottingham and Bryan Adams (photo) spends a gazillion weeks at No. 1 with an earworm theme song; *Robin Hood: Prince of Thieves*, released 19th July, is a monster hit. It's a hugely entertaining, rip-roaring adventure, blending the swashbuckling of Errol Flynn-era Robin Hood with a historic authenticity (except, perhaps, Kevin Costner's mullet).

Rock *Bottom*
Bottom features Rik Mayall and Ade Edmondson as Richie and Eddie, two revoting losers who share a flat in Hammersmith where they are on a perpetually unsuccessful quest to sleep with women. Building on the relationship between Rick and Vyvyan in *The Young Ones* and their own friendship, *Bottom* is puerile, nihilistic, but undeniably funny. It comes to an end in 1995 after Mayall explains, 'We'd already hit each other with everything in the flat.'

Misery
Kathy Bates wins a Best Actress Academy Award for her portrayal of Annie, the obsessive fiction fan who rescues but then holds best-selling author Paul (James Caan) captive in her remote Colorado cabin when she discovers he plans to write off her favourite character, Misery Chastain. Paul's injuries and the film's violence increase in tandem with Annie's escalating mania and one scene involving a sledgehammer and Paul's feet makes audiences let out a shocked groan in unison. Stephen King offers *Misery* as one of his favourites among the many film adaptations of his books.

Creature Comforts
The *Creature Comforts* advertisements for the electricity board win Best Commercial of the Year. *Creature Comforts* features a variety of plasticine animals voiced by ordinary people with different regional accents. The endearing combination of the Aardman creatures with everyday human dialogue (complete with ums and aahs) is completed by a concluding voiceover from the king of funny animal voices, Johnny Morris.

Sega Game Gear
The Game Gear, Sega's riposte to Nintendo's Game boy is launched this year. It lacks the neat dimensions of the Gameboy and guzzles batteries but is redeemed by a strong selection of software to choose from with popular games including *Sonic the Hedgehog 2, Gunstar Heroes* and *Prince of Persia*.

Thelma and Louise

Ridley Scott's cinematic eye gives *Thelma and Louise* a majestic backdrop, but it's the relationship of the two women whose road trip goes badly wrong that is the lynchpin of this groundbreaking film. Louise (Geena Davis) is a pretty but downtrodden housewife, Thelma (Susan Sarandon), her older, wiser waitress friend. As they hit the road in a bid to get away from it all, the men they meet along the way are the catalysts for a spiralling chain of disastrous events that turn Thelma and Louise into criminals on the run.

House of Eliot

31 August 1991 Fans of vintage fashion and the 1920s are in for a treat with *House of Eliot*, BBC1's new period drama. Beatrice and Evangeline Eliot are enterprising sisters with a talent for sewing and a passion for fashion. When their domineering father dies leaving them penniless, they turn their hobby into a dressmaking business that eventually, over three series, grows and flourishes into a successful couture house.

MUSIC

Billion dollar deal

11th March 1991 The deals keep getting bigger and bigger. Michael Jackson signs for Sony for one billion dollars just days after sister Janet signs for Virgin for $30 million, making her the highest paid female recording star ever. No doubt taking note is Mariah Carey, Columbia's top signing of 1990, who reaches No. 1 with her self-titled debut album. Meanwhile, old stagers the Rolling Stones conclude a comparatively modest $20 million deal with Virgin.

Silence of the Lambs

Anthony Hopkins creates one of cinema's most complex and memorable monsters when he pulls on a boilersuit and transforms into Hannibal 'the Cannibal' Lecter in this year's massive screen event, *Silence of the Lambs*. Trainee FBI agent Clarice Starling (Jodie Foster) must enlist the help of Lector, an incarcerated intellectual with a taste for human flesh, in her bid to track down a killer. Their uneasy relationship is compelling, while the more gruesome scenes have cinema audiences jumping in their seats before they go home vowing to avoid fava beans and a nice glass of chianti in future.

Nat and Natalie

27th July 1991 As part of an album tribute to her late father Nat King Cole, Natalie Cole records his signature song, *Unforgettable*, interwoven with his original 1951 recording. It is the first 'virtual duet' in recording history.

Seattle spirit

24th September 1991 'Grunge' goes international with the release of Nirvana's album *Nevermind*. Grunge is a blend of punk rock and heavy metal created by a handful of alternative bands from the Seattle area. Though interpreted as a teen anthem for the 90s, the single *Smells Like Teen Spirit* is more a song about not being ready to leave your teens behind.

REM go mainstream

REM, for so long the Georgia-based kings of small-scale, stripped-down US alternative rock, move into the big time with the album *Out of Time* and two breakthrough singles, *Losing My Religion* and the sunshine-fuelled *Shiny Happy People* featuring Kate Pierson from the B-52s. Their jangled, angular sound and Michael Stipe's intense vocals won't change but the scale of their success will.

Freddie's gone

24th November 1991 Freddie Mercury of Queen dies from bronchial pneumonia resulting from AIDS. Though there has been plenty of conjecture, his condition has been kept secret from fans and the media. His death explains why there was such a retrospective character to the last Queen album, *Innuendo*, released in February. Songs such as *The Show Must Go On* and *These are the Days of Our Lives* now sound like epitaphs. *Bohemian Rhapsody* is re-released and spends five weeks at No. 1.

Trip hop

While Happy Mondays, the Stone Roses and the Charlatans keep eyes fixed on Manchester, the Bristol club scene offers a different psychedelic/electronic hip hop fusion - 'trip hop'. The scene's leaders are Massive Attack, a collective built around Adrian 'Tricky' Thaws. Signature single *Unfinished Sympathy* has an almost Gothic grandeur enhanced by a full orchestra recorded at Abbey Road.

KLF calling

Nobody knows what KLF - the Kopyright Liberation Front - will do next. Bill Drummond and Jimmy Cauty's idea is to embarrass the music industry at every opportunity, whether by sampling all and sundry without permission or creating havoc at the BRIT Awards. This year's stunt - their last under the KLF banner - is to make a nonsense record, *Justified and Ancient*, with country music queen Tammy Wynette. Only *Bohemian Rhapsody* prevents it from reaching No. 1.

Take That formed

23rd November 1991 Wanting to create a UK New Kids on the Block, music entrepreneur Nigel Martin-Smith launches a five-piece boy band. Initially called Kick It but renamed Take That, they make their chart debut with *Promises*.

MY FIRST 18 YEARS TOP10 1991

1. **Smells Like Teen Spirit** *Nirvana*
2. **Sit Down** *James*
3. **Promise Me** *Beverley Craven*
4. **Gypsy Woman** *Crystal Waters*
5. **Whole of the Moon** *The Waterboys*
6. **This is Your Life** *Banderas*
7. **Fall at Your Feet** *Crowded House*
8. **Get Here** *Oleta Adams*
9. **Losing My Religion** *REM*
10. **The One and Only** *Chesney Hawkes*

Open | Search | Scan

Miles Davis

28th September 1991 Miles Davis, the most admired and influential figure in post-war jazz, dies of a stroke at 65.

They're too sexy

Pure raunchy fun is the best way to describe the fashion world send-up *I'm Too Sexy*, which sticks at No. 2 in the UK for weeks on end without ever dislodging the incumbent No. 1 by Bryan Adams. It's the inspired work of brothers Fred and Richard Fairbrass and guitarist Rob Manzoli in the guise of Right Said Fred.

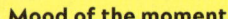

Mood of the moment

With profound changes underway to the geo-politics of Europe, two records capture the times. *Right Here, Right Now* by Jesus Jones was written while the band were in Romania shortly after the fall of Ceausescu. *Wind of Change* from veteran German rockers the Scorpions (photo) hits the European charts during a summer in which the Soviet Union disintegrates and Cold War fears seem to be banished forever.

SPORT

Shots down
25th March 1992 Aldershot Town - nicknamed 'the Shots' - face bankruptcy and resign from the Football League. They are followed five months later by Maidstone United whose debts mean that they cannot fulfil their fixtures. Both clubs are relaunched by groups of fans but have to start again in the lower leagues of the English football pyramid.

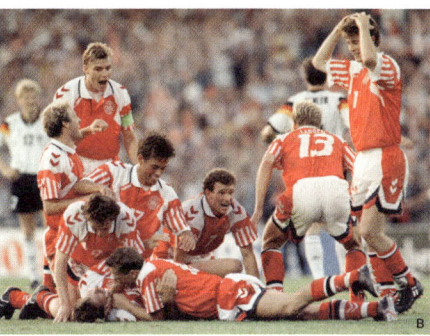

Euro 1992
10th - 26th June 1992 England and Scotland both qualify for the 1992 European Championships, hosted by Sweden, but fail to progress beyond the group stage. The tournament is won by outsiders Denmark who defeat Germany 2-0. Denmark were a late addition to the competition following the exclusion of Yugoslavia due to the conflict there.

Botham joins Durham
25th April 1992 England's legendary all-rounder Ian Botham makes his first County Championship appearance for Durham versus Leicestershire, in his new club's debut season in the competition. Although Durham finish bottom of the Championship table, glory days await - notably in the late 2000s, when they win the Championship twice in consecutive seasons.

Barcelona Olympics
25th July - 9th August 1992 British athletes perform well at the Olympic Games in Barcelona, taking a total of five golds, three silvers and twelve bronze medals. The high points from a UK point of view are on the track and on the water: Linford Christie's gold in the 100 metres and Sally Gunnell's in the 400 metres hurdles, with Mathew Pinsent and Steve Redgrave winning the coxless pairs and Garry Herbert and Greg and Jonny Searle victorious in the men's coxed pair. The most moving moment in the whole two weeks comes when UK runner Derek Redmond tears his hamstring in the 400 metres semi-final yet insists on hobbling to the end. He completes the final lap with the help of his father. The crowd responds with a standing ovation.

Premier League kicks off
15th August 1992 Just three weeks before the inaugural season of the Premier League begins, Alan Shearer becomes the most expensive footballer in UK history when he signs for Blackburn Rovers from Southampton for £3.6 million.

---

16 JAN 1992

Eric Clapton performs on MTV's *Unplugged*, the recording of which becomes the best selling live album of all time.

15 FEB 1992

Jeffrey Dahmer found guilty of killing 15 men.

26 MAR 1992

Mike Tyson sentenced to ten years for rape of Desiree Washington.

1992

Mansell retires at the top

13th September 1992 Having won the Formula One season with five races to spare just a month before - so becoming the first Brit to take the title since James Hunt in 1976 - British driver Nigel Mansell ends an outstanding career by announcing his retirement from Formula One.

DOMESTIC NEWS

Death of Leonard Cheshire

31st July 1992 Leonard Cheshire dies in Suffolk at the age of 74. One of the most decorated of all the RAF's wartime pilots, he founded the disability charity that bore his name and was married to fellow disabled champion Sue Ryder.

More bloodshed in Ulster

17th January 1992 At the start of another turbulent year in Northern Ireland, a Provisional IRA bomb kills eight Protestants working on a British Army construction project at Teebane. In a reprisal attack on 5th February, loyalist gunmen kill five Catholics in a Belfast betting shop. The Belfast shootings come during a first-ever visit to the six counties by a serving President of Ireland, Mary Robinson.

Baltic Exchange bombed

10th April 1992 One day after the General Election, the IRA bombing campaign against London continues. Three people are killed and 91 injured when the Baltic Exchange building in the City is targeted at 9.20am. It is the single most powerful bomb to strike London since the wartime Blitz. During the following night a bomb badly damages a major traffic intersection at Staples Corner in North London.

Welcome, Super Mario

11th April 1992 The Super Nintendo home video game console is launched in the UK along with the best selling Super Mario World game.

New banknotes issued

29th April 1992 A new ten-pound banknote is issued by the Bank of England depicting the author Charles Dickens, one of a
new series of notes honouring great Victorians. It remains in circulation for eleven years.

12 APR 1992

Euro Disney Paris opens.

9 MAY 1992

37th Eurovision Song Contest; Linda Martin representing Ireland wins singing '*Why Me*' in Malmo.

30 JUN 1992

Margaret Thatcher enters House of Lords as Baroness Thatcher of Kesteven.

Fairtrade UK
26th June 1992 The Fairtrade Foundation is launched in the UK as an arm of the global Fairtrade movement. The Co-Op becomes the first supermarket to market a Fairtrade product - Cafedirect coffee.

Classic FM on the air
7th September 1992 With a policy of playing only classical music, Classic FM becomes the very first national commercial radio station to open in the UK. It is the brainchild of the Great Western Radio (GWR) group and Andrew Lloyd Webber's Really Useful Group.

ROYALTY & POLITICS

Coal mine closures
13th October 1992 Trade Secretary Michael Heseltine announces the closures of 31 of the 50 remaining UK coal mines. With memories of the recent miners' strike still sharp, the decision is seen even by sections of the Conservative press as a betrayal. One hundred thousand march in London against the closures a week later.

Women can be priests
11th November 1992 In a momentous and far-reaching decision taken after many hours of intense debate, the General Synod of the Church of England votes to allow women to be ordained into the priesthood.

'Annus horribilis'
6th February 1992 As the Queen celebrates four decades since her accession to the throne, 1992 becomes what she will later call an 'annus horribilis' (miserable year). In June, Andrew Morton's book *Diana: Her True Story* is published with revelations of adulterous behaviour by Prince Charles and Diana's five suicide attempts. In March, the Duke and Duchess of York separate after five years of marriage. In April, Princess Anne announces her divorce from Captain Mark Phillips after nineteen years. In November, a major fire destroys part of Windsor Castle and controversy follows over whether taxpayers should pay for the repairs. In December, it is confirmed that Charles and Diana have separated but have no plans for divorce. To cap it all, the Queen is now obliged to pay tax for the first time.

10 JUL 1992
Albert Pierrepoint, the UK's long-time official hangman, dies aged 87.

1 AUG 1992
Sexual Offences (Amendment) Act 1992 becomes law, giving lifelong anonymity to victims of sex crimes.

30 SEP 1992
A new, smaller 10p coin enters circulation.

1992

Election '92

9th April 1992 John Major's Conservatives win the General Election with a majority of 21 seats. The party secures the highest vote - over fourteen million - ever attained by any party in British electoral history. The final figures are 336 Conservative seats, 220 for Labour and 22 for the Liberal Democrats.

Kinnock resigns

13th April 1992 Following Labour's election defeat, party leader Neil Kinnock resigns. The process of electing a new leader begins, ending with the victory of Shadow Chancellor of the Exchequer John Smith in the final ballot on 17th July. He defeats fellow candidate Bryan Gould with over 90 per cent of the vote.

Blue helmets

Under its new Secretary General, the Egyptian Boutros Boutros-Ghali, the United Nations blue helmeted peacekeepers are active in more regions and countries than ever. The blue helmets operate in the conflict zones of the Middle East, India, Angola, Somalia, Mozambique and Cambodia. On 21st February, the UN Security Council approves Resolution 743 to send a peacekeeping force to Yugoslavia.

Maastricht Treaty

7th February 1992 With the signing of the new Maastricht Treaty, the EEC becomes the European Community (EC), a partnership with common foreign and security policies and justice and home affairs policies. The European Parliament will have more legislative and supervisory power.

Black Wednesday

16th September 1992 On a day destined to be remembered as 'Black Wednesday', the government faces a humiliating climbdown when it is forced to withdraw sterling from the European Exchange Rate Mechanism (ERM) after insisting it would not do so. The withdrawal causes real damage to the Conservatives' reputation for safe handling of the UK economy, leading to a decline in the opinion polls and eventual electoral defeat in 1997.

26 OCT 1992
The last Russian troops leave Poland.

25 NOV 1992
Czechoslovakia votes to split the country into two separate nations, the Czech Republic and Slovakia.

31 DEC 1992
Breakfast television company TV-am makes its final broadcast.

Civil war in Bosnia
5th April 1992 After Slovenia and Croatia, Bosnia-Herzegovina declares its independence from Yugoslavia. Just as in Croatia, this leads to civil war. The Serbian minority declares its own Serbian Republic which, under the control of Radovan Karadžić and Radkol Mladić and with the support of the Yugoslav army, besieges Sarajevo and commits mass murders in villages and towns in eastern Bosnia to 'cleanse' the region. Bosnian Muslims and Croats are mistreated, starved, abused and murdered.

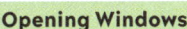

Rodney King riots
29th April 1992 The acquittal of four Los Angeles police officers, on trial for beating up an unarmed black man, Rodney King, in March 1991, sparks six days of rioting, causing 63 deaths.

Clinton and Bush
3rd November 1992 In the US Presidential election, the incumbent George H. W. Bush (photo right) is defeated by Democratic Party candidate and Arkansas Governor Bill Clinton (photo left). The charismatic Clinton wins the elections by a huge margin and becomes the 42nd President.

First text message
3rd December 1992 Vodafone employee Richard Jarvis is sipping a drink when he receives the first ever text message on his mobile phone. The message says 'Merry Christmas' and comes from software programmer Neil Papworth of tech company Sema Group, which has been hired by Vodafone to develop a messaging service for pagers and mobile phones. What we now know as SMS - the Short Message Service - is born.

ENTERTAINMENT

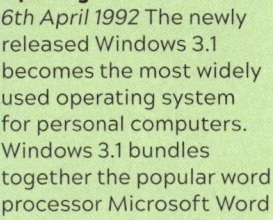

Opening Windows
6th April 1992 The newly released Windows 3.1 becomes the most widely used operating system for personal computers. Windows 3.1 bundles together the popular word processor Microsoft Word with Microsoft Excel, Microsoft PowerPoint and Microsoft Mail.

You've been Tango'd
'Orange Man' the advertising campaign for Tango fizzy orange drink airs this year. The citrussy taste sensation is personified by an impudent bald, orange man who appears out of nowhere to give Tango drinkers a sloppy kiss or a slap around the chops. 'You know when you've been Tango'd' becomes part of common parlance used especially to describe anyone who has overdone the fake tan!

Who shot JFK?

24th January 1992 Writer and director Oliver Stone isn't afraid to tackle America's big questions. He explored the ordinary man's experience of the Vietnam War in *Platoon* and *Born on the Fourth of July* and this year, in *JFK*, he asks perhaps the biggest question of all - who killed John F. Kennedy? He asks it already knowing there will be no answer. Nevertheless, with Kevin Costner as dogged New Orleans district attorney Jim Garrison, and Gary Oldman as Lee Harvey Oswald, *JFK* sums up the frustrations, paranoia and mystery surrounding one of the twentieth century's defining events. A gripping and brilliantly crafted piece of filmmaking.

Gladiators...Ready!

10th October 1992 Can you feel the power of the *Gladiators*? UK audiences certainly can as ITV's *Gladiators* pits have-a-go contestants against twentieth-century Gladiators - a toned and honed assembly of musclemen and Amazons - ready to scupper the mere mortals as they scamper through a series of obstacle courses and challenges in the gladiatorial arena. Footballer John Fashanu and ex-TV-am weather girl Ulrika Johnson keep the energy high octane as hosts and stoke up the screaming audience.

Where's my Willy?

Eastenders says goodbye to one of its most loyal cast members on 14th May when Willy, the pet pug belonging to Ethel Skinner, is diagnosed with cancer and Ethel makes the heartbreaking decision to have him put down. Having served on *Eastenders* since its first episode, Willy dies in real life just two weeks after his final scene.

Eldoradon't

After much fanfare, what will turn out to be one of the BBC's most expensive and embarrassing misfires begins on 6th July. *Eldorado* is a new soap, hoping to capture the sun-soaked success of *Neighbours* with a dash of *Dynasty* glamour. With a largely inexperienced cast, much of the acting is wooden, the storylines cringe-worthy and the setting of an ex-pat community in Spain fails to engage audiences who prefer the homely familiarity of East End cockneys, or Manchester landladies. *Eldorado* limps on for just 156 episodes.

Men Behaving Badly

If 'laddish' behaviour is becoming a defining feature of the 1990s, then *Men Behaving Badly*, written by Simon Nye, is the flagship for the movement. The first series, beginning on 18th February, pairs Gary (Martin Clunes) with flatmate Dermot (Harry Enfield) but Dermot is replaced in series 2 by Tony (Neil Morrissey), and the sitcom transfers to BBC1 where a later, post-watershed slot allows some colourful language and mild sexual content alongside the boozing and carousing. The result is one of the most popular comedies of the decade. As teenage boys in grown men's bodies, Gary and Tony, whose long-suffering love interests are Dorothy (Caroline Quentin) and Deborah (Leslie Ash), are the Likely Lads for a bolder, brasher era.

Nude is *The Word*

Channel 4's live, late-night show *The Word* has courted controversy from its launch in 1990 but its dubious reputation reaches new highs (or lows?) this year when all-female grunge band L7 perform their single *Pretend You're Dead* and singer and guitarist Donita Sparks pulls down her jeans and knickers and carries on the performance naked from the waist down. Presenter Terry Christian remarks afterwards, 'It's gonna be one of those shows innit?'. Often tasteless but never dull, *The Word* is essential post-pub viewing and provides many a watercooler moment with its rich tapestry of outrageous moments. In 1995, *The Word* has the last word and comes to an end.

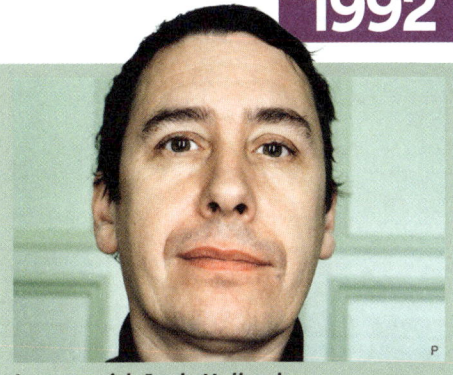

Later... with Jools Holland

Originally the music strand of *The Late Show*, *Later... with Jools Holland* begins on 8th October. Holland has a relaxed but efficient presenting style as he introduces around five musical acts, of different genres, who take turns to play live, sometimes accompanied by Holland on the piano. *Later...* continues to bring both established and undiscovered music acts to TV screens for the next 30 years, while the show's annual *Hootenany* is a New Year's Eve tradition.

In a *Heartbeat*

10th April 1992 Nick Berry had set hearts a-flutter as Simon Wicks in *Eastenders* and sealed his star status with a no. 1 single, *Every Loser Wins* in 1986. His next move is to fill the lead role in ITV's new period drama *Heartbeart* as PC Nick Rowan, alongside Niamh Cusack as Rowan's doctor wife. Set in the North Riding of Yorkshire around the fictional village of Aidensfield, it stays for eighteen series, attracting audiences of over 13 million at the peak of its popularity.

DO YOU REMEMBER THIS?

Raider

The Crying Game

30th October 1992 Neil Jordan wins the Oscar for Best Screenplay for his low-budget indie sleeper hit, *The Crying Game*. Set in Northern Ireland, Stephen Rea is an IRA operative whose capture and role in the death of a British soldier (Forest Whitaker) leads to him seeking out the man's lover. Complex, multi-layered and sexually subversive, *The Crying Game* surprises with a story that meanders unexpectedly off course and an ending that nobody sees coming.

Blobby blunders in

Mr Blobby makes his debut on BBC1's *Noel's House Party* on 24th October as Noel Edmonds' sidekick and chief troublemaker. An over-sized, goggle-eyed, yellow spotted avacado-shaped figure the colour of pink blancmange, Blobby's unintelligible language (he can only say 'Blobby') makes him sound like he's drowning, and his main talents appear to be bumping into everything and falling on top of everyone. Inexplicably, Mr. Blobby becomes a huge star and even has a No. 1 Christmas single in 1993 with, *Mr. Blobby*. A nadir in the cultural history of Western civilisation.

Party on!

22nd May 1992 Wayne's World developed from a short sketch on the American show *Saturday Night Live*. The film's two leads, Wayne and Garth, coining a whole new collection of universally copied catchphrases from 'Schwing!' to 'Party on!' and 'We're not worth, we're not worthy!' The film's most famous scene, when Wayne and Garth head bang along to Queen's '*Bohemian Rhapsody*' while driving an AMC Pacer, propels the song to No. 2 in America and reignites interest in the band despite the death of Freddie Mercury.

The Big Breakfast

Channel 4 launch weekday morning show *The Big Breakfast* on 28th September, aiming to pull in a younger audience with its light-hearted and fast-paced format. Broadcast from a real house in Bow, east London, presenters Chris Evans and Gaby Roslin are joined by puppets Zig and Zag, and Paula Yates who conducts flirtatious celebrity interviews on a double bed, including a notorious 1994 chat with INXS sexpot Michael Hutchence that has the nation yelling, 'Get a room!'

Ab Fab

PR guru, neurotic hypochondriac and Christian Lacroix devotee Edina 'Eddie' Monsoon (Jennifer Saunders) is introduced to audiences for the first time on 12th November with the start of *Absolutely Fabulous* on BBC2. Together with her best friend Patsy Stone (Joanna Lumley), Eddie attempts to keep up with the cool kids, spends lavishly at 'Harvey Nicks', tries every New Age fad going, and mostly leaves the running of her company to her spaced-out PA, Bubble (Jane Horrocks) all under the disapproving gaze of sensible daughter Saffie (Julia Sawalha). Quickly established as a comedy classic, *Ab Fab* is a mischievous and outrageous send-up of the fickle world of fashion and celebrity.

Reimagining the Western

Some might say Clint Eastwood has made the Western his speciality but as director and star, he brings an unprecedented depth and darkness to *Unforgiven*, a brooding reinvention of the genre, released in cinemas on 18th September. As William Munny, he's a grizzled ex-mercenary riding out to claim one last bounty with his sidekick Ned (Morgan Freeman) as he takes up the cause of women in a brothel who seek vengeance for a knifed and disfigured young prostitute. Critically acclaimed, *Unforgiven* wins Eastwood two Oscars for Best Picture and Best Director while Gene Hackman gains one as Best Supporting Actor for his turn as the callous sheriff, Little Bill.

Remembering Freddie

20th April 1992 The stars gather at Wembley Stadium to pay tribute to the late Freddie Mercury, with all profits going to a new Mercury Phoenix Trust in aid of AIDS research. Performers include Elton John, David Bowie, George Michael, Annie Lennox and Guns N' Roses.

MUSIC

Bodyguard bonanza

The biggest song of 1992 is actually twenty years old. Dolly Parton's *I Will Always Love You* is the centrepiece of the Whitney Houston-Kevin Costner movie *The Bodyguard*. A hugely powerful vocal performance, Whitney's single tops the US chart for fourteen weeks and the UK chart for ten, while the soundtrack becomes the top selling movie album ever at 45 million plus.

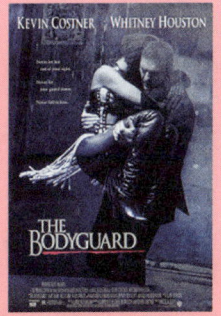

Clampdown on raves

22nd - 29th May 1992 As unauthorised rave events mushroom in warehouses and on farmland, the chaos at a week-long free festival at Castlemorton Common in the Malvern Hills prompts government action. A bill is introduced in Parliament to make illegal outdoor festivals which play 'sounds wholly or predominantly characterised by the emission of a succession of repetitive beats'. The Criminal Justice and Public Order Act becomes law in 1994.

Sex by Madonna

20th April 1992 Madonna signs a seven year multimedia deal worth $60 million with Time Warner, making her the most powerful woman in global entertainment. Her activities this year include a new album, *Erotica*, and a coffee table book of erotic self-portraits simply titled *Sex*.

Madness at Madstock

8th August 1992 Madness re-form and headline a 'Madstock' concert in Finsbury Park, close to their Camden Town stamping ground. Supporting act Morrissey, now solo after leaving the Smiths, is bombarded with coins and cans when he sings *National Front Disco* wrapped in a Union Jack.

Nirvana at Reading

30th August 1992 Nirvana play a muddy Reading Festival in front of 40,000 fans. It will be their last live performance in the UK. Despite the media storm surrounding the Cobain-Love marriage and drug use, drummer Dave Grohl describes it as 'a wonderful show - and it healed us for a little while'.

First Mercury Prize

9th September 1992 The prestigious Mercury Prize is awarded for the first time. Conceived to honour the most innovative UK or Irish album of the year, it goes to Scottish rock band Primal Scream for *Screamadelica*. They proceed to lose their £20,000 prize cheque in the celebrations.

Sinead controversy

3rd October 1992 Sinead O'Connor incurs the wrath of American Catholics by tearing up a picture of Pope John Paul II on the *Saturday Night Live* show. She explains that it was a statement against child abuse in the Catholic church.

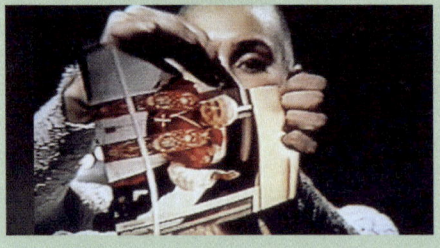

MY FIRST 18 YEARS
TOP 10   1992

1. **Under the Bridge** *Red Hot Chili Peppers*
2. **I Can't Dance** *Genesis*
3. **Winter** *Tori Amos*
4. **Friday I'm in Love** *The Cure*
5. **Would I Lie to You** *Charles and Eddie*
6. **Sleeping Satellite** *Tamsin Archer*
7. **Walking on Broken Glass** *Annie Lennox*
8. **Damn I Wish I was Your Lover** *Sophie B. Hawkins*
9. **The Days of Pearly Spencer** *Marc Almond*
10. **It Must Be Love** *Madness*

Open 🟢 | Search 🔍 | Scan 📷

Country matters

23rd November 1992 Billy Ray Cyrus's dippy line-dancing tune *Achy Breaky Heart* is one of the biggest global hits of the year. Elsewhere, veteran Willie Nelson is selling better than ever despite owing enormous sums in unpaid tax, while names like Joe Ely, Iris Dement, Vince Gill and especially Garth Brooks - fifth best selling act of 1992 at ten million albums - are leading country's new wave.

Mariah and the MiniDisc

7th December 1992 Challenging the compact disc is a new music format - the MiniDisc, developed by Sony. Released today is the format's first commercial release, Mariah Carey's *Unplugged*, comprising live recordings from her recent MTV show. The MiniDisc never takes off.

SPORT

Last BDO Championship

7th January 1993 The game of darts has been rising in stature and popularity since the early 1980s thanks to increased television exposure and the emergence of great personalities like Eric Bristow (photo) and his protégé Phil Taylor. As a split looms between the leading stars and darts administration body the British Darts Organisation (BDO), the very last BDO World Darts Championship sees all the big-name darts stars of the time - Bristow, Taylor, Dennis Priestley and Jocky Wilson included - knocked out before the final. The title is won by John Owen, who beats Alan Warriner 3-6.

National chaos

3rd April 1993 The Grand National at Aintree is cancelled after a chaotic false start in which 30 of the 39 horses keep running and seven even complete the course. Bookmakers are forced to repay the £75 million bets placed on the race. The official starter, Keith Brown, was taking charge of his last Grand National before retiring.

Seles stabbed

30th April 1993 World number one Monica Seles is stabbed between her shoulder blades by a spectator during a match in a World Tennis Association tournament in Hamburg. She will not play again for two years.

Giants of the game

British football mourns the loss of two giants of the game. Bobby Moore, the only player to captain England to World Cup victory, dies of cancer aged 53 on 24th February. Danny Blanchflower, whose death is announced on 9th December, was a Northern Ireland international who captained Tottenham Hotspur's famous double winning side in 1961 and later moved into journalism.

Ball of the century

4th June 1993 The England-Australia summer Test series sees the visitors retain the Ashes by winning four matches to England's one, with one match drawn. The most memorable moment comes on the second day of the first Test, when Australian spin bowler Shane Warne bowls out Mike Gatting with an extraordinary delivery that is soon named 'the ball of the century'.

World Cup misery

17th November 1993 England fail to qualify for the 1994 FIFA World Cup, in spite of beating San Marino 7-1 in their last qualification game. The damage was done in an earlier 2-0 defeat at the hands of the Netherlands. Manager Graham Taylor resigns eight days later. Wales also miss out on qualifying with a 2-1 defeat to Romania.

20 JAN 1993	6 FEB 1993	12 MAR 1993
Bill Clinton is inaugurated as the 42nd US President.	Tennis superstar Arthur Ashe dies from HIV contracted through a blood transfusion.	317 killed by bomb attacks in Bombay.

DOMESTIC
NEWS

Target Warrington
February - March 1993 Warrington in Cheshire becomes the new focus of Provisional IRA attacks on the British mainland. Bombs explode destroying gas holders while devices planted in the town centre kill three-year-old Jonathan Ball and twelve-year-old Timothy Parry. Attacks on the City of London resume on 24th April, when a truck bomb kills a photographer and causes huge damage to Bishopsgate and the Natwest Tower.

Stephen Lawrence
22nd April 1993 The murder of black teen-ager Stephen Lawrence at a bus shelter in Eltham, South London, has ramifications that are still being felt over 30 years later. Six suspects are arrested but not charged, leading to a private prosecution of the alleged perpetrators by Stephen's family that fails to achieve convictions. An enquiry into the handling of the case by the Metropolitan Police and the Criminal Prosecution Service delivers a damning report in 1998.

Braer oil spill
5th January 1993 The Liberian oil tanker MV *Braer* hits rocks on the south coast of Shetland, causing a massive oil spill - 84,700 tonnes of crude oil - and threatening wildlife. The ship breaks up five days later during a ferocious North Atlantic storm. The upturned bow remains visible from the coast for years after.

Virgin bites back
11th January 1993 British Airways apologises to Virgin Atlantic for undertaking a 'dirty tricks' campaign against the company to disrupt its commercial operations. Legal action by Virgin boss Richard Branson against BA results in an out of court settlement in his favour, leaving BA with a bill of over £3.5 million.

Bulger murder
12th February 1993 In one of the most distressing child murder cases in years, two-year-old James Bulger is abducted and killed by two ten-year-old boys in Bootle, Merseyside. At the end of their trial in November, the boys - Robert Thompson and Jon Venables - become the youngest convicted murderers in British legal history.

19 APR 1993
A 51-day stand-off at Waco, Texas, between FBI agents and Branch Davidian followers ends in 76 deaths.

17 MAY 1993
Rebecca Stephens is the first UK woman to reach the summit of Everest.

15 JUN 1993
James Hunt, 1976 Formula 1 World Drivers' Champion, dies of a heart attack at 45.

Hotel collapse
4th June 1993 A huge coastal landslide at Scarborough, North Yorkshire, causes a large section of the Holbeck Hall Hotel to collapse into the sea. Some of the collapse is seen live on television during an edition of Yorkshire TV's *Calendar* news programme. Nobody is hurt and what remains of the building is demolished safely.

ROYALTY & POLITICS

Royal doors open
29th April 1993 In a new spirit of openness and accountability to the public, Buckingham Palace announces that the Queen will allow part of the building to be opened to visitors during the summer months.

Lamont sacked
27th May 1993 In a reshuffle of his Cabinet prompted by his government's recent poor showing in the Newbury by-election, John Major sacks Norman Lamont and makes Kenneth Clarke his new Chancellor of the Exchequer. He refuses the offer of a lesser post as Secretary of State for the Environment and becomes a severe critic of Major's policies and a fierce Eurosceptic.

Tunnel vision
20th June 1993 The first high-speed train journey through the Channel Tunnel takes place ahead of its official opening in 1994.

Equal status for Welsh
21st October 1993 The Welsh Language Act 1993 is passed into law, giving Welsh equal status with English in all aspects of public life in Wales. The most immediate impact is a visible one: all road signage in Wales will from now on be bilingual.

BNP takes council seat
17th September 1993 The right-wing anti-immigration British National Party (BNP) wins its first ever council seat, in Tower Hamlets in East London.

M40 minibus crash
18th November 1993 In what has been described as the UK's worst ever motorway accident, twelve children from Hagley Roman Catholic High School and their teacher Eleanor Fry are killed in a late-night minibus crash on the M40 near Warwick. They were returning home from a concert at the Royal Albert Hall.

4 JUL 1993
Pete Sampras beats fellow American Jim Courier in four sets, for his first of seven Wimbledon titles.

30 AUG 1993
The Eiffel Tower welcomes its 150 millionth paying visitor.

10 SEP 1993
Mystery sci-fi series *The X Files* debuts on US TV.

Diana withdraws
3rd December 1993 Although there is still no sign of the Prince and Princess of Wales divorcing after their separation, Diana announces her intention to withdraw from public life in a speech at London's Hilton Hotel.

Air Max
In the 1990s, the popularity of the Nike Air Max explodes. A true Air Max hunt spreads across the world and leads to bizarre scenes in stores. The shoe is popular with almost every subculture.

Downing Street Declaration
15th December 1993 A glimmer of hope for the peace process in Northern Ireland: Prime Minister John Major and Irish premier Albert Reynolds sign the Downing Street Declaration affirming the right of the people of Ireland to self-determination and that Northern Ireland would be transferred to the Republic of Ireland from the UK only if a majority of its population was in favour. It signifies a subtle but important change of policy and opens up the prospect of republican party Sinn Fein joining negotiations.

World Trade Center bombed
26th February 1993 A bomb explodes in a van parked below the north tower in the World Trade Center in New York, an attack by terrorists linked to Al-Qaeda. Their aim is to blow down the north tower against the south tower, so that the symbol of international trade disappears in one fell swoop. The attack kills six people and injures more than a thousand others, but it fails in its objective. The towers remain standing - at least for now.

1 OCT 1992

In defence of his heavyweight boxing title Lennox Lewis beats Frank Bruno by TKO in round 7.

30 NOV 1992

Toy giants Mattel and Fisher-Price complete a $15 million merger.

31 DEC 1992

Figures show there are now fifteen million users of the Internet and 623 websites.

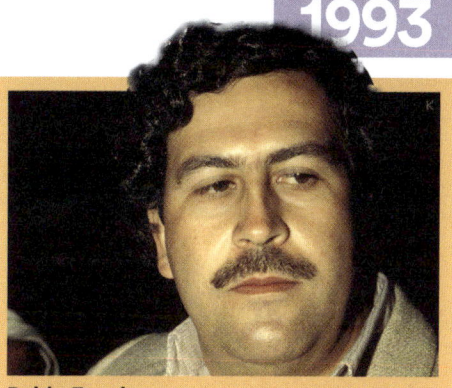

Spamming accident
31st March 1993 By mistake, software developer Richard Depew sends the same message two hundred times to a newsgroup on Usenet. The enormous amount of messages frustrates other users, who are turning to the newsgroup to discuss the progress of the web. One of the users, Joel Furr, is the first to give the message explosion a name: spam!

Srebrenica
16th April 1993 In Bosnia, the civil war is raging between Serbs and the Bosniaks and Croats. Tens of thousands of Muslim Bosnians who survived the massacres in their villages and towns are fleeing to enclaves where the Bosnian army has managed to hold back the Serbs. One of those enclaves is the city of Srebrenica, which is today declared a UN-protected 'safe area'.

Pablo Escobar
2nd December 1993 Colombian Pablo Escobar is the most feared drug baron in the world. The head of the infamous Medellín cartel controls about 80 per cent of the global cocaine trade, earning him more than $70 million a day in the best years. Escobar has a hand in thousands of murders to protect himself and his business, which makes him untouchable in Colombia and one of the richest yet also one of the most wanted people on earth. Escobar's fate is determined when, after several escapes from prison, the Colombian police investigation team trace him to his hideout in Medellín, where he is shot dead on the roof of his house.

Oslo Accords
13th September 1993 In the utmost secrecy, Israel and the PLO are negotiating a solution to their mutual conflict. In Oslo, out of sight of the cameras and international interference, an agreement is reached in which the Palestinians will be given self-government and can establish a Palestinian Authority. The formal signing by Prime Minister Yitzchak Rabin and PLO head Yasser Arafat will take place in Washington DC.

 **ENTERTAINMENT**

Morning motivation
Attired in eye-popping, multi-coloured lycra, Mr Motivator (real name Derrick Evans), becomes a regular on *GMTV* this year, encouraging the nation to get moving with his upbeat keep fit routines.

First browser
Mosaic becomes the first popular Internet browser. It is easy to install and for the first time images can be shown between the text on the web pages. In Mosaic you can also see which websites you have visited and save pages to view later.

Reservoir Dogs

Quentin Tarantino announces his arrival on the scene in 1992 when his heist-gone-wrong movie *Reservoir Dogs* is first shown at the Sundance Film Festival. The UK must wait until 15th January this year to see it, and then, due to a clamp down on film violence in the UK, another two and a half years before a VHS is available, during which time it firmly establishes itself as a cult classic. The film's poster, featuring the male cast in matching black suits and shades below a blood-spattered title, presages the unique blend of style and violence that will typify Tarantino's work. So too does the 1970s soundtrack, carefully curated by the director himself.

Thunderbirds are glued

After BBC2 repeats old episodes of *Thunderbirds* in 1992 there is a revival of interest in the retro puppet-led adventure show, and Matchbox Toys' Tracey Island playset sells out. But *Blue Peter* comes to the rescue on 7th January as presenter Anthea Turner shows viewers how to create their own Tracy Island out of cereal packets, drinking straws and sawdust. There are over 10,000 requests for the printed instructions published by the BBC.

DO YOU REMEMBER THIS?

VHS videocamera

Film according to French and Saunders

A highlight of comedy duo *French and Saunders'* sketch show is their regular film spoof segment. This year, Dawn becomes Hannibal Lecter and Jennifer, Clarice Starling in their own version of *Silence of the Lambs*. No films are safe from their clutches and *Thelma and Louise*, *Titanic* (Dawn plays Jack), *Gentlemen Prefer Blondes*, *Star Wars*, *Lord of the Rings* and *The Exorcist* all get the *French and Saunders* treatment over the years.

Wallace and Gromit – The Wrong Trousers

Aired on Boxing Day, Wensleydale cheese-loving inventor Wallace (voiced with gentle charm by Peter Sallis), his watchful dog Gromit and some robotic trousers get involved in foiling a diamond heist, masterminded by Wallace's new lodger, a dead-eyed criminal penguin, in this hilarious plasticine stop-motion animation adventure, created by 'claymation' genius, Nick Park.

Supermarket Sweep

Perma-tanned charmer Dale Winton hosts *Supermarket Sweep*, the ITV daytime quiz show where contestants answer questions and dash around a (mock-up) supermarket filling their trolleys and building up time or cash. The fun begins on 6th September.

Groundhog Day

Often cited as one of cinema's most perfect comedies, *Groundhog Day* has its UK release on 7th May. Bill Murray is bored, curmudgeonly weatherman Phil Connors, sent with his producer (Andie MacDowell) to the Pennsylvania town of Punxsutawney to report on the Groundhog Day ceremony (a genuine tradition in the US), only to then wake up on the same day, again, and again, and again... and again in a smart and mind-bending concept. Phil goes through confusion, delight, bitterness, and despair before eventually using his predicament for good and emerging a better human being.

Gone too soon?

The lives of two young actors are cut tragically short this year. Brandon Lee (photo), son of Bruce Lee, is shot in a freak accident on the set of *The Crow* on 31st March. On 31st October, River Phoenix dies of a drug-induced heart attack outside The Viper Room in Los Angeles. He is just 23 years old.

Monster movie

Steven Spielberg uses every visual effect trick in the book in what may well be the movie event of the decade - *Jurassic Park*. Seamlessly blending animatronics and live action with lightly applied computer-generated effects, audiences are transported to the ultimate theme park where eccentric millionaire John Hammond (Richard Attenborough) has brought dinosaurs back to life using DNA found in amber. Inevitably, things go badly wrong in this prehistoric paradise when a storm sets loose its most dangerous, and very hungry, inmates. Sam Neill, Laura Dern and Jeff Goldblum are among the specially selected group invited to preview the park and who go from cuddling herbivores to running for their lives from velociraptors and T-Rex. A terrifying, thrilling rollercoaster of a film.

Sleepless in Seattle

Tom Hanks and Meg Ryan star in Norah Ephron's whimsical long-distance love story, *Sleepless in Seattle*, released in the UK on 24th September. It's notable in that the two romantic leads, widower Sam and journalist Annie, spend just two minutes on screen together.

Cracker

Robbie Coltrane plays one of TV's most charismatic characters in Jimmy McGovern's *Cracker*, which begins on ITV on 27th September. As Edward 'Fitz' Fitzgerald, he's a criminal psychologist, brought in to help profile suspects for Greater Manchester Police. Larger-than-life, Fitz is a flawed genius, admitting in one episode; 'I drink too much, I smoke too much, I gamble too much, I am too much.' Some scorching storylines and an assemblage of brilliant acting talent make *Cracker* a huge success. Among Coltrane's co-stars are Robert Carlyle and Christopher Eccleston, the DCI whose final scenes after being stabbed are seared into viewers' memories.

Lard questions

On 4th June, ex-Deputy Leader of the Labour Party Roy Hattersley fails to appear as a panellist on satirical news show *Have I Got News For You*. It is the third time Hattersley has cancelled at the last minute and the furious producers replace him with a tub of lard, stating that, 'they possessed the same qualities and were likely to give similar performances'. Despite his team-mate being The Rt. Hon. Tub of Lard, M.P., Paul Merton still wins the show.

Eurotrash

The 1990s appetite for outrageous and titillating entertainment shows no sign of dimming and so *Eurotrash*, which begins on Channel 4 on 24th September, fits right in. Presented by the suave Antoine de Caunes, and the enfant terrible of French fashion, Jean Paul Gaultier, *Eurotrash* feeds us with a smorgasbord of film clips offering snapshots of strange and bizarre behaviour from our European neighbours. Lily Savage enjoying the delights of a male naked cleaning service in Berlin, or Michael Winner visiting a Paris restaurant staffed by drag queens is all standard fare in the world of *Eurotrash*.

MUSIC

Bill bows out

7th January 1993 Bill Wyman confirms his departure from the Rolling Stones. He has not played or recorded with the band since 1990.

Mick is 50

26th July 1993 The unthinkable has happened. Mick Jagger is 50. He and 300 guests celebrate at a fancy dress birthday bash on a French Revolution theme.

Suede make the grade

10th April 1993 Formed in Haywards Heath in 1990 and now releasing their self-titled debut album, Suede are a new critics' favourite. Sporting a provocative cover picture of a gender-undefined couple kissing, the glam-rock influenced set enters the chart at No. 1 and wins the 1993 Mercury Prize.

Ronson is dead
29th April 1993 Mick Ronson, David Bowie's ever-reliable Spider from Mars throughout his Ziggy Stardust period, dies of cancer aged 46.

Prince changes his name
7th June 1993 Prince is 35 today. To mark the occasion he announces that he will no longer be known by that name but by a squiggle-like symbol. From now he is referred to as The Artist Formerly Known as Prince. The move isn't quite as eccentric as it seems, as he and Warner Brothers are in dispute. The record label effectively owns the Prince name, so a new identity is a clever ruse to challenge his contract and gain greater control over his releases.

Goodbye Bruce
28th August 1993 Heavy metal aristocrats Iron Maiden say goodbye to singer Bruce Dickinson at their final gig together, a BBC show at Pinewood Studios. His replacement is Blaze Bayley from Wolfsbane. Dickinson rejoins in 1999.

Jackson abuse allegations
14th September 1993 A civil law suit is filed against Michael Jackson by the parents of thirteen-year-old Jordan Chandler alleging abuse. Jackson refutes the claims in a public statement issued in December.

Slivers of reggae
Two chart toppers prove that reggae is still a force. In March, Jamaican-born Shaggy matches a 1950s ska tune to a sample from Henry Mancini's film theme Peter Gunn and creates *Oh Carolina*. Three months later, UB40 (photo) add a reggae rhythm to the Elvis classic *Can't Help Falling in Love with You*. Both tracks are featured on the soundtrack of the Sharon Stone thriller *Sliver*.

Take That at the top
17th July 1993 Take That enjoy their first UK No. 1 with *Pray*. Becoming Britain's top boy band has not been a totally smooth ride, with their management's initial concentration on an older gay market rather than teenage girls now looking misplaced. After establishing themselves with two cover records - of Tavares' *It Only Takes a Minute* and Barry Manilow's *Could it be Magic* - they are now trusting the songwriting to Gary Barlow's Elton John-like facility for creating tunes to order.

Meat Loaf is back

23rd October 1993 After the runaway success of *Bat Out of Hell* in the late 70s, Meat Loaf's career was derailed by poor health and legal problems. Now he's back working with songwriter Jim Steinman on a sequel, *Bat Out of Hell II: Back into Hell*, which they introduce with the chart topping *I'd Do Anything for Love (But I Won't Do That)*. It's like the last sixteen years had never happened.

MY FIRST 18 YEARS
TOP10   1993

1. **Dreams** *Gabrielle*
2. **All That She Wants** *Ace of Base*
3. **Play Dead** *Bjork*
4. **Constant Craving** *k. d. lang*
5. **Pray** *Take That*
6. **The River of Dreams** *Billy Joel*
7. **Rubberband Girl** *Kate Bush*
8. **Fields of Gold** *Sting*
9. **Ordinary World** *Duran Duran*
10. **Moving On Up** *M People*

Open | Search | Scan

Rick retires

The polite, self-effacing and ever-spruce Rick Astley never looked comfortable with all the trappings of pop stardom. It's no real surprise, then, that he has chosen to retire from performing and recording at the grand old age of 27 after selling 40 million records worldwide. He stays true to his word for the next nine years.

Sugar-free Bjork

A national treasure in her native Iceland, Bjork has now left the Sugarcubes to release her solo album. The album *Debut* is a box of delights mixing trippy beats, new age atmospherics, Bond theme-like orchestral flourishes and even a looping Bollywood backing on the lovely *Venus as a Boy*. She has a voice that can go from a whisper to a roar in two seconds.

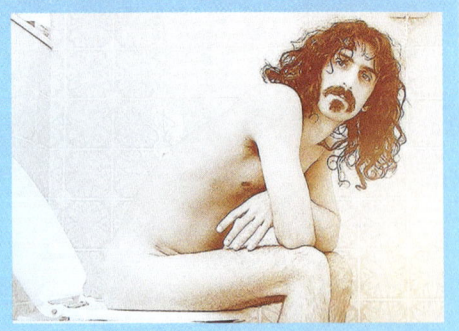

Zappa dies

4th December 1993 Frank Zappa, founder of the Mothers of Invention and one of rock music's great iconoclasts, dies of cancer aged 52. A favourite Zappa quote: 'Without deviation from the norm, progress is not possible.'

SPORT

Busby dies
8th January 1994 Former Manchester United manager Sir Matt Busby, who survived the 1958 Munich air disaster to rebuild the team and guide them to winning the European Cup in 1968, dies aged 84. Appropriately, United end the season by winning the 'double' as Premier League and FA Cup champions - the first side to do so since Arsenal in 1971.

Lara's record
6th June 1994 Brian Lara scores an unbeaten 501 runs off 427 balls in 474 minutes batting for Warwickshire against Durham. It creates a new first class cricket record for a highest score that still stands 30 years later. This is unquestionably his year: he breaks the world Test batting record by scoring 375 for the West Indies versus England in April and helps to steer his county to a treble of trophies - County Championship, Benson & Hedges Cup and Sunday League.

Bowing out with bronze
21st February 1994 Former gold medal winners Jayne Torvill and Christopher Dean announce their retirement from competition after taking bronze in the ice dancing at the Winter Olympics in Lillehammer.

World Cup 1994
17th June - 17th July 1994
The FIFA World Cup stirs temporary 'soccer' fever in host country the US, with well over three million people attending the matches. Brazil (photo) beat Italy on penalties in the final after the game ends 0-0, with poster boy player Roberto Baggio missing his deciding spot kick. With none of the UK nations participating, most home interest centres on Ireland, managed by ex-England international Jack Charlton. The Irish cause a sensation in their first group match by beating Italy 1-0. A real tragedy of the tournament is the fate of Colombia's Andres Escobar, who is shot dead on 2nd July in his home city of Medellín in apparent revenge for scoring an own goal.

17 JAN 1994
Yahoo!, the world's first search engine, is launched.

8 FEB 1994
With 432 Test wickets to his name, India's Kapil Dev sets a new world record.

16 MAR 1994
American figure skater Tonya Harding pleads guilty to attacking former Olympic teammate Nancy Kerrigan.

Hill pays tribute to Senna

11th December 1994 British driver Damon Hill is voted BBC Sports Personality of the Year at the end of a tumultuous year in motor racing. Hill had the responsibility of taking over as head driver of the Williams team after the death of Brazil's Ayrton Senna in the San Marino Grand Prix in May. In his acceptance speech at the BBC awards, Hill pays warm tribute to his former teammate. Hill's award is recognition for his triumph in the British Grand Prix at Silverstone, his six out of sixteen Formula One wins and his second place in the drivers' championship behind Michael Schumacher.

South Africa tour again

21st July - 21st August 1994 After 21 years in the wilderness, unable to compete internationally because of the country's apartheid policy, South Africa continue their return to Test match cricket with a series against England. The team is led by veteran Kepler Wessels, who during the long hiatus played 24 Tests for Australia. The series is drawn 1-1 but marred by accusations of ball tampering against England captain Michael Atherton.

DO YOU REMEMBER THIS?

Beeper

Rover sold

31st January 1994 BMW's acquisition of British Aerospace's 80 per cent stake in Rover leaves the UK without its own independent high-volume car manufacturer. Three weeks later, Honda sells its twenty per cent stake in Rover to BMW, giving the latter full ownership. The new Rover Group becomes the seventh largest carmaker in Europe.

Porn cinema fire

26th February 1994 An arson attack on an unlicensed adult cinema in Clerkenwell, London, kills eleven men. A homeless man nicknamed 'Deaf Dave' who had been refused entry is convicted after giving himself in to police. Four firefighters receive awards for their life-saving actions.

Cromwell Street murders

28th February 1994 Soon to be revealed as one of the UK's most notorious serial killers, Fred West is charged with murdering his daughter Heather and eighteen-year-old Shirley Robinson. Excavations at his house at 25 Cromwell Street, Gloucester, lead to discoveries of multiple bodies and the arrest of his wife Rose on 20th April. The couple are brought before Gloucester magistrates court on 30th June and charged with twelve murders.

22 APR 1994	19 MAY 1994	14 JUN 1994
Former US President Richard Nixon dies at 81.	Death of Jacqueline Onassis, former US First Lady.	UK holiday company Sunseeker Leisure collapses.

Heathrow attacks

9th - 13th March 1994 The IRA delivers a series of mortar attacks on Heathrow Airport, causing heavy disruption to flights but no casualties.

Channel Tunnel opens

6th May 1994 The 35-mile-long Channel Tunnel is officially opened by the Queen and President Mitterrand after six years of construction. Linking the UK and France, it is the longest undersea tunnel in the world. The new five-platform terminus for Eurostar services to Paris and Brussels via the Channel Tunnel opens at London's Waterloo Station on 14th November.

Equipped for the streets

20th June 1994 As part of a far-reaching series of changes to UK policing, the traditional police truncheon is replaced with a US-style baton. Over the next few years, the 'bobby on the beat' virtually disappears, police community support officers (PCSOs) take over non-arresting duties, Tasers are introduced and police uniforms evolve into something straight out of Robocop. Many forces withdraw the century-old 'custodian helmet' in favour of peaked caps, though the Metropolitan Police retains the old school headwear for ceremonial duties.

Bottled up

4th August 1994 Famous for such slogans as 'drinka pinta milka day' and 'milk has got a lotta bottle', the Milk Marketing Board is set for closure after 61 years following deregulation of the UK's milk market under the new Agriculture Act.

Changes to criminal law

3rd November 1994 The Criminal Justice and Public Order Act becomes law, increasing police powers to stop and search suspects, criminalising some civil offences, tightening the obscenity laws and lowering the age of consent for homosexual acts to 18.

Tattoos and piercings

As body art becomes increasingly popular, tattoos are no longer reserved for rough sailors but are increasingly seen decorating arms, backs, shoulders and legs. First seen in the punk era of the late 70s, piercings are now a fashion item. In the music video for Aerosmith's *Cryin'*, teen idol Alicia Silverstone has a belly button piercing as well as a tattoo! Many teenage girls follow her example and show off their navel piercings under a short shirt. Ears, lips, tongues, noses, eyebrows and nipples are fair game, too. Some even get a piercing in more intimate places, to provide extra stimulation during sex.

2 JUL 1994
Mass trespass by anti-road activists at Twyford Down motorway construction site.

1 AUG 1994
Jordan and Israel end a 46-year-long state of war.

3 SEP 1994
Former England and Wolves captain Billy Wright dies aged 70.

IRA ceasefire

31st August 1994 The IRA announces a ceasefire, which the UK government greets with scepticism. As a gesture of good faith, the government ends the long-time broadcasting ban on Sinn Fein and exclusion orders on the party's leaders, Gerry Adams and Martin McGuinness. In October, the Combined Loyalist Military Command (CLMC), representing all Loyalist paramilitary organisations, declares its own ceasefire.

'Release the balls!'

19th November 1994 The first National Lottery draw takes place on live television, during a show presented by Noel Edmonds who gives the famous instruction to 'Release the balls!' The lottery is operated by the Camelot Group under franchise, with proceeds going towards approved charitable and heritage projects. Seven winners share the opening jackpot, each scooping a cool £839,254.

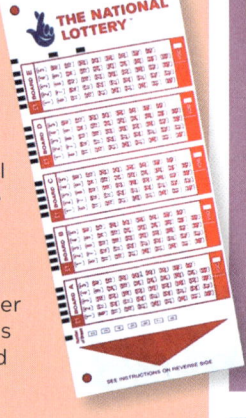

Labour leadership race

12th May 1994 Labour Party leader John Smith dies of a heart attack aged 55. His death triggers a leadership race won on 22nd July by Tony Blair, who beats John Prescott and Margaret Beckett. Prescott becomes Deputy Leader. Gordon Brown, seen by many as a contender himself, backs Blair's campaign, allegedly in return for a promise of becoming Chancellor of the Exchequer in a Labour Government and taking over from Blair as Prime Minister after ten years.

Cash for questions

20th October 1994 A major political scandal erupts after *The Guardian* alleges that Conservative MPs Neil Hamilton and Tim Smith have taken bribes from Harrods owner Mohamed Al-Fayed to ask questions on their behalf in Parliament. This follows a *Sunday Times* report in July that Conservative MPs Graham Riddick and David Treddinick had accepted payment for tabling a question, resulting in their suspension from Parliament. Smith resigns while Hamilton begins a libel action against *The Guardian*.

ROYALTY & POLITICS

MP's mystery death

7th February 1994 Conservative MP Stephen Milligan is found dead at his Chiswick home aged 45. Forensic tests later reveal that he died of asphyxiation during an auto-erotic act. The eventual inquest verdict is death by misadventure.

6 OKT 1994
The NHS launches a central register for potential organ donors to join.

28 NOV 1994
Norway follows Finland and Sweden in voting for European Union membership.

2 DEC 1994
Yitzhak Rabin, Shimon Peres and Yasser Arafat receive Nobel Peace Prize.

Charles admits adultery

29th June 1994 As the war of words between Prince Charles and Princess Diana gathers momentum, Prince Charles is interviewed by his biographer Jonathan Dimbleby about the failure of his marriage. The programme is called *Charles: The Private Man, The Public Role*. Charles states that he was 'faithful and honourable' to Diana until the marriage broke down - a stark admittance of adultery. On the night of transmission and with the eyes of the world on her, Diana attends an event at the Serpentine Gallery in Kensington Gardens wearing what the press instantly dub her 'revenge' dress - a striking black off-the-shoulder number.

FOREIGN
NEWS

Scream theft

12th February 1994 Edvard Munch's painting of *The Scream* is stolen from the National Gallery in Oslo. A ransom demand is made but the painting is recovered intact on 7th May during a sting operation. Four men are charged.

Rwandan genocide

6th April 1994 An attack on a plane that kills the Rwandan and Burundian Presidents is the starting signal for a gruesome genocide. Hutu militias slaughter about three-quarters of the Tutsi minority in a hundred days. Tutsis are beheaded with machetes, shot or killed with grenades. Exterminated villages are then razed to the ground with bulldozers and set on fire. About one million Tutsis and moderate Hutus die. Another two million Rwandans flee the country. In July, the Rwandan Patriotic Front force the interim government into Zaire and the genocide ends.

President Mandela

27th April 1994 The first free and racially unrestricted elections in South Africa yield a landslide victory for the African National Congress (ANC) led by 75-year-old Nelson Mandela, the man who was imprisoned for 27 years in the fight against apartheid. Mandela becomes the first black President of South Africa. South Africa rejoins the Commonwealth in June, having left in 1961.

Republican clean sweep

8th November 1994 In a mid-term congressional election triumph that has political commentators talking of a 'Republican revolution' in the US, the party takes control of both the House of Representatives and the Senate. In Texas, George W. Bush, son of the former President, is elected Governor.

Bezos founds Amazon

5th July 1994 Seattle-based science graduate Jeff Bezos starts an online book store from a rented garage in Bellevue, Washington. He initially calls the store Cadabra but soon changes the name to Amazon. Within three years, the company is ready to go public.

Chasing O. J.

17th June 1994 Accused of murdering his ex-wife and one of her acquaintances five days before, American football star-turned-actor O. J. Simpson is the subject of a huge manhunt. Escaping as police arrive to question him, he is seen sitting in the back seat of a white Bronco with a gun to his head. Police give chase as the Bronco proceeds at low speed on Interstate 405, with every moment broadcast live to a television audience of millions. A whole hour passes before Simpson is finally arrested arriving at his home.

Heaviest human

18th July 1994 According to her then boyfriend, Carol Yager weighed 727 kilos at her heaviest. This makes her the heaviest person who 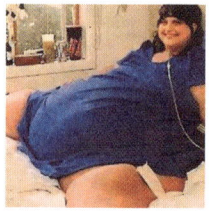 has ever lived. With that bizarre weight, health problems are obvious. Yager is hospitalised and loses 236 kilos within three months. She dies today from the effects of morbid obesity.

'Great Leader' is no more

8th July 1994 All North Koreans are crying, whether forced to or not. Their 'Great Leader' Kim Il-sung is no more. Kim Il-sung (photo left) is succeeded by his son Kim Jong-il (photo right).

Estonia disaster

28th September 1994 The worst European shipping disaster since the Second World War occurs in the Baltic Sea between Estonia and Finland. The ferry *Estonia* sinks on its way to Stockholm when the car deck suddenly takes on water. 852 passengers die in the cold water. A hole in the hull found in the wreck points to a possible collision with a submarine.

ENTERTAINMENT

Forrest Gump

7th October 1994 'Life is like a box of chocolates, you never know what you're gonna get'. So says the simple yet sage Forrest Gump, as he reflects on an extraordinary life. Tom Hanks perfects an innocent charm as Forrest, an idiot savant, who despite his shortcomings finds himself at the centre of American history, becoming a football star, meeting JFK and heroically saving the grumpy Lieutenant Dan during the Vietnam War. *Forrest Gump* wins six Oscars, including Best Picture and Best Actor for Hanks.

Schindler's List

18th February 1994 Steven Spielberg's *Schindler's List* is a harrowing, absorbing film about Oskar Schindler, the Nazi businessman who saved 1,200 Jews from concentration camps during the Holocaust by employing them in his factories. Liam Neesom is the charming Schindler while Ralph Fiennes is spectacularly unbalanced as sadistic camp commandant Amon Göth. Shot in black and white, *Schindler's List* is powerful, unflinching, and often horrifying, exposing the best and worst of humanity.

Sapphic moment

Brookside sets the nation talking when its 14th January episode features the first pre-watershed lesbian kiss on TV, between Beth Jordache (Anna Friel) and Margaret Clemence (Nicola Stephenson), a landmark LGBT moment in television history.

Pulp Fiction

Pulp Fiction, Quentin Tarantino's lurid patchwork of interlocking crime stories, is released in the UK on 21st October. Inspired by a variety of film and pop culture references, from kung fu and film noir to *Saturday Night Fever*, it's kitsch, flamboyant and packed with attitude. John Travolta's role as a hitman, opposite Samuel L. Jackson, is career-reviving. He even slips on his dancing shoes for an iconic dance scene with Uma Thurman to Chuck Berry's *You Never Can Tell*.

Hello boys

Drivers crash their cars and pedestrians walk into lamp posts this year, all because of a distracting 48-sheet poster. Model Eva Herzigova stars in an advertising campaign for Playtex Wonderbra, where she marvels at the cleavage oomph achieved with a little bit of lingerie lift. Accompanied by the slogan, 'Hello boys'. the advert is a sensation, Wonderbra sales soar and boobs are back, big time.

Mrs Doubtfire

Following in the stilettoes of other cross-dressing comedies such as *Some Like It Hot* and *Tootsie*, *Mrs Doubtfire* hits cinemas on 28th January, with Robin Williams on top form as a voice actor who, following his divorce, impersonates an elderly Scottish nanny in order to spend time with his kids. Williams sits for four hours in make-up every day to transform into an entirely plausible 60-year-old woman.

The X Files

19th September 1994 FBI super sleuths Fox Mulder (David Duchovny) and Dana Scully (Gillian Anderson), are given the mysterious cases nobody else can solve as each week they dive into the world of paranormal phenomena with the odd monster thrown in. *The X Files*, first shown on BBC2, is a sci-fi hit, partly due to the charismatic pairing of Duchovny and Anderson, and the dynamic of their characters, but also because the supernatural storylines are inventive, creepy, and often genuinely terrifying.

Four weddings, a funeral and THAT dress
Everybody loves a wedding and this quirky British film has four, as well as a funeral to provide a poignant interlude amid the marriage mayhem. Hugh Grant is Charles, a seasoned, and occasionally jaded attendee of endless nuptials, who along with his posh pals, dashes around country lanes and Scottish castles, bumping into neurotic ex-girlfriends and amorous newlyweds. When sophisticated American fashion editor (Andie Macdowell) falls for his awkward, floppy-haired charm, it looks as if Charles may also be heading for the altar. Made for under £3 million, *Four Weddings and a Funeral* is an unexpected box office smash, making £245 million globally. It confirms Grant's A-list status, and when he attends the 11th May premiere in London with his girlfriend, Elizabeth Hurley, wearing a revealing Versace safety pin dress, his stock rises even higher.

Ready, Steady, Cook
Afternoons get gourmet from 24th October with the arrival of the fun cooking show, *Ready, Steady, Cook* on BBC1. Presented by Fern Britton, two professional chefs are provided with a bag of random ingredients valued at £5, from which they must concoct a delicious meal. After the dishes have been served up, audience members vote for either the red tomato or green pepper team. *Ready, Steady, Cook* not only offers culinary inspiration, but makes the participating chefs, including Ainsley Harriott, Anthony Worrall-Thompson and Nick Nairn, household names.

The Lion King
7th October 1994 *The Lion King* becomes an instant and much-loved classic. The story of Simba, the lion cub who witnesses the death of his father at the paws of his evil uncle Scar, is one of laughter and tragedy, terror and joy, with the African Savannah and its panoply of beasts brought wonderfully to life by Disney's animation team and a glorious soundtrack courtesy of Elton John and Tim Rice. Broadly appealing to young and old, it's the *Circle of Life* right there in front of us.

This week, I have been mostly watching *The Fast Show*
27th September 1994 Paul Whitehouse, Charlie Higson and crew launch their sketch show on BBC2, introducing a cast of vividly drawn, comic characters.

MUSIC

Kurt Cobain

5th April 1994 Kurt Cobain of Nirvana shoots himself at his home in Seattle. His body is found three days later with a suicide note quoting a line from a Neil Young song, 'It's better to burn out than fade away.' He had been hospitalised a month earlier after an apparent suicide attempt and had been missing since walking out of a drug recovery centre in Los Angeles on 31st March. He was 27.

Riverdance at Eurovision

30th April 1994 Ireland hosts the Eurovision Song Contest and becomes the first country ever to win three years in a row, with *Rock'n'Roll Kids* by Paul Harrington and Charlie McGettigan. The show also launches the Riverdance phenomenon, when Michael Flatley and his dance company perform in the interlude before the votes are announced.

Michael and Lisa

26th May 1994 It is a romantic match that nobody could have predicted. Michael Jackson marries Lisa Marie Presley, daughter of Elvis and Priscilla, in the Dominican Republic. The marriage lasts two years.

Professional slavery

1st June 1994 George Michael's action against Sony Records concludes at the High Court in London. He loses the case and faces legal costs of up to four million pounds. Just as significant is the damage done to his career by putting all recording and releasing on hold.

Go Wets

4th June 1994 Wet Wet Wet begin a mammoth fifteen weeks at No. 1 with a revival of the Troggs' 1967 hit *Love is All Around*, recorded for the soundtrack of the rom-com movie *Four Weddings and a Funeral*. The band insist on the single's withdrawal from sale before it can top the chart for a further week and equal Bryan Adams' record for chart-topping longevity set in 1991.

Holiday hit

16th September 1994 European-made records often become hits in the UK after holidaymakers hear them in the discos and tavernas and seek them out back in Blighty. The latest is *Saturday Night* by Danish model-turned-singer Whigfield, which has shot to No. 1 in the UK its first week of release.

Money to burn

23rd August 1994 Stunt masters and music industry baiters the KLF are not done yet. Officially retired, they burn a million pounds in sterling on the Scottish island of Jura and video the event.

1994

Woodstock '94

12th - 14th August 1994 An attempt to re-create the spirit of Woodstock 1969 is made in upstate New York where thousands gather for Woodstock '94. Bad weather and gate crashers mark the occasion but performers include Aerosmith, Bob Dylan, Peter Gabriel, Red Hot Chili Peppers and the new stars of Irish rock, the Cranberries led by Dolores O'Riordan.

M People

17th September 1994 Another surprise from the Mercury Music Prize panel. Although the hot favourites are Pulp and Blur, this year's award goes to *Elegant Slumming* by M People, a Manchester dance collective with the most soulful voice in current UK music - Heather Small.

Hello boyz

10th December 1994 There's a new name in the charts with a long career ahead of them. Boyzone are a five-piece boy band from Ireland fronted by Ronan Keating and Stephen Gateley. They debut with *Love Me for a Reason*, a cover of an Osmonds No. 1 from 1974. On the same day, a boy band with a much tougher attitude claims the top spot - East 17 (photo) with *Stay Another Day*. They're a foursome from Walthamstow whose image is everything that Boyzone's isn't - sullen, streetwise and dressed like rappers.

MY FIRST 18 YEARS
TOP 10 — 1994

1. **Girls and Boys** *Blur*
2. **Kiss from a Rose** *Seal*
3. **Marvellous** *The Lightning Seeds*
4. **Linger** *The Cranberries*
5. **7 Seconds** *Youssou N'Dour, Neneh Cherry*
6. **Patience of Angels** *Eddi Reader*
7. **All I Wanna Do** *Sheryl Crow*
8. **Think Twice** *Celine Dion*
9. **Cigarettes and Alcohol** *Oasis*
10. **Good as Gold** *The Beautiful South*

Open | Search | Scan

What a carry on

The biggest selling album of the year by a UK act is a surprise. It's *Carry On Up the Charts*, a collection of all the spiky domestic drama hits to date by the low-profile and decidedly unhip Beautiful South. Its million-plus sales make Paul Heaton and writing partner Dave Rotheray the UK's most successful songwriting partnership since Lennon and McCartney.

SPORT

Transfer records

A sign of the impact that the Premier League is making is the breaking of the UK transfer record three times in nine months, by Andy Cole (Newcastle to Manchester United, £7 million), Dennis Bergkamp (Inter Milan to Arsenal, £7.5 million) and Stan Collymore (Nottingham Forest to Liverpool, £8.5 million).

Perry dies

2nd February 1995 Tennis great Fred Perry, the last British player to win Wimbledon, dies following a fall in Melbourne, Australia, aged 85.

DO YOU REMEMBER THIS?

Scented pens

Phil powers to victory

2nd January 1995 Darts superstar Phil 'The Power' Taylor begins his domination of the World Darts Championship with a 6-2 victory in the final over Rod Harrington. He goes on to win eleven of the next twelve championship finals and countless other titles before his retirement in 2018.

Rugby goes professional

27th August 1995 Rugby Union will never be quite the same again as the International Rugby Football Board, meeting in Paris, votes to allow payment to players. The switch to professionalism comes under the threat of a breakaway competition funded by satellite television. It allows elite players to focus on training and playing rugby full-time, improving their skills and overall performance, and greatly increases the marketability of the sport.

Cantona's kick

25th January 1995 In an away game at Crystal Palace in January, Manchester United's enigmatic French forward Eric Cantona is sent off and literally kicks out kung fu-style at a spectator who abuses him verbally. He is given an eight-month ban by the FA, while police bring an assault charge that leaves him facing 120 hours of community service.

18 JAN 1995	**10 FEB** 1995	**5 MAR** 1995
Pope John Paul II begins his visit to Australia.	£267 million compensation set for members of Maxwell pension fund.	Graves of murdered Czar Nicholas and family found in St Petersburg.

1995

Champion Frank
2nd September 1995 For decades, British heavyweight boxers have been regarded as cannon fodder for the all-conquering Americans. Lennox

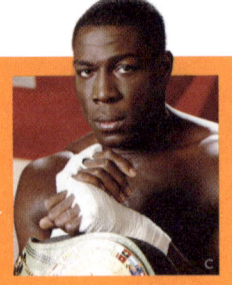

Lewis started to change that perception by becoming the World Boxing Council (WBC) champion in 1993. Now Frank Bruno has achieved what many thought was impossible by outpointing reigning champion Oliver McCall. Frank's reign as world's best is brief, ending with defeat to a resurgent Mike Tyson in 1996 and his retirement from the ring.

Rugby League World Cup
28th October 1995 The eleventh Rugby League World Cup climaxes at Wembley Stadium with a 16-8 victory for holders Australia versus England.

DOMESTIC
NEWS

M3 completed
1st January 1995 The M3 motorway between London and Southampton is now fully open following the completion of the Twyford Down section that was the focus of so many environmental protests during its construction. Six lanes of traffic now cut through what was once one of Hampshire's most scenic areas of downland.

Fred West suicide
1st January 1995 Accused of twelve murders, the Gloucester builder Fred West is found hanged in his cell at Winson Green Prison in Birmingham. His wife Rose stands trial for ten murders in October and is found guilty on all counts. She is sentenced to life imprisonment without parole.

Rumbelows closes
7th February 1995 A familiar high street name since the 1950s and now part of Thorn Electrical Industries, electrical chain store Rumbelows closes all its 311 outlets due to dwindling sales.

MG brand revived
17th February 1995 The Rover Group announces the revival of the MG sports car, due for re-launch in September.

Barings Bank fails
26th February 1995 The UK's oldest merchant bank, Barings, collapses. The blame is levelled at a derivatives trader in the bank's Singapore office named Nick Leeson, who accumulated $140 million of losses. Leeson flees but is later arrested in Frankfurt and extradited for trial. In December he is convicted of fraud by a Singapore court and sentenced to six years in prison.

Damon Hill fined for speeding
1st March 1995 Formula One star Damon Hill is convicted of speeding at over 100 mph on the M40 in Oxfordshire. Admitting the charge, he is banned from driving for seven days by Bicester magistrates, fined £350 and ordered to pay court costs.

---

4 APR 1995

Radio and TV personality Kenny Everett dies at 50 of an AIDS-related illness.

20 MAY 1995

Kevin Moran of Manchester United is first player sent off in an FA Cup Final.

27 JUN 1995

Chechen rebels seize hundreds of hostages in Russian hospital.

Ronnie Kray is dead

17th March 1995 Ronnie Kray, who with his brother Reggie led a notorious East London crime operation in the 1960s, dies of a heart attack aged 61. He had been a Category A prisoner at Broadmoor since being committed in 1979.

50 years since VE Day

8th May 1995 The May Day bank holiday is moved from the first Monday in May to a Friday for the first time to allow UK citizens to mark the 50th anniversary of the end of the Second World War in Europe. Services, commemorations, festivals, fetes and air displays are held up and down the country.

Campaign against ecstasy

9th October 1995 Teenager Leah Betts dies four days after taking the recreational drug MDMA ('ecstasy') and drinking seven litres of water. Her death triggers a high-profile media campaign against the tablets and their suppliers led by Leah's family.

Over the sea to Skye

16th October 1995 The arch-shaped Skye Bridge one and a half miles in length is opened, linking the Isle of Skye to the Scottish mainland at Kyle of Lochalsh. It remains a toll bridge until 2004, when it is purchased by the Scottish government and becomes toll-free.

Hirst wins the Turner Prize

29th November 1995 Controversial artist Damien Hirst reinforces his growing reputation and notoriety by winning the Turner Prize with *Mother and Child, Divided*, a sculpture made up of four glass tanks containing the two halves of a cow and calf preserved in formaldehyde.

Headteacher murdered

8th December 1995 Headteacher Philip Lawrence is fatally stabbed outside his school, St George's Roman Catholic Secondary School, while trying to protect a pupil from an attack by a gang from a neighbouring school. He is posthumously awarded the Queen's Gallantry Medal in 1997.

10 JUL 1995

Imprisoned Burmese opposition leader Aung San Suu Kyi released.

17 AUG 1995

Alison Hargreaves, who climbed Everest without oxygen in May, is killed in avalanche on K2.

8 SEP 1995

David Trimble voted new leader of Ulster Unionists.

1995

ROYALTY & POLITICS

Kinnock leaves Parliament
16th February 1995 Former Labour leader Neil Kinnock resigns his Islwyn seat as an MP to become a European Commissioner and sparks a by-election which his party wins comfortably.

The Queen in Armagh
9th March 1995 With the IRA ceasefire in place but amid high security, the Queen and the Duke of Edinburgh make a rare one-day visit to Northern Ireland to open the City of Armagh High School and meet Cardinal Cathal Daly.

South African visit
19th - 25th March 1995 The Queen and the Duke of Edinburgh make their first visit to South Africa for nearly 50 years as guests of President Nelson Mandela.

Major challenges his doubters
22nd June 1995 Fed up with criticism from his own MPs and even from within the Cabinet, John Major tells them it is time 'to put up or shut up' and resigns as leader of the Conservatives to stand again in a leadership ballot. The only senior MP prepared to take him on is Secretary of State for Wales John Redwood, who is defeated on 4th July by 89 votes to Major's 218.

Diana states her case
20th November 1995 Princess Diana gives an astonishingly frank interview to BBC reporter Martin Bashir in which she discusses her marriage to Prince Charles, her own adultery and depression, and her struggles with bulimia. A month after the interview, the Queen writes to Charles and Diana advising them to seek a divorce.

FOREIGN NEWS

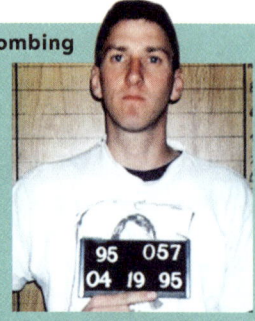

Oklahoma City bombing
19th April 1995 A total of 168 people including 19 children are killed by a huge truck bomb left outside the Alfred P. Murrah Federal Building in Oklahoma City. The worst terrorist atrocity ever committed on US soil to this point, it is the work of anti-government extremists Timothy McVeigh, a Gulf War veteran, and Terry Nichols.

---

18 OCT 1995
Death of legendary horse Red Rum, winner of three Grand Nationals.

19 NOV 1995
Lech Walesa defeated in Polish presidential election.

29 DEC 1995
Emma Nicolson is second Tory MP this year to defect to opposition benches.

Agreement in Dayton

July - December 1995 More than 8,000 Bosnian Muslims are massacred by Bosnian Serbs when they overrun the UN's 'safe haven' of Srebrenica. In August, after Bosnian Serb forces refuse to move weaponry out of Sarajevo, NATO begins a bombing campaign against Serb positions in Bosnia-Herzegovina. Negotiations between all parties involved to end the conflict finally begin in Dayton, Ohio, in November and are concluded on 14th December. Signed by the leaders of Bosnia, Serbia and Croatia, the agreement recognises Bosnia-Herzegovina as a complete state, fixes new boundaries and sets elections for 1996.

That's rich

17th July 1995 Forbes magazine names Microsoft co-founder Bill Gates as the world's richest man with a net worth of $12.9 billion.

eBay

3rd September 1995 In California's Silicon Valley, French-born Iranian American Pierre Omidyar (photo left) offers a broken laser pointer for sale through his own website. To his own surprise, a collector wants to buy it for almost fifteen dollars. It gives Omidyar an idea. He builds the first website on which people can bid on other people's items: AuctionWeb. The auction site soon changes its name to eBay and grows into the largest trading site in the world.

PlayStation launches

9th September 1995 Sony's PlayStation is launched in the US and Europe after a trial launch in Japan a year earlier. The PS1 is, literally, a game-changer, spawning over 7,900 individual games and selling over 100 million units and 960 million games over time.

Simpson on trial

3rd October 1995 The exhaustively televised trial of O. J. Simpson for the murders of his wife Nicole Brown Simpson and her friend Ronald Goldman puts American life on hold for months and concludes on its 133rd day with his acquittal on both counts.

Rabin murdered

4th November 1995 Israeli Prime Minister Yitzhak Rabin is assassinated in Tel Aviv. Not by a Palestinian or Arab terrorist, but by a Jewish extremist appalled by the Oslo Accords between Israel and Palestine. Conservative Benjamin Netanyahu wins the next elections. Peace between Israel and the Arab world seems further away than ever.

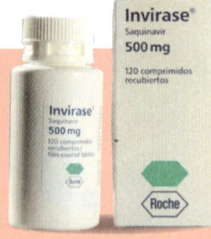

Saquinivar approved

6th December 1995
On the day that President Clinton hosts the first White House conference on HIV/AIDS, the US Food and Drug Administration gives approval to Saquinivir, the first inhibitor medication to treat the disease. Figures released two years later show a decrease in the number of deaths from AIDS from 50,000 to around 18,000.

ENTERTAINMENT

The Shawshank Redemption

17th February 1995 When *The Shawshank Redemption* is first released in the USA it makes a paltry $16 million at the box office, but seven Academy Award nominations and word of mouth soon change its fortunes. Tim Robbins is Andy, the accountant serving a life sentence for the alleged murder of his wife and her lover, whose financial skills are exploited by corrupt prison management for money laundering purposes. Morgan Freeman is Red, the sagacious inmate, doing time for contraband smuggling, who befriends him. A tough watch in places, the definitions of good and evil are intentionally skewed but hope prevails with Andy and Red finding the redemption promised in the film's title, while retribution awaits those who abuse their power.

Making *Friends*

22nd April 1995 UK viewers first meet Ross, Phoebe, Monica, Rachel, Chandler and Joey, aka *Friends*, when Channel 4 airs the pilot episode. Hailed as the defining sitcom of the '90s, these twenty-something New Yorkers quickly charm us as we invest in Ross and Rachel's on-off romance, sing along to Phoebe's *Smelly Cat* song, wonder if Chandler could be any more adorable and swoon at Joey asking, 'How are you doin?' *Friends* is a phenomenon and an addiction; it even launches the hairdo of the decade as every woman requests the swingy, shaggy Rachel cut, as worn by Jennifer Aniston.

ER

US medical drama *ER* begins on Channel 4 on 1st February, socking it to British viewers who struggle to keep up with the frenetic pace as they watch patients shocked back to life by doctors who speak unintelligible rapid-fire medicalese. Writing in

The Times, Libby Purves opines, 'It makes our own dear *Casualty* look like a wistful mood piece by Alan Bennett.' But as the show's characters begin to fully form, we acclimatise and can't wait for our next appointment. Compulsive viewing, *ER* is the shot in the arm we all need.

Hollyoaks

Hollyoaks, a new Chester-set soap opera conceived by Phil Redmond and aimed at a youthful audience, begins on Channel 4 on 23rd October.

Shallow Grave

Made in just one month on a shoestring budget, Danny Boyle's directorial debut *Shallow Grave* stars Christopher Eccleston, Ewan McGregor and Kerry Fox as Edinburgh flatmates who find their just-moved-in fourth housemate (Keith Allen) mysteriously dead and conspire to dis-member and dispose of his body to keep the huge stash of cash found in his room. Paranoia and suspicion send their plan spiralling out of control in a blacker-than-black comedy that becomes the most successful British-made film of 1995 and establishes Boyle as a name to watch.

They'll never take our freedom!

8th September 1995 Mel Gibson has a habit of making films that emphasise the perfidious English as invaders, conquer-ors and occupiers, and *Braveheart* is no exception. Still, it's impossible not to root for him as he daubs on the woad, twirls in his kilt and gives some rousing pre-battle pep talks as William Wallace, the Scot-tish freedom fighter who is ultimately betrayed. It's passionate, swashbuckling, and stunning to look at with a cast of sword-wielding thousands expertly cho-reographed in thrilling - and often gory - battle scenes.

Pocahontas

8th September 1995 Disney's *Pocahontas* is an idealised retelling of the relationship between the Native American princess and English settler Captain John Smith. Glen Keane, the animator responsible for drawing Ariel in *The Little Mermaid,* is drafted in to create the face of Poca-hontas and uses two of her descendants as blueprints with further inspiration provided by supermodels such as Naomi Campbell and Kate Moss.

Goldeneye

It's all change at MI6 when, after a six-year hiatus, Bond is back in *Goldeneye*, a suave, silly but enormously successful rebooted Bond for the '90s. Donning the well-worn tuxedo for the first time is the devilishly handsome Pierce Brosnan, who many believe revives Sean Connery's lethal charm. Judi Dench becomes the first woman in the role of M, and Saman-tha Bond is Miss Moneypenny although veteran cast member Desmond Llewelyn returns as gadget boffin, Q. In its first week, *Goldeneye* becomes the third most successful film in UK box office history.

Don't Forget Your Toothbrush

The final episode of Chris Evans' audacious, high-energy entertainment show *Don't Forget Your Toothbrush* airs on Channel 4, and, determined to go out on a high, studio contestants can play a game to win either a Ferrari 308 or a fish finger. Over two series, the show has a reputation for big prizes and memorable stunts. Celebrity guests from Cher to Tony ('We love you madly') Hadley take part in a head-to-head quiz about themselves with a selected superfan, and usually come out the loser.

Austen power

24th September heralds the beginning of BBC1's flagship costume drama, *Pride and Prejudice*, written by Andrew Davies. This new version is replete with gorgeous Regency frocks, stunning locations and a cast that includes Jennifer Ehle as Elizabeth Bennett and Colin Firth as the brooding Mr. Darcy. But what might Jane Austen have thought of the scene in episode 3 where Elizabeth bumps

into Mr. Darcy just as he emerges from a quick swim in the lake at his country pile, Pemberley? With his dark locks dripping and wet shirt clinging to his well-defined torso, the nation's ladies collectively reach for the smelling salts, lest they be overcome.

Brad obsession

America's most-read magazine, *People* magazine (readership around 45 million) puts Brad Pitt, star of *Se7en* and *Twelve Monkeys* this year, on the cover of its 30th January issue with the headline 'The Sexiest Man Alive!' Who are we to argue?

Father Ted

Set on the fictional Craggy Island off the west coast of Ireland, sitcom *Father Ted* is sweet, surreal, and occasionally wicked, as three Roman Catholic priests, banished to this remote outpost for various misdemeanours, entertain us with their scrapes and misadventures. There is the titular Ted (Dermot Morgan), perpetually in deep water and frustrated by his idiotic housemates; wide-eyed innocent Father Dougal (Ardal O'Hanlon); and unrepentant alcoholic Father Jack (Frank Kelly), not forgetting their attentive housekeeper, Mrs Doyle (Pauline McLynn), compulsive feeder and server of tea, urging guests at the parochial home to, 'go on, go on, go on'. *Father Ted* goes on to inspire an annual Ted Fest festival in Ireland, and even a set of Irish stamps.

Babe

15th December 1995 Co-producer and writer George Miller first fell in love with Dick King-Smith's delightful children's book, *The Sheep-Pig* back in the mid-1980s, but finally brings *Babe* to the screen this year, at a point when animatronics and other magical special effects are sufficiently developed to leave audiences almost believing they are truly watching animals talk. *Babe*, the tale of the little piglet with the tuft of hair who becomes a champion sheep herder is simply enchanting and leads many to contemplate vegetarianism as they leave the cinema.

MUSIC

Richey Edwards disappears

1st February 1995 Richey Edwards of Welsh rock band Manic Street Preachers goes missing. His car is found abandoned two weeks later at a motorway services close to the Severn Bridge. His body is never found.

REM's bad luck tour
1st January 1995 REM's very first world tour seems cursed. The misfortune begins in Lausanne, Switzerland, when drummer Bill Berry is forced to leave the stage with what he thinks is a severe migraine. Two days later he has major surgery to treat a brain aneurysm. In July, bassist Mike Mills has an emergency operation to remove an intestinal tumour, while two teenagers drown in the River Boyne while trying to reach the band's concert at Slane Castle. In August, Michael Stipe has hernia surgery prior to performing in Prague.

Tommy Lee weds Baywatch star
14th February 1995 Tommy Lee of US hard rock band Motley Crüe marries actress Pamela Anderson of *Baywatch* fame on a Mexican beach.

Robson and Jerome
20th May 1995 Riding high with the first of three consecutive No. 1s are Robson Green and Jerome Flynn, stars of the ITV drama *Soldier, Soldier*. A young executive at RCA named Simon Cowell spotted them singing *Unchained Melody* in the show and offered them a recording deal, with Mike Stock and Matt Aitken. All three of their subsequent double-sided hits are songs at least 30 years old.

Jagged Little Pill
13th June 1995 A hallmark album for the 90s is released - Alanis Morisette's *Jagged Little Pill*. Bracketed with Tori Amos and Sheryl Crow, 21-year-old Alanis writes brutally frank material with a streak of venom. Topping the US charts in October, it becomes the third best selling album of the 90s at fifteen million sales, just behind Metallica's *Metallica* and Shania Twain's *Come On Over*.

Pulp faction
24th June 1995 Replacing the Stone Roses as headliners, Sheffield band Pulp light up Glastonbury with one of the festival's classic performances. Fronted by Jarvis Cocker, they've been together since 1983 without making much progress. With Britpop dawning, their blend of smart, acerbic lyrics and an updated glam rock sound is showcased brilliantly on their Mercury Prize-winning *Different Class* album.

Robbie sacked
17th July 1995 Distraught Take That fans take in the news that youngest member Robbie Williams is leaving the band. His behaviour is starting to cause friction within the group and manager Nigel Martin-Smith has had enough. The group's latest No. 1 single *Never Forget* - produced by Jim Steinman - shows they can do perfectly well without him, while general opinion is that Robbie will struggle on his own. But is there a goodbye message to the fans in the song? How long can the Take That juggernaut last?

Breaking Windows
24th August 1995 The Rolling Stones are paid a reported twelve million dollars by Microsoft for the use of *Start Me Up* in television ads promoting the new Windows 95 software.

Oh what a Knight
25th October 1995 Cliff Richard is knighted by the Queen at Buckingham Palace. He is the first figure from the British pop world to be so honoured.

Which side are you on?
26th August 1995 The battle lines are drawn. On one side are Blur, Essex boys whose *Parklife* album is the last word in chirpy, knowing art school pop in the tradition of the Small Faces and the Kinks. On the other are Oasis, swaggering Manchester lads with chips on their shoulders whose songs on *Definitely Maybe* are anthemic and Beatle-like. Months of mutual sniping lead to the equivalent of a shoot-out at dawn: Blur issue *Country House* in the same week that Oasis release *Roll with It*. Blur's track goes straight in at No. 1 while *Roll with It* enters at No. 2. In the long term Oasis have the last laugh: *What's the Story, Morning Glory*, released in October, becomes the third best selling album of all time.

MY FIRST 18 YEARS TOP10 1995
1. **Wonderwall** *Oasis*
2. **Missing** *Everything but the Girl*
3. **Love Can Build a Bridge** *Cher, Chrissie Hynde ...*
4. **Back for Good** *Take That*
5. **Wake Up Boo** *The Boo Radleys*
6. **A Girl Like You** *Edwyn Collins*
7. **Boombastic** *Shaggy*
8. **Gangsta's Paradise** *Coolio*
9. **Disco 2000** *Pulp*
10. **Waterfalls** *TLC*

Open | Search | Scan

Beatles reunited
10th December 1995 At the end of a year that sees the release of *The Beatles Anthology* containing numerous unreleased studio and radio recordings, a tape of an unfinished John Lennon song, *Free as a Bird*, is completed by Paul, Ringo and George and reaches No. 2 in the UK.

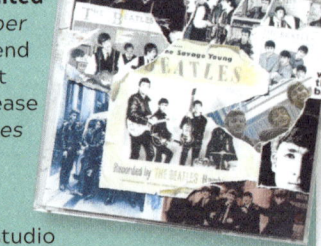

Death of Dino
25th December 1995 Dean Martin dies at his home in Beverly Hills aged 78. His last years have been tough, burdened by divorce, poor health, the death of his son and a falling out with Frank Sinatra when he left a Rat Pack reunion tour. Though he disliked rock, Dean's easy-going, effortless vocal style was a model for Elvis, while his top-rated television show gave Americans their first glimpse of the Rolling Stones in 1964.

SPORT

Super League launched
29th March 1996 A new era in rugby league begins with the first match in the Super League, a reconstituted elite league of England's top teams plus French side Paris Saint-Germain. With Sky Sports coverage and a switch from a winter to a summer season, the new league kicks off with all guns blazing as PSG beat Sheffield Eagles 30-24. St Helens finish the inaugural season as champions.

United's double glory
11th May 1996 Manchester United's run of glory continues as they win the Premier League for the third time in four seasons and beat Liverpool 1-0 to win the FA Cup. In so doing they become the only team to date to win the famous 'double' of League title and FA Cup twice.

Germany on penalties - again
8th - 30th June 1996 The chant on every England fan's lips is 'football's coming home' as the 1996 European Championships - known as Euro 96 - are held for the first time in the country that gave football to the world. After an indifferent start, England's performances improve game on game, reaching a peak with a 4-1 demolition of the Netherlands. Negotiating a tricky quarter final with Spain, England and Germany play out a tense semi-final match. The match ends 1-1 but, once again, England suffer the heartbreak of a penalty shootout when Gareth Southgate misses his spot kick. Germany go on to win the tournament with a 2-1 victory over the Czech Republic.

Dickie Bird retires
20th - 24th June 1996 The much loved Dickie Bird umpires his last Test match before retirement - England v India at Lord's - and receives a guard of honour from the players as he takes to the pitch.

Atlanta Olympics
19th July - 2nd August 1996 The Olympic Games in Atlanta, Georgia, produce a modest return for British athletes, the only gold coming in the men's coxless pairs for Matthew Pinsent and Steve Redgrave. Linford Christie's attempt to retain the 100 metres Olympic crown he won four years earlier is ruined by two false starts and disqualification in the final. The home star of the Games is Michael Johnson, winner of the 200 metres and 400 metres and Carl Lewis winning his fourth gold on the long jump. As expected, the US tops the medal table with 101 in total.

3 JAN 1996	**15 FEB** 1996	**21 MAR** 1996
The Motorola StarTAC goes on sale - the world's first flip mobile phone.	Pembrokeshire beaches are heavily polluted after oil tanker runs aground.	Death of Rev. Wilbert Awdry, creator of *Thomas the Tank Engine*.

Frankie's magnificent seven
28th September 1996 UK-based Italian-born jockey Frankie Dettori - the reigning Champion Jockey - creates racing history by riding all seven winners in the British Festival of Racing at Ascot. Dettori's achievement is said to have lost the UK betting industry around £40 million.

Champion Hill
13th October 1996 In Formula One's 50th season, Damon Hill's win in the Japanese Grand Prix in Suzuka secures him his first and only Drivers' World Championship. In December he becomes the first sports star since Henry Cooper to win the BBC Sports Personality of the Year twice.

Last *Titanic* passenger
14th February 1996 Eva Hart, the last living survivor of the *Titanic* maritime disaster in 1912, dies at the age of 91.

Dunblane massacre
13th March 1996 One-time Scout leader Thomas Hamilton enters a primary school in Dunblane near Stirling, Scotland, and shoots dead sixteen children and a teacher before turning one of his four guns on himself. The horrific events shock the world and lead to immediate calls to make possession of handguns illegal in the UK. It emerges that Hamilton had grievances against individuals and local organisations over rumours about his inappropriate behaviour towards young boys, and that he blamed them for the loss of his business in 1993. It also emerges that his guns were legally held.

DOMESTIC NEWS

DO YOU REMEMBER THIS?

Bacardi Breezer

IRA breaks its ceasefire
9th February 1996 A huge truck bomb explodes in South Quays, Docklands, kills two and signals the end of the Provisional IRA ceasefire after seventeen months. Damage to the area is estimated at £150 million. Nine days later a bus bomb detonates prematurely and kills an IRA operative in Aldwych, London.

3 APR 1996
In the US Theodore Kaczynski the 'UnaBomber' is arrested.

18 MAY 1996
Dublin-born singer Aimear Quinn wins the 41st Eurovision Song Contest.

15 JUN 1996
Ella Fitzgerald, jazz vocalist and song interpreter supreme, dies at the age of 79.

Legoland opens
17th March 1996 Legoland Windsor opens, becoming the second Legoland theme park in Europe.

Mad cow disease
20th March 1996 The crisis over 'mad cow disease' or bovine spongiform encephalopathy (BSE), which has been growing since the late 1980s, takes another turn as Secretary of State for Health Stephen Dorrell announces that eating BSE-infected beef can cause the fatal Creutzfeld-Jakobs disease (vCJD) in humans. The issue is linked to the practice of feeding meat and bone meal to cattle, which was widespread in UK farming prior to being banned in 1988. European Union, Japanese and US bans follow on importing UK beef. At home, beef sales drop by nearly a third. The cost to the UK economy of the whole crisis is estimated at approaching £4 billion.

Goodbye, Christopher Robin
20th - 23rd April 1996 Two major figures of children's literature pass away within days of each other - Christopher Robin Milne (76), the boy hero of his father's *Winnie the Pooh* books, and P. J. Travers (97), creator of *Mary Poppins*.

Dome site selected
19th June 1996 On the south side of the River Thames from the Isle of Dogs, the Greenwich peninsula is chosen as the site for the construction of the new Millennium Dome, set to open at the start of 2000. No specific use for the building has yet been determined.

Hello Dolly
5th July 1996 Although the news does not emerge until February 1997, the first mammal to be cloned from an adult cell is born at the Roslin Institute, a research department of Edinburgh University. The animal in question is a sheep named Dolly after singer Dolly Parton. Dolly began life as a single cell in a test tube from the mammary gland of a Finn Dorset sheep and an egg cell from a Scottish Blackface sheep. The embryo was then transferred to a surrogate mother. Dolly's birth represents a landmark on the road to producing genetically modified livestock. She lives for six years.

Severn wonder
5th June 1996 A second toll bridge over the River Severn is opened by Prince Charles, carrying the M4 motorway from England to Wales. Unlike the first Severn crossing, opened in 1966 and now part of the M48, it is a cable-stayed bridge rather than a suspension bridge and bears six lanes of traffic rather than four.

4 JUL 1996
Hotmail is launched as a free email service.

21 AUG 1996
The reconstructed Globe Theatre opens on the south bank of the Thames.

1 SEP 1996
David Beckham makes his England debut in World Cup qualifier versus Moldova.

1996

Ossie Clark murdered
6th August 1996 Fashion designer Ossie Clark is stabbed to death by his lover Diego Cogolato, who is later convicted of manslaughter and jailed for six years.

'House of horrors' torn down
12th October 1996 Amid tight security to deter souvenir hunters, the house of serial killers Fred and Rose West - 25 Cromwell Street, Gloucester - is demolished and all its contents destroyed.

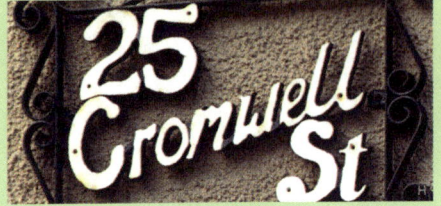

ROYALTY &
POLITICS

Scargill's new party
13th January 1996 Appalled by the reformist tendencies of the Labour Party's new leadership, National Union of Miners leader Arthur Scargill announces the formation of a Socialist Labour Party to fight the next election on an unapologetically left-wing platform.

Charles and Diana divorce
28th August 1996 The divorce agreed between Prince Charles and Princess Diana is now final. Diana will continue to hold the title of Princess of Wales but will lose the title of Her Royal Highness. The divorce follows that of Charles's brother Andrew, Duke of York, from Sarah, Duchess of York, in May.

Education, education, education
1st October 1996 Labour leader Tony Blair makes one of the most memorable speeches of his political career, telling his party's conference at Blackpool that his three main priorities once elected will be 'education, education, education'.

McAlpine defects
6th October 1996 A former adviser to Margaret Thatcher, Conservative Party treasurer and a key party fundraiser, construction magnate Lord McAlpine, defects from the Tories to James Goldsmith's Referendum Party, which is campaigning for a referendum on the UK's continued membership of the European Union.

FOREIGN
NEWS

Mitterrand dies
8th January 1996 Former President of France François Mitterrand dies of prostate cancer just six months after leaving office, aged 79.

22 OCT 1996
Chelsea FC executive Matthew Harding among five killed in helicopter crash.

5 NOV 1996
Bill Clinton re-elected as US President.

5 DEC 1996
NASA's first Mars Rover is launched.

ANC in control
9th May 1996 In South Africa, the National Party withdraws from the coalition government it formed with the African National Congress, leaving the ANC to govern alone.

A gorilla's tenderness
16th August 1996 A three-year-old boy falls 24 feet into the gorilla enclosure at Brookfield Zoo, Chicago. Astonished visitors watch as a female gorilla named Binti Jua sits and tends to the unconscious boy until he is rescued.

Tasmanian devil
28th April 1996 The deadliest massacre in Australian history occurs in the tourist centre of Port Arthur, Tasmania, where Martin Bryant kills 35 people and wounds 23 others in a shooting spree with two semi-automatic rifles. The murders lead to an instant tightening of Australian gun laws.

Olympic Games attack
27th July 1996 A pipe bomb attack on visitors gathering at the Centennial Olympic Park in Atlanta, Georgia, kills one and injures over a hundred others. The park was being evacuated when the bomb exploded. When the perpetrator, anti-government activist Michael udolph, is arrested in 2003 he is charged with the Atlanta bombing and three subsequent bomb attacks.

Whitewater fraud
28th May 1996 James and Susan McDougal and Arkansas Governor Jim Guy Tucker are convicted of fraud relating to a $200,000 housing development near the Whitewater

rapids in Arkansas. Public and media interest in the case centers on the investment made in the project by the current US President Bill Clinton during his own spell as Arkansas Governor. Although they are never prosecuted, the doggedness of lawyer Kenneth Starr in pursuing the Clintons will lead to revelations about a much more damaging affair - the President's dalliance or otherwise with White House intern Monica Lewinsky.

Yeltsin re-elected
3rd July 1996 Despite a series of health scares and an undisclosed heart attack that leaves him very close to death, Boris Yeltsin defeats his Communist Party challenger Gennady Zyuganov and is re-elected as President of Russia.

Taliban takeover

27th September 1996 Radical Islamic group the Taliban reinforce their hold on Afghanistan by ousting President Burhanuddin Rabbani, executing former leader Mohammad Najibullah and capturing the capital city of Kabul. They are also giving refuge to members of the Al-Qaeda terrorist network, notably Osama Bin Laden, who just weeks before had issued a chilling declaration of Jihad 'on the Americans occupying the Country of the Two Sacred Places', meaning the US military presence in his homeland of Saudi Arabia.

O. J. back in court

23rd October 1996 O. J. Simpson enters court in California accused of the 'wrongful death' of his wife Nicole and her friend Ron Goldman. Although cleared of the charges in 1995 (photo), he is now the subject of a civil suit brought by her parents and Goldman's father. The trial lasts until February 1997.

ENTERTAINMENT

Toy Story

The world's first computer-generated animation, *Toy Story*, opens at British cinemas on 22 March. Created by Pixar Animations and directed by John Lasseter, his first Pixar short, *Tin Toy*, which won an Oscar in 1988, caught the attention of Disney, who eventually asked Pixar to make a feature-length film on the subject of toys. The result is a film that is perfect in almost every way, with undeniable cross-generational appeal. Puppet cowboy Woody (voiced by Tom Hanks) and Buzz Lightyear (Tim Allen), the space toy who usurps Woody in his owner's affection, soon take their place among the ranks of much-loved cartoon characters, kicking off a franchise which is one of the most successful in cinema history. Animation will never be the same again.

Our Friends in the North

Landmark dramas don't get much better than *Our Friends in the North*, which begins on BBC2 on 15th January. Peter Flannery's sprawling, state-of-the-nation saga (originating from his play for the RSC) traces the lives of four friends from the north-east through thirty years from 1964 to the present day, with major, real-life events such as the miners' strike punctuating their personal stories. The four leads - Mark Strong, Gina McKee, Christopher Eccleston, and a certain Daniel Craig - all go on to become major TV and feature film stars.

Ballykissangel

The arrival of a Manchester priest in a small, rural Irish community is the premise for *Ballykissangel*, which begins on 11th February on BBC1. Starring Stephen Tomkinson as Father Peter Clifford and Dervla Kirwan as pub landlady Assumpta Fitzgerald, *Ballykissangel* runs for five series and is watched by ten million at the peak of its popularity.

Sense and Sensibility
23rd February 1996 The 1990s taste for all things Jane Austen continues with this film adaptation of her 1811 novel, *Sense and Sensibility*. Emma Thompson writes the screenplay and stars as Elinor Dashwood, elder sister to Kate Winslet's passionate Marianne, while their male co-stars are Hugh Grant, Greg Wise as the dashing yet despicable Willoughby and Alan Rickman, playing the wise and loyal Colonel Brandon. A delight from beginning to end, *Sense and Sensibility* is a box office success and wins Thompson an Oscar for Best Adapted Screenplay.

Ladette culture
As the decade's lad culture reaches its pinnacle, 1990s women refuse to take a back seat and the 'ladette' is born. *The Girlie Show* and its four rookie presenters, including Sara

Cox in her first TV role, takes the ladette concept and runs with it in a programme first shown on 26th January on Channel 4. *The Girlie Show* follows in the edgy tradition of *The Word*, doing its best to court controversy with segments like 'Wanker of the Week' and 'Naked Apes' featuring a group of Sunderland lads, getting up to various lager-fuelled stunts. *The Girlie Show* feels amateurish and often cringeworthy but captures a moment and is notable for an early TV appearance of a group of females who really can be said to represent Girl Power - the Spice Girls.

Trainspotting
Brutal, squalid, and boisterously funny, Danny Boyle's film version of Irvine Welsh's 1993 novel *Trainspotting* opens at cinemas on 26th February. Skilfully treading a fine line between the glorification and condemnation of heroin use, drugs may be the running thread through *Trainspotting*, but it's the characters that are etched into cinematic legend. Ewan McGregor loses two stone to play addict Renton and even considers (but decides against) trying heroin to better understand the character. Robert Carlyle is uncertain he has the right physique to play psychopathic loose cannon Begbie. Joining them are Ewen Bremner as likeable loser Spud, Jonny Lee Miller as Sick Boy and Kelly McDonald (in her first role) as schoolgirl seductress Diane. All leer out of the iconic posters plastered around the UK, a rogues' gallery of misfits from one of Britain's finest, era-defining films.

TFI Friday
Court jester Chris Evans seems unstoppable and after skipping from *The Big Breakfast* to *Don't Forget Your Toothbrush*, his next project is *TFI Friday*, made by his own company, Ginger Productions. Its matey vibe, in-jokes and who's who of music special guests tap into the Cool Britannia zeitgeist. The audience spend most of the time in the studio bar where celebs also hang out in between performing or chatting to Chris. Habitual swearing by guests lands the show in trouble. But a little notoriety goes a long way, and *TFI Friday* with its Britpop tunes and laddish high jinks makes every night in feel like a night out.

The English Patient

15th November 1996 The English Patient is an epic wartime romance adapted from the novel by Michael Ondaatje. Ralph Fiennes is the patient of the title, an air crash survivor burned beyond recognition and nursed by Nina (Juliette Binoche) as he slowly pieces together the story of his doomed love affair with Katharine Clifton (Kristin Scott Thomas). *The English Patient* is a triumph, both critically and commercially, and dominates the 1997 Oscars by winning nine awards in total.

Body count

We begin to spend more time in morgues than is probably acceptable when *Silent Witness* begins on BBC1 on 21st February. Differing from usual crime dramas, it follows forensic pathologist Dr Sam Ryan (Amanda Burton) and her team who are the key to solving cases. Dr Ryan's manner is calm and unruffled as she goes about carving up cadavers hoping they'll spill the beans along with their brains and intestines.

Changing Rooms

Stippling, stencilling, and other paint effect terms all become part of daily parlance after *Changing Rooms* begins on BBC2 on 4th September. Friends or neighbours swap homes for a couple of days and with the help of a top interior designer and ever-helpful chippy, 'Handy' Andy, give a room a complete makeover, hoping the transformation will delight rather than displease. It's edge of your seat stuff.

MUSIC

Take That split

12th February 1996 Confirmed today is the news that Take That are disbanding. For their last single they choose the Bee Gees' *How Deep is Your Love*, which duly tops the UK chart during March. Their parting gift to their fans is a *Greatest Hits* album.

DO YOU REMEMBER THIS?

Ring watergame

Fargo

Kidnaps rarely go to plan in films, but none go quite as horribly wrong as the one in *Fargo*, Joel and Ethan Coen's wickedly funny story of deception fraud, and murder in snow-covered Minnesota. Mild-mannered car salesman Jerry Lundergaard (William H. Macey) attempts to clear his debts by arranging the abduction of his wife by two thugs and it's the town's heavily pregnant police chief, Marge Gunderson (Frances McDormand) who has to sort out the mess.

All spice

When 1996 dawns, the Spice Girls are virtually unknown and are yet to have a single released. Seven months later they are not just a pop phenomenon but a national obsession, thanks not only to clever marketing and media management but also to a genuinely new and assertive spirit emerging in the UK. With their distinct personalities, images and nicknames, Geri, Victoria, Emma, Mel B and Mel C represent a cross-section of young British womanhood that female fans respond to. And the music's not bad, either: mostly self-written soul-based tracks geared to the dance floor. For the moment, this really is a Spice World and the rest of us just happen to live in it.

Jarvis objects

19th February 1996 Notorious for moments of unscheduled chaos, the 1996 BRIT Awards produce another. Enraged by Jackson's self-depiction as a Christ-like figure while performing *Earth Song*, Jarvis Cocker of Pulp jumps on to the stage to protest. Much of the incident is missed by the television cameras.

Collins leaves Genesis

28th March 1996 Phil Collins leaves Genesis to prioritise his solo career. Mike Rutherford and Tony Banks decide to continue but wait a whole year before announcing his replacement, Ray Wilson from Stiltskin.

Flint makes fire

30th March 1996 At No. 1 is the most disturbing single of the year, *Firestarter* by Essex rap band the Prodigy. Filmed in a disused tube tunnel, its video features Keith Flint dancing and snarling at the camera and sends the tabloid press into fits of rage for supposedly encouraging arson.

Pumpkin deaths

11th May 1996 Chicago rock band Smashing Pumpkins abandon their UK and Irish tour when a seventeen-year-old fan, Bernadette O'Brien, is fatally crushed during a crowd surfing incident at a Dublin concert. More tragedy follows in July when keyboard player Jonathan Melvoin dies from a heroin overdose.

Older and wiser

13th May 1996 Smarting from his ill-fated legal action against Sony, George Michael releases *Older*, his first album for Virgin. The clue is

in the title: this is George as a mature and explorative artist, tackling big emotional themes and newly influenced by Brazilian music. Although he has not yet come out as gay, the hints are there in the two No. 1 singles extracted from the album, *Fastlove* and *Jesus to a Child*.

Football Comes Home

Football's coming home

8th June 1996 As UEFA's Euro '96 tournament begins on home soil, England's hopes of progress are high. But it's not the official theme song, *We're in this Together* by Simply Red, that helps sweep the team to the semi-final. The song that captures the nation's mood is *Three Lions* by comedians Frank Skinner and David Baddiel and Ian Broudie of the Lightning Seeds. Though England's run ends in defeat to eventual winners Germany, the song reaches No. 1 and will be revived during every subsequent Euros and World Cup, as England's 'thirty years of hurt' without a trophy extends to 56 and counting.

Oasis at Knebworth

10th August 1996 Oasis fever reaches a new high point as the band play two outdoor concerts to over 350,000 at Knebworth House in Hertfordshire. A further two million apply for tickets but are disappointed.

MY FIRST 18 YEARS
TOP10　1996

1. **Don't Look Back in Anger** *Oasis*
2. **A Design for Life** *Manic Street Preachers*
3. **Killing Me Softly** *The Fugees*
4. **Macarena** *Los Del Rio*
5. **Stupid Girl** *Garbage*
6. **Virtual Insanity** *Jamiroquai*
7. **Lifted** *Lighthouse Family*
8. **How Bizarre** *OMC*
9. **Say You'll Be There** *The Spice Girls*
10. **You're Gorgeous** *Babybird*

Open ⬤ | Search 🔍 | Scan 📷

Tupac murdered
7th September 1996 Leading rapper Tupac Shakur is shot in a drive-by shooting in Las Vegas. He dies six days later. No arrest is made until 2023.

Last of the Roses?
29th October 1996 Two bands suffer personnel upheavals on the same day. In the US, guitarist Slash departs Guns N' Roses via a fax message to MTV. In the UK, Ian Brown and Gary Mounfield leave the Stone Roses, effectively dissolving the band altogether.

A knight to remember
12th November 1996 Long-time Beatles producer George Martin is knighted for services to the music industry at a Buckingham Palace investiture.

🏃 SPORT

Denis Compton RIP
23rd April 1997 A hero of English cricket's great post-war era, the debonair Denis Compton dies aged 78. He spent his whole club career with Middlesex and played in 78 Test matches, achieving a batting average of just over 50 per innings. He also played professionally for Arsenal, winning the league title with them in 1948 and the FA Cup in 1950.

FA Cup near miss, United glory
In the FA Cup, Division Two club Chesterfield make it all the way to the semi-final before losing to Middlesbrough 3-0. Chelsea, managed by ex-Netherlands star Ruud Gullit, beat Middlesbrough 2-0 to win the club's first trophy for a quarter of a century. Other major football stories of 1997 include Harrods boss Mohamed Al Fayed's purchase of Fulham, Eric Cantona's surprise retirement at 31, and an unforgettably close finish to the season as Manchester United peg back Newcastle's seemingly unstoppable race to the title and Toon manager Kevin Keegan loses his cool in an after-match rant against Alex Ferguson. Meanwhile, Scotland's top football clubs vote to create an elite league on the English model, to be called the Scottish Premier League and set to start in 1998.

A bout with bite
1st July 1997 In the aftermath of Evander Holyfield's defeat of Mike Tyson in June, in which Tyson was disqualified for biting each of Holyfield's ears, the Nevada Athletic Commission suspends Tyson, withholds his $20 million fee and fines him $3 million.

Breaking new grounds
30th July 1997 Sunderland FC's new home, the Stadium of Light, is the first of several new stadia opened in time for the new football season. It is built on the site of Monkwearmouth Colliery, which closed in 1993. Derby County's new ground at Pride Park opens on 14th August, the same day that Sir Stanley Matthews opens Stoke City's new ground, the Britannia Stadium, and the Deputy Prime Minister declares Bolton Wanderers' new Reebok Stadium open for business.

Grand National abandoned
5th April 1997 The showcase Grand National meeting at Aintree is abandoned after credible bomb threats are received just an hour before the race is due to be run. For the first time ever, the race is run on the following Monday. The winner is Lord Gyllene ridden by Tony Dobbin.

9 JAN 1997
Volkswagen settle lawsuit brought by General Motors over alleged espionage.

19 FEB 1997
Death of Chinese leader Deng Xiaoping aged 92.

26 MAR 1997
Mass suicide in San Diego by 39 members of religious cult Heaven's Gate.

Villeneuve is champion

26th October 1997 Jacques Villeneuve becomes the first Canadian to win the Formula One championship with Williams, securing the title in the last race of the season in Spain while rival Michael Schumacher is penalised for deliberately ramming Villeneuve's car.

DOMESTIC NEWS

Channel 5 launches

30th March 1997 Channel 5 is launched, the fifth terrestrial television channel in the UK. The first programme on air is *Family Affairs*, a new soap opera.

Wild about Harry

26th June 1997 Harry Potter and the Philosopher's Stone by unknown children's author J. K. Rowling is published by Bloomsbury with an initial print run of just 500 copies in hardback. The book's reputation grows steadily through word of mouth, positive reviews and winning the Smarties Book Prize.

Halifax makes history

2nd June 1997 The UK's biggest building society, the Halifax, is floated on the London Stock Exchange. Now officially a bank, its 7.5 million account holders become shareholders.

UUP agree to talks

17th September 1997 A breakthrough comes in the peace process in Northern Ireland. The Ulster Unionists, representing a large swathe of loyalist opinion, agree to take part in talks that include Sinn Fein.

Louise Woodward case

31st October 1997 After a high-profile trial that makes headlines all around the world, eighteen-year-old British au pair Louise Woodward is convicted by a Massachusetts court of murdering Matthew Eappen, an eight-month-old boy she was caring for. Two weeks later her conviction is reduced on appeal to manslaughter, and she is released having served nearly a year in prison.

Hague marries

19th December 1997 New Conservative Party leader William Hague marries Ffion Jenkins, whom he met while serving as Secretary of State for Wales.

Biggs stays in Brazil

12th November 1997 The Supreme Court in Brazil refuses the UK's request to extradite the Great Train Robber Ronnie Biggs, who escaped from Wandsworth Prison in 1965. He has been living in Brazil since 1970.

---

7 APR 1997

Steve Irwin's *The Crocodile Hunter* premieres.

27 MAY 1997

NATO-Russian co-operation charter signed in Paris.

10 JUN 1997

Pol Pot orders murder of his defence minister and eleven family members.

Britannia leaves the waves
11th December 1997 The Royal Yacht *Britannia* is formally decommissioned in a moving ceremony that brings the Queen to tears. Having transported the royal family to events and on tours since 1954, the yacht is now ageing and is too expensive to refit. Soon after coming to power, the new Labour government decides that a replacement yacht will not be provided out of the public purse.

ROYALTY &
POLITICS

Labour landslide
1st May 1997 Although Tony Blair's victory in the General Election is widely expected, its scale is stunning. The Labour Party win 418 seats, giving it a majority of 179, while the number of Conservative held seats reduces from 343 to 165. After eighteen years in government, the Conservatives lose seats in constituencies that have been 'true blue' for decades, including those of seven former Cabinet ministers and the man tipped to take over from John Major, Michael Portillo. The Conservatives lose all their seats in Scotland and Wales, while the Liberal Democrats increase their tally in the Commons from 28 seats to 46. The next day, John Major resigns as Conservative Party leader while Tony Blair enters 10 Downing Street as Prime Minister.

Labour's first measures
2nd July 1997 The new Labour government's first budget, presented to the House of Commons by Chancellor of the Exchequer Gordon Brown, focuses on boosting funding for education, healthcare and getting the long-term unemployed back into work.

Wales says 'yes' (just)
18th September 1997 A referendum in Wales on devolution produces a much closer result than that achieved by the 'yes' campaign in Scotland. Just over 50 per cent of those voting opt for the creation of a Welsh Assembly - enough to regard the 'yes' vote as carried. The Wales Act 1998 is introduced to prepare the way for elections to the new Assembly in 1999.

Scotland says 'yes'
11th September 1997 A referendum in Scotland on devolution of some powers from Westminster to a Scottish Parliament delivers a firm 'yes' vote. The final figures are 74.29 per cent for yes, 25.71 per cent for no. A second question on whether such a Parliament should have tax-raising powers is backed by a 63.48 per cent 'yes' vote.

2 JUL 1997
All-American movie great James Stewart dies aged 89.

29 AUG 1997
Netflix is founded as an online DVD rental service in California.

17 SEP 1997
A draft international landmines treaty is rejected by the US.

1997

Diana is dead

31st August 1997 The UK wakes to news of the deaths of Diana, Princess of Wales, and her companion Dodi Fayed in a high-speed car accident in a road tunnel in Paris. The focus of much media attention after their relationship blossomed during the summer, the couple were escaping photographers on scooters after leaving the Ritz in a car driven by chauffeur Henri Paul, who is also killed. Prince Charles flies to France to bring Diana's body home and normal life in the UK seems to come to a halt. An extraordinary week follows, as the flowers mount a Kensington Palace and along the Mall and criticism of the royal family's response to Diana's death grows. Guided by advice from Tony Blair and his media team, the Queen returns from Balmoral to Buckingham Palace and makes a live television tribute to Diana on the evening of 5th September.

'Goodbye, England's rose'

6th September 1997 Diana, Princess of Wales, is given a state funeral in all but name with a service at Westminster Abbey. Prince Charles, Prince Philip and Diana's brother Charles Spencer join Princes William and Harry in following the coffin on foot from Buckingham Palace to the Abbey. Charles Spencer delivers a powerful eulogy that includes a scorching rebuke of her treatment by the royal family and the media which provokes a wave of applause in the Abbey that spreads to the thousands in the streets and parks of central London. Thousands more line the route as the funeral cortege makes its way to Northamptonshire and a private burial at Althorp, the Spencers' childhood home.

FOREIGN NEWS

Looted art

27th January 1997 Research published today shows that museums in France own almost two thousand works of art stolen by the Nazis, mostly from Jewish owners, during the German Occupation. Some are even thought to be on display in the Louvre. The question of rightful ownership and the right to restitution becomes a huge issue within the international art world during the year.

Hong Kong handover

1st July 1997 After several years of negotiations and an attempt by Governor Chris Patten to strengthen democracy in Hong Kong, control of the colony is passed from the UK to the People's Republic of China. The handover of sovereignty is completed with due ceremony after the end of the 99-year lease.

---

7 OCT 1997
All-party talks on Northern Ireland begin.

1 NOV 1997
Titanic receives its world premiere at the Tokyo International Film Festival.

11 DEC 1997
Kyoto Protocol commits signatory nations to limiting greenhouse gases.

Comet Hale-Bopp

1st March 1997 Anyone looking at the starry sky in the spring will see a large and remarkably bright comet with the naked eye. Hale-Bopp, named after its two discoverers, measures 40 kilometers in diameter and provides quite a spectacle at night.

O. J. trial decision

5th February 1997 The civil law case against O. J. Simpson over the 'wrongful death' of his wife Nicole Brown Simpson and Ronald Goldman, who were murdered in 1994, is finally concluded. The jury finds Simpson responsible for both deaths and awards the families of the victims $33.5 million in damages.

Che is buried

13th July 1997 The remains of revolutionary leader Che Guevara are returned to Cuba from Bolivia, where he was executed in 1967, for burial with full military honours. A mausoleum has been built for him in Santa Clara, where he led his forces to victory during the Cuban revolution in 1958.

Land mine treaty

3rd December 1997 A treaty agreeing the prohibition of the manufacture and use of anti-personnel land mines is signed by 121 countries at a conference in the Canadian capital of Ottawa. Notable omissions from the list of signatories are the US, China, Russia and South Korea. The campaign against land mines was a cause especially close to the heart of the late Diana, Princess of Wales, who did much to bring it to international attention.

Versace murdered

15th July 1997 The great Italian fashion designer Gianni Versace is shot dead outside his home in Miami Beach, Florida. He was 50 years old. His killer Andrew Cunanan commits suicide before police find him. Versace's funeral is held at Milan Cathedral on 22nd July and attended by over 2,000 people including his close friends Elton John and Diana, Princess of Wales.

Google registered
15th September 1997 In 1996, Stanford students Larry Page and Sergey Brin devise a system to make searching the Internet easier. You enter a search term on their website, after which servers scour the Internet looking for web pages that match your search query. The results then appear neatly arranged, one below the other, on the screen. On this day, Page and Brin register the domain name google.com for their search engine, after the word 'googol' for a number composed of one followed by 100 zeros.

Kyoto Treaty
11th December 1997 In the Japanese city of Kyoto, 84 countries conclude a major climate agreement. The Kyoto Treaty stipulates that industrialised countries will significantly reduce emissions of harmful greenhouse gases that contribute to global warming.

⊳ ENTERTAINMENT

Scream
Slasher movie *Scream*, directed by Wes Craven, is released on 31st January. Unusually for a horror film it features several well-known stars including Courtney Cox and Drew Barrymore, which help to make it a screaming success and to revive what many thought a dying genre. Six *Scream* films follow this original.

Spicegirls in a Spiceworld
A year and a half after they burst onto the music scene with *Wannabe*, the Spice Girls star in their own movie, the comic romp *Spiceworld*, which opens on Boxing Day.

Show me the money
When slick sports agent Jerry McGuire has an existential crisis and writes a polemic to his colleagues about the exploitative nature of the business, he finds himself fired and left with just one client: a washed-up footballer (Cuba Gooding Junior) with an inflated ego whose pay demands outweigh his current form. Only a lone member of staff, single mother Dorothy (Renee Zellweger) agrees to join him in setting up his own venture. Cruise is at his best in a role that requires him to fit in but break free of the machismo of sports management, while Zellweger, who nobody has heard of before, is charming as his love interest, especially as she's given that killer line, 'You had me at hello.' Jonathan Lipnicki is cute as a button as her son Ray and Gooding Junior wins an Oscar for Best Supporting Actor as Rod Stillwell. A hugely likeable and heartwarming film, even if American football leaves you cold.

This Life

This Life, the BBC2 drama about four law graduates sharing a London house (and each other's beds) first aired in 1996 yet passed largely under the radar. But a new series this year warrants a repeat of the first, beginning 2nd January, and suddenly, the antics of Miles, Egg, Millie, Anna and co have us hooked. *This Life* reflects twentysomething life in the big smoke in all its messy, messed-up glamour and grunginess. They sleep around, have massive hangovers, and take ecstasy or cocaine in between arguing over the phone bill and losing the house keys - all part and parcel of 'this life'. Soundtracked with music from Blur, Oasis and Elastica, this is water cooler TV for the Cool Britannia brigade.

Mrs Brown

5th September 1997 Judi Dench takes on the role of the grieving, reclusive Queen Victoria in *Mrs Brown*, her first lead film role, despite decades of television and stage credits. Comedian Billy Connolly is cast as John Brown, her Highland ghillie, aggressively loyal to his mistress with a brusqueness that makes him enemies among courtiers, royal family members and the press. Dench receives a Best Actress Oscar nomination and wins a BAFTA and Golden Globe for her subtle portrayal of the imperious yet vulnerable monarch.

L.A. Confidential

31st October 1997 A stylish homage to film noir, *L.A. Confidential* is a sizzling tale of bent cops, mobsters, and classy dames. Director Curtis Hanson chooses two relatively unknown Australians - Guy Pearce and Russell Crowe - to star in this adaptation of James Ellroy's 1990 novel, alongside Kevin Spacey and Kim Basinger.

Eh-oh! It's the Teletubbies

31st March 1997 Tinky-Winky, Dipsy, Laa-laa and Po, aka the *Teletubbies*, wave at us from Teletubbieland on BBC2. There has never been anything quite like them. Four brightly coloured, human-sized, toddler-shaped creatures with antennae and a liking for pink custard, they speak in gibberish, have screens in their bellies and clean up any mess with the help of a vacuum cleaner called Noo-noo. Teletubbieland is a tranquil green land of rolling hillocks where rabbits hop around peacefully, as the Teletubbies potter. Dipsy has a hat, Po a scooter, Laa-Laa an orange ball, and the metrosexual Tiny-Winky has a handbag. All their antics take place under a shining sun with the face of a delighted, chuckling baby. The *Teletubbies* are HUGE and soft toys are in short supply this Christmas when everybody wants one to help them go 'Tubby-bye-bye'.

Yeh, baby!

Shamelessly lampooning the spy thrillers of the 1960s, Mike Myers is *Austin Powers, International Man of Mystery*, a toothy secret agent and serial lothario, who, cryogenically frozen, brings swinging London to the present day as he tries to save the world from his arch-nemesis , Dr Evil (also Myers). Myers created Powers in tribute to his late, British-born father, who he says introduced him to 'James Bond, Peter Sellers, The Beatles, The Goodies, Peter Cook and Dudley Moore'.

Liam and Patsy wed

7th April 1997 Liam Gallagher marries actress Patsy Kensit at Westminster Register Office.

Ground Force

19th September 1997 After the success of home makeover show *Changing Rooms*, BBC2 executives figure that garden makeovers might prove just as popular. And they do, with *Ground Force* deploying a crack team of gardening wizards who descend on a house for the weekend, while the unsuspecting owner is bundled away for the duration. The result? Tears of gratitude and gasps of appreciation at the end of the show, as cracked patios give way to smart decking, and weed-choked beds are transformed into blooming beautiful borders.

Men in Black

1st August 1997 Agent J and Agent K (Will Smith and a deadpan Tommy Lee Jones), dressed in shades and sharp suits, are the *Men in Black*, part of an ultra-secret government organisation responsible for hunting down earth-dwelling aliens. Aliens employ all kinds of trickery to disguise their true selves, but if the public do witness extra-terrestrial activity, the MIB deploy neutralisers to wipe their memory instantly. Accompanied by a hit single courtesy of Smith, *Men in Black* is the megahit of the summer.

Gotcha Tamagotchi

Tamagotchi, little egg-shaped digital pets, are the latest fad from Japan and become the best-selling toy this Christmas. Requiring some responsibility on the part of the owner, it's important to keep an eye on your Tamagotchi's health, food, activities and behaviour to ensure it thrives. Whether or not a Tamagotchi survives until next Christmas is an excellent litmus test to see if your offspring really will look after that puppy they've been pleading for.

Titanic

James Cameron's film about the sinking of the *Titanic* cost a whopping $200 million and is filmmaking on an epic scale. The result is a movie layered with romance, drama, tragedy, stunning period details and awesome special effects. The pairing of Leonardo di Caprio and Kate Winslet as Jack and Rose, the couple who find love across the class divide, creates some of cinema's most memorable moments and by the end, we're so carried away with the story, as Jack slips into the icy depths of the Atlantic we want to reach across and pull him back out again.

MUSIC

Harvey sacked

18th February 1997 Brian Harvey is sacked from East 17 after defending the drug ecstasy in a radio interview. With their chart fortunes faltering, he is invited back during 1998 when the group relaunches itself as E-17.

The Full Monty

In 1996, *Brassed Off*, a film about a Yorkshire colliery band, took the decline of the mining industry as its backdrop. This year's *The Full Monty*, released 29th August, has as its setting Sheffield steel. On the dole, and losing hope, ex-steel worker Gaz (Robert Carlyle) has a money-making idea and auditions a motley assortment of male hopefuls to form a striptease act, which promises to go 'the full monty'. As jolly as it is, the film also explores several more serious issues including depression and fathers' rights, but the male protagonists come through the process with a renewed sense of purpose and self-esteem restored. Feelgood is an overused term in the world of film, but *The Full Monty* IS guaranteed to leave you with a smile on your face.

Knight fever

11th March 1997 Paul McCartney is knighted by the Queen at Buckingham Palace.

Bitter sweet Verve

13th September 1997 Wigan five-piece the Verve have endured one disbandment and a reconciliation before finally coming good with the *Urban Hymns* album. However, legal action over the sampling of the Rolling Stones' *The Last Time* on *Bitter Sweet Symphony* accounts for most of the profits. A second track from the album, *The Drugs Don't Work* – which, contrary to tabloid reports, concerns medical drugs, not the recreational kind – reaches No. 1. Another break-up follows as gifted but prickly front man Richard Ashcroft begins a solo career.

Radiohead rules OK

21st May 1997 Critics' favourites Radiohead make their big leap towards Pink Floyd-type sanctity with the multi-award winning *OK Computer*, an experimental album triggered by Miles Davis' *Bitches Brew* and blending ambient and electronic elements with lyrics about a dystopian future. An appearance at Glastonbury boosts their live reputation. They also become one of the first bands in the UK to start a website.

UK wins Eurovision

3rd May 1997 The UK entry wins the Eurovision Song Contest for only the fifth time, though Katrina Leskanich of Katrina and the Waves is actually American. *Love Shine a Light* is written by band member Kimberley Rew.

Another rap murder

9th March 1997 It's another bleak day for the US rap scene as gang violence claims another victim. Chris Wallace aka Biggie Smalls aka Notorious B.I.G. is shot dead in Los Angeles. Fellow rapper Puff Daddy records a tribute to him, *I'll Be Missing You*, with Notorious B.I.G.'s widow Faith Evans. The track is a reworking of *Every Breath You Take* by the Police and tops the US and UK listings in June.

Elton's tribute

6th September 1997 Following the shocking death of Diana, Princess of Wales in a car crash in Paris, Elton John is asked to sing a tribute at her funeral in Westminster Abbey. In front of a television audience estimated at over two billion people, he performs his song *Candle in the Wind*, with lyrics revised for the occasion by Bernie Taupin. Released as a single, it becomes the biggest global seller ever - eclipsing even Bing Crosby's *White Christmas* - at 33 million, with proceeds going to the Memorial Fund.

Denver dies

12th October 1997 Singer-songwriter John Denver, best known for *Annie's Song*, *Leavin' on a Jet Plane* and *Take Me Home Country Roads*, is killed when the aircraft he is piloting crashes into Monterey Bay in California.

Hutchence suicide

22nd November 1997 INXS singer Michael Hutchence commits suicide at a hotel in Sydney. He had never fully recovered from a fist fight with a taxi driver in 1992 that left him without a sense of taste or smell. Alcohol and drug problems followed, worsened by a decline in the band's popularity and the fallout from his relationship with Paula Yates, with whom he had a daughter, Tiger Lily. The final straw seems to have been the custody battle between Yates and husband Bob Geldof, which prevented Tiger Lily from coming to Australia.

MY FIRST 18 YEARS
TOP10   1997

1. **Song 2** *Blur*
2. **Say What You Want** *Texas*
3. **Brimful of Asha** *Cornershop*
4. **Men in Black** *Will Smith*
5. **Never Ever** *All Saints*
6. **Don't Speak** *No Doubt*
7. **Tubthumping** *Chumbawamba*
8. **Where Have All the Cowboys Gone?** *Paula Cole*
9. **Torn** *Natalie Umbruglia*
10. **Stand By Me** *Oasis*

Open | Search | Scan

Barbie barbs

1st November 1997 Danish band Aqua, currently at No. 1 in the UK with the satirical *Barbie Girl*, are threatened with a law suit by Barbie doll manufacturer Mattel. Agreement is eventually reached to include a sticker on the single making clear that it is not a Mattel-endorsed product.

Bee Gees storm off

30th October 1997 The Bee Gees walk out of a television interview with chat show host Clive Anderson when he calls them 'tossers'. Nobody had told them that insulting his guests is a big part of Anderson's style.

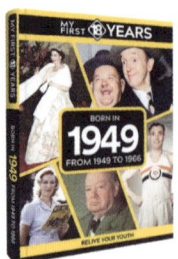

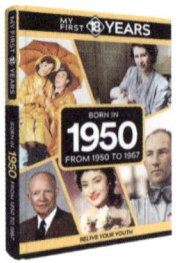

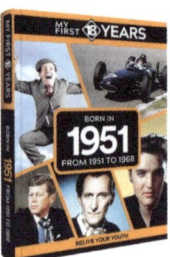

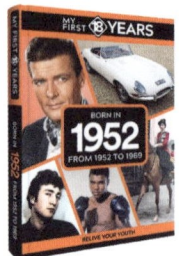

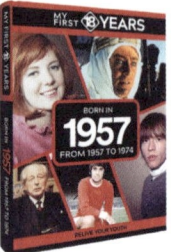

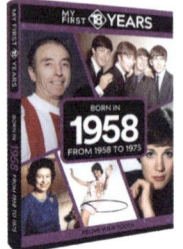

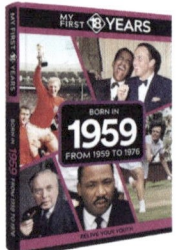

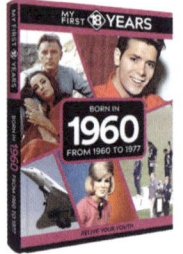

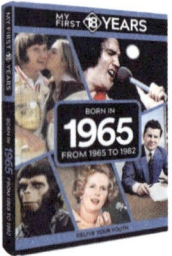

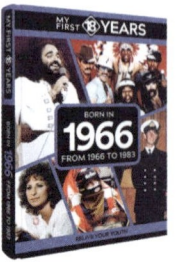

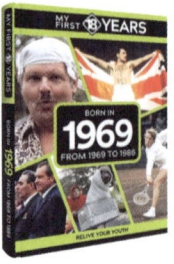

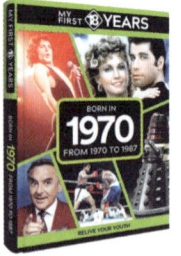

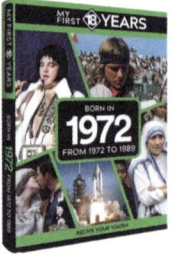

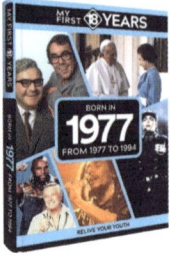

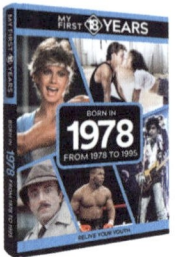

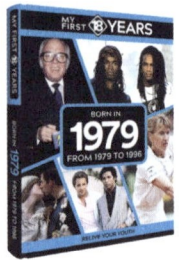

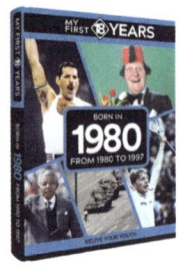